THE 1998 ANNUAL: Volume 2 Consulting

(The Thirty-First Annual)

Jossey-Bass
Pfeiffer

THE
1998 ANNUAL:
Volume 2
Consulting

(The Thirty-First Annual)

Jossey-Bass
Pfeiffer

San Francisco

PREFACE

One of the keys to the success of the *Annual* series is its continuing ability to meet the needs of human resource development (HRD) practitioners— be they trainers, consultants, performance-improvement technologists, facilitators, or educators. The contents of each *Annual* focus on increasing the reader's professional competence by providing materials of immediate, practical use.

In 1995, Pfeiffer began publishing two volumes of the *Annual:* Volume 1, focusing on training, and Volume 2, focusing on consulting. For the purposes of the *Annuals,* we consider training that which has an impact on individuals, and consulting that which has an impact on organizations. Feedback from you, our readers, has let us know that you welcome and use both volumes. It is difficult, in some cases, to place materials strictly in one category or the other, so there is some overlap in what the two volumes cover.

The 1998 Annual: Volume 2, Consulting reflects our intention to continue to publish materials that help you stay on the cutting edge of your profession. In keeping with this objective, you may duplicate and modify materials from the *Annuals,* as long as each copy includes the credit statement printed on the copyright page of the particular volume. However, reproducing materials in publications for sale or for large-scale distribution (more than 100 copies in 12 months) requires prior written permission. Reproduction of material that is copyrighted by another source (as indicated in a footnote) requires written permission from the designated copyright holder. Also, reproduction on computer disk, or by any other electronic means, requires written permission.

We at Jossey-Bass/Pfeiffer encourage you to submit materials for publication. For the *Annuals,* we are interested in receiving presentation and discussion resources (articles that include theory along with practical application); inventories, questionnaires, and surveys (paper-and-pencil inventories, rating scales, and other response tools); and experiential learning activities (group learning designs based on the five stages of the experiential learning cycle: experiencing, publishing, processing, generalizing, and applying). Contact the Jossey-Bass/Pfeiffer Editorial Department at the address listed on the copyright page for copies of our guidelines for contributors. Send submissions to the *Annual* editor at the same address.

I want to thank the dedicated people at Jossey-Bass/Pfeiffer who produced the *Annuals* this year: Kathleen Dolan Davies, Dawn Kilgore, Arlette Ballew, Carol Nolde, Susan Rachmeler, and Rebecca Taff. Special thanks go to Josh Blatter, who took on the extremely important task of securing the materials that make up both volumes. I am grateful to Dr. Beverly Robinson, who once again reviewed all the experiential learning activities and contributed her perspective as a facilitator. I also want to thank Elaine Biech, our new consulting editor, for reinforcing our connection to you, the practitioner. Finally, I want to express our gratitude to our authors for sharing their professional ideas, techniques, and materials so that other HRD practitioners may benefit.

Lawrence E. Alexander
Publisher

About Jossey-Bass/Pfeiffer

Jossey-Bass/Pfeiffer is actively engaged in publishing insightful human resource development (HRD) materials. The organization has earned an international reputation as the leading source of practical resources that are immediately useful to today's consultants, trainers, facilitators, and managers in a variety of industries. All materials are designed by practicing professionals who are continually experimenting with new techniques. Thus, readers and users benefit from the fresh and thoughtful approach that underlies Jossey-Bass/Pfeiffer's experientially based materials, books, workbooks, instruments, and other learning resources and programs. This broad range of products is designed to help human resource practitioners increase individual, group, and organizational effectiveness and provide a variety of training and intervention technologies as well as background in the field.

CONTENTS

*See Experiential Learning Activities Categories, p. 5, for an explanation of the numbering system.

GENERAL INTRODUCTION
TO THE 1998 ANNUAL

The 1998 Annual: Volume 2, Consulting is the thirty-first volume in the *Annual* series. Each *Annual* has three main sections: twelve *experiential learning activities;* three or four *inventories, questionnaires, and surveys;* and a series of *presentation and discussion resources.* Each of the pieces is classified in one of the following categories: Individual Development, Communication, Problem Solving, Groups, Teams, Consulting, Facilitating, and Leadership. Within each category, pieces are further classified into logical subcategories, which are explained in the introductions to the three sections.

The *Annual* series is a collection of practical and useful materials for professionals in the broad area described as human resource development (HRD). These materials are written by and for professionals, including trainers, organization-development/effectiveness consultants, performance-improvement technologists, educators, instructional designers, and others. As such, the series continues to provide a publication outlet for HRD professionals who wish to share their experiences, their viewpoints, and their procedures with their colleagues. To that end, Jossey-Bass/Pfeiffer publishes guidelines for potential authors. These guidelines, revised in 1996, are available from the Pfeiffer editorial department at Jossey-Bass Inc., Publishers, in San Francisco, California.

Materials are selected for the *Annuals* based on the quality of the ideas, applicability to real-world concerns, relevance to current HRD issues, clarity of presentation, and ability to enhance our readers' professional development. In addition, we choose experiential learning activities that will create a high degree of enthusiasm among the participants and add enjoyment to the learning process. As in the past several years, the contents of each *Annual* span a range of subject matter, reflecting the range of interests of our readers.

A list of contributors to the *Annual* can be found at the end of the volume, including their names, affiliations, addresses, telephone numbers, facsimile numbers, and e-mail addresses (if available). Readers will find this list of contributors useful if they wish to locate the authors of specific pieces for feedback, comments, or questions. Further information is presented in a brief biographical sketch of each contributor that appears at the conclusion of his or her article. These elements are intended to contribute to the "networking" function that is so valuable in the field of human resource development.

The editorial staff continues to be pleased with the high quality of materials submitted for publication. Nevertheless, just as we cannot publish every manuscript we receive, readers may find that not all the works included in a particular *Annual* are equally useful to them. We invite ideas, materials, and suggestions that will help us to make subsequent *Annuals* as useful as possible to our readers.

Introduction
to the Experiental Learning Activities Section

Experiential learning activities are extremely varied. They should be selected according to the needs of the participants and the abilities of the facilitator. Many different activities might accomplish similar goals. However,
if the activity is to address the participants' unique needs, the facilitator must
be able to assist the participants in processing the data from that experience.

Each experiential learning activity in this *Annual* includes a description of the goals of the activity, the size of the group and/or subgroups that
can be accommodated, the time required to do and process[1] the activity, a
list of the materials and handouts required, the physical setting, step-by-step
instructions for facilitating the experiential task and discussion phases of
the activity, and variations of the design that the facilitator might find useful.
All of these activities are complete; the content of all handouts is provided.

The 1998 Annual: Volume 2, Consulting includes twelve activities, in the
following categories:

Problem Solving: Consensus/Synergy

605. Councils to the President: Achieving Consensus on Complex
Issues by Michele Stimac

606. New-Member Welcome: Experimenting with Individual, Pair,
and Group-Consensus Tasks by Andrew Kimball

Groups: How Groups Work

607. Innovative Meetings: Creative Communication Tools
by M.K. Key and Jennifer Nordloh

---

[1]It would be redundant to print here a caveat for the use of experiential learning activities,
but HRD professionals who are not experienced in the use of this training technology are strongly
urged to read the "Introduction" to the *Reference Guide to Handbooks and Annuals* (1997 Edition).
This article presents the theory behind the experiential-learning cycle and explains the necessity
of adequately completing each phase of the cycle to allow effective learning to occur.

608. No Strings Attached: Learning How Groups Organize
To Complete Tasks by Jeyakar Vedamanickam

Groups: Competition/Collaboration

609. Allied Circuits: An Empowerment Role Play
by Barbara Pate Glacel and Emile A. Robert, Jr.

610. The Forest vs. the Trees: Understanding Preferences for
the Big Picture or the Details by Bonnie Jameson

Teams: Problem Solving/Decision Making

611. News Room: A Group-Consensus Task by Heidi Ann Campbell
and Heather Jean Campbell

Teams: Feedback

612. Enablers and Barriers: Assessing Your Team
by Karen Vander Linde

Consulting: Awareness

613. System Review: Preparing for Strategic Planning
by Wayne Reschke

Leadership: Ethics

614. Ethics in Action: Aligning Decisions with Organizational Values
by Jean G. Lamkin

Leadership: Interviewing/Appraisal

615. Sign Here: Assessing an Appraisal System by Nancy Jackson

Leadership: Motivation

616. Managerial Perceptions: What Do Employees Really Want?
by John Sample

Other activities that address certain goals can be located using the "Experiential Learning Activities Categories" chart that follows or by using our comprehensive *Reference Guide to Handbooks and Annuals.* The *Reference Guide,* which is updated regularly, indexes the contents of all *Annuals* and *Handbooks of Structured Experiences* that we have published to date. With each revision, the *Reference Guide* becomes a complete, up-to-date, and easy-to-use resource for selecting appropriate materials from all of the *Annuals* and *Handbooks.*

EXPERIENTIAL LEARNING ACTIVITIES CATEGORIES

Vol. Page

INDIVIDUAL DEVELOPMENT

Sensory Awareness

Feelings & Defenses (56)	III	31
Lemons (71)	III	94
Growth & Name Fantasy (85)	'72	59
Group Exploration (119)	IV	92
Relaxation & Perceptual Awareness (136)	'74	84
T'ai Chi Chuan (199)	VI	10
Roles Impact Feelings (214)	VI	102
Projections (300)	VIII	30
Mastering the Deadline Demon (593)	'98–1	9

Self-Disclosure

Johari Window (13)	I	65
Graphics (20)	I	88
Personal Journal (74)	III	109
Make Your Own Bag (90)	'73	13
Growth Cards (109)	IV	30
Expressing Anger (122)	IV	104
Stretching (123)	IV	107
Forced-Choice Identity (129)	'74	20
Boasting (181)	'76	49
The Other You (182)	'76	51
Praise (306)	VIII	61
Introjection (321)	'82	29
Personality Traits (349)	IX	158
Understanding the Need for Approval (438)	'88	21
The Golden Egg Award (448)	'88	89
Adventures at Work (521)	'95–1	9
That's Me (522)	'95–1	17

Sex Roles

Polarization (62)	III	57
Sex-Role Stereotyping (95)	'73	26
Sex-Role Attributes (184)	'76	63
Who Gets Hired? (215)	VI	106
Sexual Assessment (226)	'78	36
Alpha II (248)	VII	19
Sexual Values (249)	VII	24
Sex-Role Attitudes (258)	VII	85
Sexual Values in Organizations (268)	VII	146
Sexual Attraction (272)	'80	26

Vol. Page

Sexism in Advertisements (305)	VIII	58
The Promotion (362)	IX	152
Raising Elizabeth (415)	'86	21
The Problem with Men/ Women Is . . . (437)	'88	9
The Girl and the Sailor (450)	'89	17
Tina Carlan (466)	'90	45

Diversity

Status-Interaction Study (41)	II	85
Peer Perceptions (58)	III	41
Discrimination (63)	III	62
Traditional American Values (94)	'73	23
Growth Group Values (113)	IV	45
The In-Group (124)	IV	112
Leadership Characteristics (127)	'74	13
Group Composition (172)	V	139
Headbands (203)	VI	25
Sherlock (213)	VI	92
Negotiating Differences (217)	VI	114
Young/Old Woman (227)	'78	40
Pygmalion (229)	'78	51
Race from Outer Space (239)	'79	38
Prejudice (247)	VII	15
Physical Characteristics (262)	VII	108
Whom To Choose (267)	VII	141
Data Survey (292)	'81	57
Lifeline (298)	VIII	21
Four Cultures (338)	'83	72
All Iowans Are Naive (344)	IX	14
AIRSOPAC (364)	IX	172
Doctor, Lawyer, Indian Chief (427)	'87	21
Life Raft (462)	'90	17
Zenoland (492)	'92	69
First Impressions (509)	'94	9
Parole Board (510)	'94	17
Fourteen Dimensions (557)	'96–2	9
Adoption (569)	'97–1	9
Globalization (570)	'97–1	19
Generational Pyramids (571)	'97–1	33
People with Disabilities (594)	'98–1	15

Vol. Page

Life/Career Planning

Life Planning (46)	II	101
Banners (233)	'79	9
Wants Bombardment (261)	VII	105
Career Renewal (332)	'83	27
Life Assessment and Planning (378)	'85	15
Work-Needs Assessment (393)	X	31
The Ego-Radius Model (394)	X	41
Dropping Out (414)	'86	15
Roles (416)	'86	27
Creating Ideal Personal Futures (439)	'88	31
Pie in the Sky (461)	'90	9
What's in It for Me? (463)	'90	21
Affirmations (473)	'91	9
Supporting Cast (486)	'92	15
Career Visioning (498)	'93	13
The Hand You're Dealt (523)	'95–1	23
Living Our Values (548)	'96–1	25
Career Roads (549)	'96–1	35
Collaborating for Success (572)	'97–1	45
High Jump (573)	'97–1	57
Issues, Trends, and Goals (595)	'98–1	21
Bouncing Back (596)	'98–1	35
Work Activities (597)	'98–1	43

COMMUNICATION

Awareness

One-Way, Two-Way (4)	I	13
Think-Feel (65)	III	70
Ball Game (108)	IV	27
Re-Owning (128)	'74	18
Helping Relationships (152)	V	13
Babel (153)	V	16
Blindfolds (175)	'76	13
Letter Exchange (190)	'77	28
Dominoes (202)	VI	21
Blivet (241)	'79	46
Meanings Are in People (250)	VII	28
Mixed Messages (251)	VII	34
Gestures (286)	'81	28
Maze (307)	VIII	64

The 1998 Annual: Volume 2, Consulting/© 1998 Jossey-Bass/Pfeiffer

605. Councils to the President: Achieving Consensus on Complex Issues

Goals

- To offer participants an opportunity to experience the dynamics involved in consensus decision making.
- To encourage participants to voice their opinions and values in a group setting.

Group Size

Fifteen to thirty participants, in three to five subgroups of five or six members each.

Time Required

One hour and thirty-five to fifty-five minutes.

Materials

- A copy of the Councils to the President Situation Sheet for each participant.
- A copy of the Councils to the President Task Sheet for each participant.
- Several sheets of paper and a pencil for each participant.

Physical Setting

It is preferable to have a main meeting room for the assignment of the task and for presentations plus separate breakout rooms for the subgroups. If breakout rooms are not available, the activity may be conducted in any room large enough so that the subgroups can work without disturbing one another. A table and chairs must be provided for each subgroup.

Process

1. The facilitator announces the goals of the activity.

2. The participants are assembled into subgroups of five or six members each. The facilitator distributes copies of the situation sheet, copies of the task sheet, paper, and pencils. The participants are instructed to read both handouts. Afterward the facilitator answers any questions about the task. (Fifteen minutes.)

3. The facilitator asks each subgroup to select one or two members to present the subgroup's results later to the total group. The subgroups are told that they have forty-five minutes to complete the task—thirty-five minutes to reach consensus and ten minutes to prepare a five-minute presentation for the total group. Then the subgroups are instructed to begin. (Forty-five minutes.)

4. While the subgroups are working, the facilitator apprises them of the remaining time at intervals. When there are only ten minutes left, the facilitator asks the subgroups to stop working on the consensus part of the task and to begin filling out the task sheet for the presentation.

5. When the ten-minute period is up, the facilitator reconvenes the total group and asks the spokespersons to take turns making their presentations. (Fifteen to twenty-five minutes.)

6. The facilitator leads a concluding discussion with the following questions:

   - What was your instinctive answer to the question, before you started working with your group? How did your thoughts about the question evolve as you listened to the other members of your group?

   - How did you feel about voicing your personal opinions and values in your group? How did you react to others' opinions and values?

   - How did your group make sure that everyone's opinions were heard?

   - How do you feel about the quality of your group's decision?

   - What were your reactions to the other groups' presentations and conclusions? What insights did you gain? How did your own opinion change?

   - If you could do this task again, what would you do differently?

   - What have you learned about making a consensus decision on a complex issue? What are the advantages of consensus? What are the disadvantages?

- How can you use what you have learned in working with groups in the future?

(Twenty to thirty minutes.)

Variation

- Those councils that believe it is possible to eradicate violence may be asked to submit a plan for accomplishing the eradication.

On-Line Variation

This activity is an excellent one to conduct on-line in a distance-learning situation. The complexity of the question about eradicating violence can be examined in much greater depth, along with a number of other issues related to group functioning, values, etc.

Following is the basic design for the on-line activity:

Goals

In addition to those listed for the face-to-face activity, the goals may be expanded to include encouraging participants to challenge current paradigms, to think globally as well as domestically, and to examine their individual values about human nature and the environment. The facilitator may add other goals that are appropriate to the specific learning situation.

Group Size

The group size is more flexible; more than thirty participants can be accommodated easily. There can be more than five subgroups, and the subgroups can have as many as ten members each. In this case the task of reaching consensus is made more difficult and more time consuming.

Time Required

The activity may be conducted over several days or several weeks, depending on how the facilitator chooses to use the design, the needs and composition of the participant group, and other factors. The author generally conducts it over several weeks.

Materials

Each participant must have access to a computer with appropriate peripherals and software. The participants must be connected via a network such as Netscape so that they can gain access to virtual rooms in which they can converse with one another. They should also have access to a means of asynchronous interaction such as newsgroups or a listserv.

On-Line Instructions for Participants (Process)

The facilitator posts the following instructions on-line. Note that the on-line activity has extra steps that do not appear in the face-to-face version:

- Your assignment is to participate in a group simulation, spending as much time as needed on-line in a virtual room deliberating the question proposed in the simulation. You are expected to be genuine, honest, and sincere in stating the truth as you see it. When stating your opinions, you should feel free to cite materials you have read as well as your own work and life experience.

- Be sure to manage your time well so that you can complete the assigned task with a high level of integrity and an equally high level of precision in your deliberation and dialogue. Yet another challenge for you and your fellow group members is to work together effectively as a team.

The Situation

For some time now the President of the United States has been working on the possibility of eradicating violence worldwide. After receiving a great deal of information from various interest groups—politicians, educators, philosophers, social scientists, and psychologists—the President has come to believe that it is possible to create societies organized on a world view of *peace and partnership* rather than *violence and dominance.*

The President further believes that it is time to change basic social organizations accordingly, starting with those in the U.S., in order to facilitate this paradigm shift. However, a number of scholars have advised the President that we human beings may never be able to change our culture of violence if we believe that war is ever justified or "just." Therefore, the President has decided to appoint several councils across the nation composed of sensible people to determine if they believe that the desired paradigm shift is viable: *Is it, in fact, possible to eradicate violence worldwide?*

You have been appointed to one of these councils. As you and the other council members grapple with this question, you will want to consider some of the conflicting views that have been presented to the President:

- It is impossible to eradicate violence in a competitive world in which resources are limited, in which human beings do not live virtuously, and in which they continue to believe in the notion of "just war."

- Any individual or group has the right to defend itself and consequently the right to fight if attacked by others. This fighting is a kind of war, even if only on a small scale.

- Human-rights violations warrant a "just war," even if the war must be conducted on a global scale.

- Violence begets violence. If we justify it in any situation, it will reverberate in subsequent situations when victims retaliate.

- Violence of any kind is not without consequence.

- If we continue our violent ways, we will bring about our own annihilation, because we have the power to destroy all of humanity with atomic warfare.

- We have no chance of eradicating violence if we do not address the issues that lead to it.

- Eradicating violence can only occur as a consequence of deep internal and spiritual development of human beings who commit to a radical shift in the way they relate to one another.

In addition, you will want to consider any related questions, such as these: Can there be universal agreement on what human rights are? Can a world ethic be established?

The Task

Phase 1

Your council is to discuss the question thoroughly from all perspectives; it is extremely important that all members offer their personal views. You must come to your conclusion by consensus, meaning that *all members must be able to live with the decision.* You also must give your rationale.

The Question: Is it possible to eradicate violence worldwide?

Phase 2

At the conclusion of the consensus/deliberation period, your council chooses a representative to post your position and rationale on-line in a news group, for example, so that the other councils can read them. If your council was unable to reach consensus, your representative posts a review of the various positions discussed.

After the postings are complete, you and the other councils will review one another's postings, raising and answering questions. Each individual council member is expected to read and respond to all postings. However, the time that you personally devote to this part of the activity should not be more than about an hour. Be sure to read everyone's ideas carefully, building on them if you wish.

Phase 3

After the review period, the individual councils reconvene on-line to determine if they wish to alter their original positions based on issues raised during the dialogue with other councils. The final product from each council is an on-line posting of a position report addressed to the President's delegate (the facilitator).

The facilitator posts an on-line evaluation of each presentation and questions each council about its position. This evaluation concentrates on the quality of the council's rationale for its position and the quality of the process by which it came to that position.

Submitted by Michele Stimac.

Michele Stimac, Ed.D., is a professor in the Graduate School of Education and Psychology at Pepperdine University in Culver City, California. She received the Luckman Distinguished Professor Award in 1995, a distinction held for five years. A member of the team that created Pepperdine's first doctorate, Dr. Stimac teaches courses in leadership and management of human resources and serves as chairperson for doctoral dissertations. In the recently developed educational technology concentration of the doctoral program, she teaches the above courses on-line as well as face-to-face. She is an advocate of incorporating technology across the curriculum. Dr. Stimac has published in the areas of leadership, values, career development, peace education, conflict management, and consensus building.

COUNCILS TO THE PRESIDENT
SITUATION SHEET

For some time now the President of the United States has been working on the possibility of eradicating violence worldwide. After receiving a great deal of information from various interest groups—politicians, educators, philosophers, social scientists, and psychologists—the President has come to believe that it is possible to create societies organized on a world view of *peace and partnership* rather than *violence and dominance.*

The President further believes that it is time to change basic social organizations accordingly, starting with those in the U.S., in order to facilitate this paradigm shift. However, a number of scholars have advised the President that we human beings may never be able to change our culture of violence if we believe that war is ever justified or "just." Therefore, the President has decided to appoint several councils across the nation composed of sensible people to determine if they believe that the desired paradigm shift is viable: *Is it, in fact, possible to eradicate violence worldwide?*

You have been appointed to one of these councils. As you and the other council members grapple with this question, you will want to consider some of the conflicting views that have been presented to the President:

- It is impossible to eradicate violence in a competitive world in which resources are limited, in which human beings do not live virtuously, and in which they continue to believe in the notion of "just war."

- Any individual or group has the right to defend itself and consequently the right to fight if attacked by others. This fighting is a kind of war, even if only on a small scale.

- Human-rights violations warrant a "just war," even if the war must be conducted on a global scale.

- Violence begets violence. If we justify it in any situation, it will reverberate in subsequent situations when victims retaliate.

- Violence of any kind is not without consequence.

- If we continue our violent ways, we will bring about our own annihilation, because we have the power to destroy all of humanity with atomic warfare.

- We have no chance of eradicating violence if we do not address the issues that lead to it.

- Eradicating violence can only occur as a consequence of deep internal and spiritual development of human beings who commit to a radical shift in the way they relate to one another.

In addition, you will want to consider any related questions, such as these: Can there be universal agreement on what human rights are? Can a world ethic be established?

COUNCILS TO THE PRESIDENT
TASK SHEET

Your council is to discuss the question thoroughly from all perspectives; it is extremely important that all members offer their personal views. You must come to your conclusion by consensus, meaning that *all members must be able to live with the decision*. Afterward you will be asked to give your rationale.

The Question: Is it possible to eradicate violence worldwide?

Discussion Notes:

Our Answer:

Our Rationale:

606. NEW-MEMBER WELCOME: EXPERIMENTING WITH INDIVIDUAL, PAIR, AND GROUP-CONSENSUS TASKS

Goals

- To encourage participants to explore the differences between individual work, work done in collaboration with partners, and group work.

- To offer participants an opportunity to practice decision making by consensus.

Group Size

Three to six ongoing work teams of at least four members each.

Time Required

Approximately one hour.

Materials

- Fifty 3" x 5" or 4" x 6" index cards for each participant. (In step 1 each participant is given thirty index cards, but more are needed during later steps.)

- A pencil for each participant.

Physical Setting

A large room in which the teams can work without disturbing one another. Each team needs to have a table and movable chairs.

Process

1. The facilitator gives each participant thirty index cards and a pencil and explains the first task:

   "For the first task in this activity, you'll be working by yourself. Assume that your team is about to gain three new members. Your task is to create a checklist of things that you and your fellow teammates could do to *make these three people's entry into your team as successful as possible*. For this task, assume that you have everything available that you might need in terms of budget, resources, and information.

   "To create the checklist of items, write one action idea only on each index card. Write legibly, because your teammates will be reading your ideas. Write as many ideas as you can in the time you're given. You'll have five minutes when I say 'go.'"

   The facilitator answers questions about the task and then says "go." (Five minutes.)

2. After five minutes the participants are told to stop writing. Each participant is asked to choose a partner from his or her team. (If a team has an odd number of members, one trio may be formed.) The facilitator tells the pairs about the second task:

   "Share your ideas with your partner. As a result of this sharing, you should combine similar ideas, identify and discard duplicate ideas, and add any important ideas that you can think of. You'll have ten minutes when I say 'go.'"

   The facilitator answers questions about the task and then says "go." Additional index cards are distributed as necessary. (Ten minutes.)

3. After ten minutes the facilitator asks the participants to stop writing. The participants are instructed to assemble into their intact work groups. The facilitator gives each group a flip chart and a felt-tipped marker and explains the work-group task:

   "Go through all of the cards. When I say 'go,' you'll have fifteen minutes to make several team decisions, using consensus as your decision-making method:

   ■ Identify and discard duplicates.

   ■ Organize and categorize the remaining items.

   ■ Physically arrange them into columns on your table, assigning a heading to each column.

- Write the name of each heading on a new index card, and place the heading card at the top of the column for that category.

The facilitator answers questions about the task, says 'go,' and monitors the groups' activities. Additional index cards are distributed as necessary. (Fifteen minutes.)

4. The facilitator reconvenes the total group and leads a concluding discussion:

- What was your reaction to the individual work? To the work with a partner? To the work done in your group?

- How would you compare the products of your individual work, work with a partner, and work with your whole group?

- How did the process of consensus differ from working on your own and with a partner?

- What has this experience taught you about the value of working alone, working with a partner, and working with your whole group? Under what conditions is each of these methods most appropriate?

- What has this experience taught you about consensus? Its advantages? Its disadvantages?

- As a result of participating in this activity, what might you do differently when working on your own, with a partner, or with your whole group? What might you do differently when your group uses consensus decision making?

(Fifteen to twenty minutes.)

Variations

- A fifth step may be added in which the teams reconvene and each chooses three to five priority items from its categories. (The team members select the cards from those on the table.)

- The facilitator may ask the teams to report their priorities (from variation 1) to the total group. Then the total group could choose five priorities from all those reported. The processing would include questions about the advantages and disadvantages of working and achieving consensus in a large, heterogeneous group.

- The task may be changed to reflect an issue that each team is concerned about and may include action planning to address that issue.

- The teams may be asked to share how they used their individual and pair ideas when they approached the task in the whole team.

Submitted by Andrew Kimball.

Andrew Kimball is the founder and one of the principals of Qube Learning, LLC, an international team of veteran salespeople, sales managers, and performance specialists focused on helping clients develop sustainable, successful, values-based sales cultures. Mr. Kimball has worked with clients in over fifteen countries in Europe, North Africa, Asia, and South America. Before founding Qube Learning, Mr. Kimball was the national director of sales and marketing for the Financial Advisory Services division of Coopers & Lybrand, LLP. In addition, he has held executive sales and sales management positions with Bank of America and Citicorp. At both banks, Mr. Kimball created and trained highly successful financial services sales forces. Mr. Kimball holds an M.S. in international economics from American University in Washington, D.C., and a B.S. in economics and linguistics from the University of Maryland.

607. INNOVATIVE MEETINGS: CREATIVE COMMUNICATION TOOLS

Goals

- To learn about some new and innovative types of meetings.
- To decide which meeting style is most effective in a given situation.

Group Size

Up to thirty people, in subgroups of five to ten.

Time Required

Forty-five minutes to one and one-half hours.

Materials

- A newsprint flip chart and markers for the facilitator.
- An overhead projector and a transparency of the Innovative Meetings Description Sheet.
- One copy of the Innovative Meetings Description Sheet for each participant.
- One copy of the Innovative Meetings Scenario Sheet for each participant.
- One copy of the Innovative Meetings Answer Key Sheet for the facilitator.

Physical Setting

A room that can accommodate all subgroups without interference.

Process

1. The facilitator begins the session by saying that information is the greatest human need during times of great change. People must learn to meet and communicate in new ways to fill the gap.

2. The facilitator then describes the activity as a way for participants to learn about some innovative meeting styles that could potentially help them to communicate more effectively and to craft the most effective types of meetings to get the results they want. (Five minutes.)

3. The facilitator displays the Innovative Meetings Description Sheet on the overhead projector and reviews the sheet. (The overhead may remain on display throughout the activity or copies may be handed out to all participants for reference.) (Five minutes.)

4. The facilitator divides the participants into subgroups of five to ten members each, hands out copies of the Innovative Meetings Scenario Sheet to each person, and instructs each group to work together to decide the most appropriate style from the Innovative Meetings Description Sheet to fit each scenario. The facilitator says that each group must provide a rationale for its decisions and says that they will have fifteen minutes to complete the task. (Twenty minutes.)

5. After fifteen minutes, the facilitator checks to see whether all groups are finished and allows more time if necessary. The large group reconvenes to report the results of the subgroup sessions, which the facilitator records on the flip chart in a format such as the following:

	Group A Choices	Group B Choices	Group C Choices
Scenario			
#1			
#2			

(Ten to fifteen minutes.)

6. After all groups have reported their results for each scenario, the facilitator leads a discussion of the rationale behind using each particular type of meeting, asking the group to provide pros and cons of using it, and giving the "best" answers and rationale from the Innovative Meetings Answer Key Sheet. (Ten minutes.)

7. The facilitator concludes by stressing the importance of using the appropriate type of meeting to achieve the desired results, using the following questions as discussion starters:

■ What was easy about this activity? What was difficult?

■ What insights have you had about new types of meetings? About fitting the meetings to the situation?

- How do these meetings compare to those with which you are currently involved?

- What is one thing you can do differently in regard to meetings at your place of work?

(Ten to fifteen minutes.)

Variations

- Participants may be asked to brainstorm other situations from their own experiences that called for an innovative meeting style, and the group can suggest the appropriate style to use.

- With smaller groups, the entire activity may be done through group discussion led by the facilitator.

Submitted by M.K. Key and Jennifer Nordloh.

M.K. Key, Ph.D., is a licensed psychologist and owns her own consulting firm, Key Associates LLC. She was most recently vice president of the Center for Continuous Improvement at Quorum Health Resources, Inc. In her twenty-five-year tenure in the health-care field, she has written and spoken about leadership, human and organization development, mediation, communication, creativity, and corporate celebration. She serves as an adjunct professor in the Department of Human and Organization Development at Vanderbilt University.

Jennifer Nordloh is an intern at Quorum Health Resources and a graduate student in the Department of Human and Organizational Development at Vanderbilt University.

INNOVATIVE MEETINGS DESCRIPTION SHEET

A. *Ask Me Meetings* (Leebov & Scott, 1990): Basic question-and-answer sessions.

B. *CEO Assembly "Viewpoint Sessions"* (O'Donnell, 1992): Meetings with a large number of participants to allow individuals to voice concerns, raise questions, and share ideas with the CEO of the organization.

C. *Greenhouse Meetings* (Leebov & Scott, 1990): Meetings held to tackle difficult problems and to come up with innovative solutions that managers are responsible for implementing.

D. *Marathon Meetings* (Leebov & Scott, 1990): Meetings held to eliminate the cycle of repeating the content from previous meetings by keeping participants at the meeting until a decision has been reached.

E. *Problem-Finding Meetings* (Beckhard & Pritchard, 1992): Less structured meetings held to identify problems and issues rather than to develop specific action plans.

F. *Results Review Meetings* (Leebov & Scott, 1990): Meetings in which specific results are presented as a basis for drawing conclusions and planning for the future.

G. *Sound Off Meetings* (Leebov & Scott, 1990): Meetings to allow participants time to "vent" their feelings, with the following guidelines: no name calling, participation by all, listening to others, and accepting others' feelings.

H. *Vertical Meetings* (Kriegel & Patler, 1991): Brief meetings held without chairs, i.e., standing up.

I. *Walking Meetings* (J. Bingham & P. Miles, personal communication, 1992): Meetings that involve movement or exercise and that typically cause decisions to be made more quickly and creatively.

J. *Workout Meetings* (P. Block, personal communication, 1993): Longer meetings focused on the evaluation of organizational practices and the elimination of unnecessary work.

INNOVATIVE MEETINGS SCENARIO SHEET

1. The situation at work has been extremely stressful all week. You have been unable to meet with a colleague to discuss the recycling project you are supposed to be working on together. Your colleague has said that he/she has little time to meet at the office. How can you get the project rolling?

2. The Accounting Department has been briefed on its new mission statement. How the mission will be accomplished has not been addressed, and you and other members of the department have some questions regarding your roles in furthering the mission. The head of the department seems the most logical source for clarification and guidance. How can you meet with him/her?

3. You are one of four managers at a community grocery store who have received feedback about and noticed a decrease in customer satisfaction. There has also been a higher than normal level of employee turnover at the store. All four of you agree that these are the most critical problems facing the store, but you have made no plans to alleviate them. How can you meet with the other managers to propose solutions?

4. You and other employees in the Purchasing Department at Parkview Hospital spend much of your time completing what seems to be useless paperwork and very little time on actual projects. Your CEO has determined that in order to save time, the number of suppliers must be reduced, with only those of highest quality being kept. Although it may take a long period of time, the CEO would like to gather all of Parkview's employees to determine which suppliers should be kept. What type of meeting should be called?

5. The Board of Directors at Aken Bank has been occupied with "business as usual" and has not had any pressing issues to deal with. Because of this, the Board has not met for over six weeks. The chairperson for the Board believes that she should call a meeting, if only to increase group cohesion and identify specific issues and projects to improve the quality of service to customers. Because there is no need for immediate action, what type of meeting should be called?

6. Members of a manufacturing firm have begun work for the day and the factory floor is full of activity. Administrators must meet with the factory workers briefly to let them know some information that would normally have been published in the company's newsletter, which will be quite late this month. Unfortunately, there is not a large enough room available to accommodate all the employees at once. What type of meeting would work in this situation?

7. Gossip has been a problem within M.T. Consulting. Many people have felt hurt or been upset about certain rumors, but nothing has been done to address the problem. Some members of the firm believe that there should be a meeting to allow people to vent their resentment, but they are uncertain how to be sure that everyone participates in a professional manner. What type of meeting might work in this situation?

8. The owner of a restaurant chain has prepared annual reports on profit, marketing results, new positions, promotions, and the results of a customer survey about new menu items and overall satisfaction. These reports must be shared with all restaurant managers and discussed in order to plan for the next year. What type of meeting should the owner call?

9. Matrix Marketing's management team has discussed the acquisition of a smaller firm for several months. If they do not make a decision soon, the smaller company is in danger of being taken over by another marketing firm. So much time is being spent discussing the potential acquisition that other important projects have been ignored. What type of meeting should be called?

10. The CEO of West Pharmaceutical wants to develop a plan for a major restructuring of the organization. He would like input from other members of the company's staff before taking any action. What type of meeting should he call?

INNOVATE MEETINGS ANSWER KEY SHEET

Meeting	Choice of Styles	Rationale
1	I, H	Time constraints
2	A	Questions for the CEO
3	C, E, or J	Critical problems to solve
4	B, J	Administrative issues to be resolved
5	E	Problem identification (action not urgently needed)
6	H	Space problem; need for speed and brevity
7	G	Need to vent feelings
8	F	Review of results
9	D	Need for haste and focus
10	B	CEO needs input

References

Beckhard, R., & Pritchard, W. (1992). *Changing the essence: The art of creativity and leading fundamental change in organizations.* San Francisco: Jossey-Bass.

Kriegel, R.J., & Patler, L. (1991). *If it ain't broke. . .break it!* New York: Warner.

Leebov, W., & Scott, G. (1990). *Health care managers in transition.* San Francisco, CA: Jossey-Bass.

O'Donnell, R.L. (1992). *Nurturing leadership.* Little Rock, AR: August House.

608. No Strings Attached: Learning How Groups Organize To Complete Tasks

---

Goal

- To give participants an opportunity to experience how group members organize themselves to accomplish a task.

Group Size

Three or four subgroups of five to eight members each.

Time Required

One hour and five to fifteen minutes.

Materials

- A copy of the No Strings Attached Prework Sheet for each subgroup.
- A copy of the No Strings Attached Answer Sheet for each subgroup.
- A copy of the No Strings Attached Observer Sheet for each subgroup's observer.
- Two pieces of string, each sixty inches long, for each subgroup.
- A pencil for each subgroup's observer.
- A clipboard or other portable writing surface for each subgroup's observer.

Physical Setting

A large room with plenty of space to separate the subgroups so that they do not disturb one another. If possible, furniture should be moved against the walls and out of the participants' way.

Process

1. The facilitator assembles subgroups of five to eight members each and asks each subgroup to select one member to serve as an observer. Each subgroup is given a copy of the prework sheet and two strings. Each observer is given a copy of the observer sheet, a pencil, and a clipboard or other portable writing surface. (Five minutes.)

2. Each subgroup is instructed to connect two persons with the strings, as indicated in step 1 on the prework sheet. The facilitator monitors this step, ensuring that people are connected with strings as intended. (Five minutes.)

3. The facilitator announces the task for each subgroup:

   "Without breaking the strings or tampering with any knot, untangle the two people from each other. This is a group task, so anyone in your group except the observer is free to help in any way."

   If the participants ask questions, the facilitator repeats the task and recommends soliciting help from the other subgroup members. After stating that the subgroups have twenty minutes, the facilitator asks them to begin. (Five minutes.)

4. After twenty minutes, the facilitator asks the subgroups to stop working on the task. Each subgroup is given a copy of the answer sheet. (To save time and to ensure that the participants do not become fixated on the task, the facilitator may demonstrate the solution with two participants.) (Twenty-five minutes.)

5. The facilitator reconvenes the total group and asks the observers to report: First the observers take turns reporting their answers to item 1 on the observer sheet, then item 2, and so on. (Ten to fifteen minutes.)

6. The facilitator leads a concluding discussion based on the following questions:

   - How do you feel about what your group achieved or did not achieve? What helped or hindered?

   - How do you feel about how your group organized itself to accomplish the task?

   - If you were to try a similar task again, what would you do differently?

   - What parallels do you see between what happened in your group and what happens in other groups that you belong to?

- What have you learned about how groups organize that you can use in the future to help accomplish group tasks?

(Fifteen to twenty minutes.)

Variations

- The task may be completed in pairs, with one observer per pair.
- The subgroups may be asked to compete to finish first. The facilitator would then process what the effect was of the competition.

Submitted by Jeyakar Vedamanickam.

Jeyakar Vedamanickam is on the senior faculty at the Hindustan Aeronautics Ltd. (HAL) Staff College in Bangalore, India. He combines his expertise as a plant engineer with experience as a trainer to offer a variety of training programs. Mr. Vedamanickam's areas of interest include creativity and innovation, value engineering, decision analysis, team building through adventure experiences, and computer-simulated business gaming. He is a member of Mensa and has conducted more than 120 workshops on creativity and innovation for diverse groups of managers and designers.

No Strings Attached Prework Sheet

Instructions: Tie the two strings to connect two volunteers of your group as shown in the figure below. *Be careful not to tie the strings too tightly around the hands.*

Volunteer 1

Right Hand   Left Hand

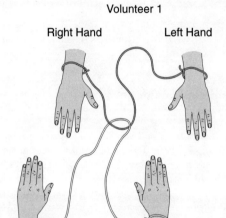

Left Hand   Right Hand

Volunteer 2

No Strings Attached Answer Sheet

Step 1

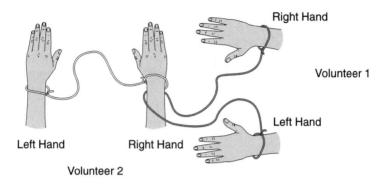

Right Hand

Volunteer 1

Left Hand

Left Hand

Right Hand

Volunteer 2

Step 2

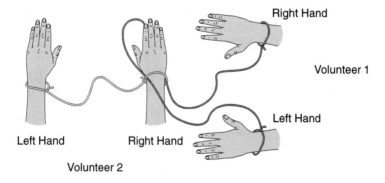

Right Hand

Volunteer 1

Left Hand

Left Hand

Right Hand

Volunteer 2

Step 3

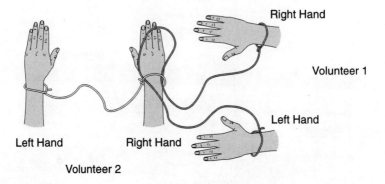

Right Hand

Volunteer 1

Left Hand

Left Hand

Right Hand

Volunteer 2

Step 4

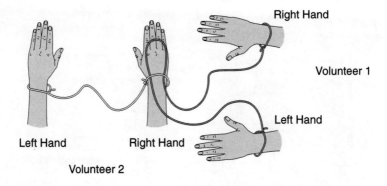

Right Hand

Volunteer 1

Left Hand

Left Hand

Right Hand

Volunteer 2

No Strings Attached Observer Sheet

Instructions: Observe the members of your group as they strive to untangle the two people attached by strings and write answers to the following questions:

1. How are the group members organizing themselves to accomplish the task?

2. What kind of leadership is evolving? How does it evolve? How does the leadership affect task accomplishment? How does it change as the members keep working on the task?

3. How would you describe the communication between group members? What helps their communication? What hinders it?

4. What difficulties arise? How do the members deal with those difficulties?

609. ALLIED CIRCUITS: AN EMPOWERMENT ROLE PLAY

Goals

- To demonstrate the difficulty of putting empowerment into practice.

- To demonstrate some of the different definitions and viewpoints about empowerment.

- To allow open discussion and problem solving about what empowerment means in an organizational setting.

Group Size

Thirty to forty participants in subgroups of six to eight participants. There are five roles in the case study, a "company trainer" to facilitate the discussion, and one or two observers.

Time Required

Approximately one and one-half hours.

Materials

- One copy of the Allied Circuits Situation Sheet for each participant.

- One set of the Allied Circuits Role Sheets for each subgroup.

- One set of the Allied Circuits Role Sheets for each observer.

- One copy of the Allied Circuits Observer Sheet for each observer.

- One copy of the Allied Circuits Discussion Questions Sheet for each participant.

- Pencils or pens for participants.

- A newsprint flip chart, masking tape, and felt-tipped markers for each subgroup.

Physical Setting

A room large enough so that all subgroups can work without disturbing one another. A round table for each group works well.

Process

1. The facilitator gives a brief overview of the goals of the activity and says:

   "Whenever a group of people comes together in the workplace, there are as many perceptions of the task as there are people, because individuals have their personal goals, aspirations, and agendas. Other factors outside the workplace also influence how a group works together. Only by discussing their different perceptions of the group's goals can people work synergistically to produce high-quality results.

   "The case study we are about to use is based on an actual situation in which the individuals had a clear organizational mission but different views as to how to attain that mission. By considering how each of the people views his or her goal, we will see how real organizations deal with conflicts and that managing relationships among people is the key to high performance."

2. The facilitator distributes copies of the Allied Circuits Situation Sheet to each participant and gives them time to read it. (Five minutes.)

3. The facilitator forms subgroups with six to eight members each and distributes one set of Allied Circuits Role Sheets to each group, asking that one person in each group volunteer to play the role of "company trainer" to facilitate the discussion.

4. Next, five members of each group are asked to choose one role-play sheet at random and then to read their roles carefully and plan what they will say in the upcoming discussion. Additional group members are designated as observers of the process and given copies of the Allied Circuits Observer Sheet and one set of role sheets per observer. (Five minutes.)

5. The facilitator instructs the designated "company trainers" to lead a discussion, with each subgroup member in role, attempting to reach consensus on the following question:

   In a hierarchical organization structure, what does empowerment mean?

   "Company trainers" post the definitions on newsprint. (Fifteen minutes.)

6. When fifteen minutes have passed, the facilitator asks observers to report their observations to their subgroups, after which the "company trainer" will lead a discussion of the observations. (Fifteen minutes.)

7. After fifteen minutes, the facilitator distributes the Allied Circuits Discussion Questions Sheet to each person and asks the groups to answer the questions from an organizational perspective, keeping each individual's perspective in mind, but no longer playing the roles. (Twenty minutes.)

8. The facilitator calls the total group together and asks them to share their answers. After all groups have reported, the facilitator asks the following questions:

   ■ What reactions did you have to your role? To others' roles?

   ■ What are your current definitions of empowerment?

   ■ How have they changed as a result of this activity.

   ■ How can you apply what you have learned to your own organization? What modifications may you need to make because of your back-home organizational structure?

   (Fifteen minutes.)

Variations

■ If participants are hesitant to role play, each can be given all five roles to read, then discuss the situation and probable outcomes among themselves before answering the discussion questions.

■ Participants could be asked to consider whether any of the role descriptions sound familiar, i.e., similar to themselves or someone they know. This helps participants to apply the learning to their own work environments.

■ Intact work groups that are "stuck" can use the activity, openly discussing the roles each plays in the current situation.

■ Observers can be assigned to observe the consensus-seeking process, asking questions such as the following:

   ■ Note times when the group reaches consensus or when someone attempts to have the group reach consensus. What are the results each time?

   ■ Note times when the group reaches an impasse. What are the reasons for this?

■ For a shorter activity, step 7 can be eliminated.

Submitted by Barbara Pate Glacel and Emile A. Robert, Jr.

Barbara Pate Glacel, Ph.D., *is CEO of VIMA International. Dr. Glacel consults in executive and organization development for organizations such as Lockheed Martin Corporation, The MITRE Corporation, NASA, MCI Communications, and Atlantic Richfield Company in the United States, Europe, Africa, and the Pacific Rim. She is an adjunct faculty member at the Center for Creative Leadership, and a member of the Alumni Board of Directors of the College of William and Mary. She is co-author of* Light Bulbs for Leaders: A Guide Book for Team Learning *(John Wiley & Sons, 1996).*

Emile A. Robert, Jr., Ph.D., *is COO of VIMA International. He has over twenty years of experience in human resource development and administration. He is an acknowledged authority in organizational development, personnel assessment and evaluation, forecasting human resource needs, and professional development. Dr. Robert works with clients across the United States as well as in Scotland, New Zealand, Southeast Asia, and South Africa. He is an adjunct faculty member at the Center for Creative Leadership. He is co-author of* Light Bulbs for Leaders: A Guide Book for Team Learning *(John Wiley & Sons, 1996).*

ALLIED CIRCUITS SITUATION SHEET

The forty-five members of the Marketing Department at Allied Circuits have been empowered by the CEO to create and project Allied's image in the world-wide market, and they have focused all their attention on meeting the needs of their clients, both internally and externally. Internally, representatives of the various product lines of Allied Circuits have placed high demands on the Marketing Department: display advertising, direct mail campaigns, public relations efforts, image management worldwide, speech writing, conferences, and media events, all with tight deadlines. Marketing efforts have to be so well coordinated that the company seems to "speak with one voice"—not a small task for forty-five empowered employees!

The department is having a difficult time right now and people do not seem to be communicating well as they respond to the demands of a new CEO and attempts to project the changing culture and marketing focus of Allied. New, talented marketing experts have been hired recently and are being integrated with the old-timers.

The *Marketing Vice President* has taken the department through two re-organizations in the past year, although these changes have taken place on direct orders of the CEO. The Vice President is convinced that the latest proposed reorganization, moving department members physically to join the product teams they represent, will help Allied to meet client needs more effectively, but some other members of the department are resentful.

The *Company Trainer* has convened all forty-five members of the department for a day-long session. Three levels of employees are present: executive, managerial, and subordinates. Some concerns about the safety of free expression have been aired, but for the most part, people feel empowered to speak their minds.

It is obvious from the beginning that the Vice President is angry and defensive, although she has tried to control her feelings. She expresses herself by saying, "How can I get you folks on board? I asked my direct reports what they thought of this new structure several weeks ago, but I was under direct orders from the CEO to put this new plan into action to support the product teams."

The *Manager of International Relations,* responsible for crisis communication worldwide and an Allied employee for less than a year, replies, "No one asked whether we wanted to move our product-support people out into the product areas. We should have a say in where we sit and how we work. Who decided that we'll be more effective if we move? I can't function in an organization that makes arbitrary decisions!"

The new *Communication Specialist*, who had formerly been a college intern with Allied, adds, "I came to work for Allied because I thought that the employees were empowered. I should be able to tell my manager how I want to work and what I'm going to do. I wouldn't have taken the job here if I had known that I would be bossed around like this."

By now, the Vice President is seething. She had asked all her staff about the proposed move and they had discussed the pros and cons over a period of several weeks. The fact that the managers had not consulted with their people had caused all this dissension, but she struggled to remain quiet, as the company trainer had urged.

Then the *Public Relations Manager*, who has recently been placed on probation for a drop in performance, speaks up. A fifteen-year veteran of Allied and still looking like a Hippie from the Sixties, the manager says, "Our new CEO came in under the banner of empowerment. That's a refreshing change from the old style around here. Things had been getting better, but this is reverting to an autocratic style, and I don't like it."

The *Marketing Manager*, who rarely speaks up in meetings, has become exasperated and speaks up, "Come on, everyone! Our boss is the boss for a reason. She asks for our input, but she alone has to make the hard calls. There are good reasons for us to move some of our staff into the product areas."

The *International Relations Manager* flashes back with hostility: "It's the process I don't like! We need to open up the question of reorganization for discussion by all of us!"

As the Vice President ponders what she can do next and the company trainer keeps trying to have the group discuss the department's successes and weaknesses, the real question seems to be: *In a hierarchical organization, what does empowerment mean?*

ALLIED CIRCUITS ROLE SHEET ONE

Marketing Vice President

You have been Marketing Vice President for Allied Circuits for one year. You were hired by a CEO who believes in empowerment, and you have been helping the department to change from the more autocratic style of your predecessor, a hard-line old-time public relations mogul, known for his marketing prowess and his no-nonsense management style. You are the only woman on the Senior Management Committee. Your high standards demand a lot from the managers who report to you, and at the same time you need their support to improve the department's performance.

You inherited a staff that functioned in organizational silos, with competition as the motivating force. You realized that this structure was not conducive to improved internal relations. When relationships among the managers deteriorated despite your efforts, you bit the bullet, fired one dysfunctional manager and moved two others into individual contributor positions. That reorganization was barely complete when you had your annual review. The president said:

"You're too patient with your people. You need to be stronger and more decisive. Your people aren't performing up to the standards we expect. In fact, Allied's marketing efforts are behind the industry norm. You must work on that."

You were stunned by this evaluation! So you immediately called your new staff leaders together and told them that in order to improve their responsiveness and performance, the product-line marketing managers would move their offices into the various product-line areas. At the time, no opposition was raised, but now a meeting has been called by your direct reports with a company trainer facilitating the meeting.

You feel blind-sided, angry, and defensive about the way they have handled the situation, because you believe that you initially empowered your direct reports to tell you their feelings and to make suggestions by asking them their reactions to this new move. The company trainer has urged you to remain quiet and to listen to what people have to say, and you are trying to do this to keep matters from getting more out of hand, but you are not sure that you can know how to proceed after you have heard what your employees have to say. *You wonder: What else do they want me to do? I don't run a democracy! How can I keep from exploding and damaging my relationships with my subordinates?*

Stay in role during the discussion, and do not share your instructions with anyone else.

ALLIED CIRCUITS ROLE SHEET TWO

International Relations Manager

You joined Allied Circuits three months ago after holding a media support job at Telcom, Inc., a much larger company, for several years. You know more about publicity and marketing than most of the people here and wish that more people would listen to your suggestions. Compared to how Telcom's marketing department functions, Allied's is in the Dark Ages.

Your job is very important. Whenever there is a crisis in Allied's global operations, you are called to consult about the situation. You are quick to respond and have done a good job protecting Allied's corporate image worldwide.

Because you are the sort of person who responds quickly, you are impatient now with what is happening in the department. The Vice President has bungled internal communications about the move of product-support people to their product areas. You would have done it differently and wonder what the Vice President was thinking! Why didn't she ask you, a person with much more experience, how you would have moved product people out into the product groups? Although you are not directly involved in any of the upcoming moves, your experience at Telcom has given you some ideas on how the needed changes can be accomplished.

You wish that others, especially the Vice President, would consult you because you have a lot of knowledge and experience and can handle most situations very well. You believe that empowerment consists of knowing the resources of your people and using their expertise. *You wonder: How can I get others to listen to me and view me as the expert that I am, starting with this meeting?*

Stay in role during the discussion, and do not share your instructions with anyone else.

ALLIED CIRCUITS ROLE SHEET THREE

Communication Specialist

You are a bright, energetic twenty-two-year old who has recently graduated with honors from the Communications School at Kenton University. You previously served as an undergraduate marketing intern for Allied and were offered a full-time job after graduation, which you eagerly accepted.

You were always known at the university for your ambition and your quick grasp of new information. Because of your creativity and talent, the internal clients at Allied love you. You are quick to volunteer for new assignments and extra work. You are determined to be on the fast track and to keep anything from holding you back! You believe that you are in control of your own destiny, and you see empowerment as allowing people to control their own work. You believe that there is a bright future ahead if you do not let any obstacles stand in the way. *You wonder: How can I demonstrate my high potential and move firmly onto the fast track during this meeting?*

Stay in role during the discussion, and do not share your instructions with anyone else.

ALLIED CIRCUITS ROLE SHEET FOUR

Public Relations Manager

You have been with Allied Circuits for fifteen years doing traditional public relations work for the corporate staff. A product of the free-wheeling Sixties, you moved from job to job for the first fifteen years of your career, finally settling in the high-tech industry, where people could be themselves. You enjoy dressing casually among your more conservative peers. You have kept your hair long and somewhat unkempt and wear flashy jewelry as a symbol of your refusal to run with the pack.

Unfortunately, some of your coworkers, the Vice President of Marketing, and a few clients and suppliers do not accept your unusual appearance. Others in the company have become more rigid and conservative in the past few years, so that it seems to you that some have confused appearance with performance. You do not see why you cannot be yourself both inside or outside the organization, whether meeting with coworkers, agents, suppliers, or customers alike. After all, in an empowered organization, employees ought to be able to just be themselves.

A week ago, the Vice President put you on probation, saying that your work must improve to reflect the unified voice with which Allied now seeks to present itself. You feel betrayed by this turn of events. *You wonder: Why can't an employee just be himself in a supposedly empowered environment?*

Stay in role during the discussion, and do not share your instructions with anyone else.

ALLIED CIRCUITS ROLE SHEET FIVE

Marketing Manager

You have been a steady, quiet, reliable manager in Allied's marketing department for ten years. You have survived several different vice presidents' management styles, and you genuinely like the style of the current Vice President, who knows what management responsibility is and accepts it, first consulting subordinate managers such as yourself.

You do not like to express your opinions too freely and believe that managers generally speak too much and should listen more. When you do speak up, however, people listen, because you usually make good sense.

Right now, you are annoyed because the other managers seem to be whining about the vice president's decision to move product managers to the product divisions. You believe that you were consulted and had a chance for input at the meeting when the decision was announced. Even if that were not the case, vice presidents often must make the hard calls and take the heat from above for the entire department. Empowerment does not mean that you always have your own way, but that everyone has some input. You resolve to tell the company trainer privately exactly how you feel during the next break. *You wonder: Is there any chance that my peers could be made to see the matter as I do?*

Stay in role during the discussion, and do not share your instructions with anyone else.

ALLIED CIRCUITS OBSERVER SHEET

During the role play, you are to silently observe what happens in the group. See how different members of the group perceive the situation. Note their areas of agreement and disagreement.

1. What are the different definitions of empowerment?

2. What are the different points of view about empowerment in a hierarchical organization?

3. How do the roles taken affect the viewpoints and definitions?

ALLIED CIRCUITS DISCUSSION QUESTIONS SHEET

At the end of the all-day session, the company trainer asks for volunteers to serve on a task force to work on departmental communication and internal relations. The task force is charged with developing internal systems that allow employees to be empowered while meeting high performance standards expected by management.

With your present knowledge of Allied's situation, answer the following questions:

1. How can performance problems be handled in an empowered organization?

2. What can the Marketing Department do so that empowered performers have a say in the future?

3. What is the ideal balance between complete democracy and autocratic leadership in an empowered business organization?

4. What changes should be implemented at Allied so that they practice what they preach?

5. What do they want from their vice president?

6. What does she want from her staff?

7. What procedures can be put in place to make the concept of empowerment grow and change to meet new organizational demands?

610. THE FOREST VS. THE TREES: UNDERSTANDING PREFERENCES FOR THE BIG PICTURE OR THE DETAILS

Goals

- To assist participants in becoming aware of their own and others' preferences for "the forest" (the big picture) or "the trees" (the details).

- To help participants to understand that both perspectives (the forest and the trees) are valuable in a group and that both may also cause conflict in a group.

- To help participants to understand what each type of person needs from the other in order to work together.

Group Size

Sixteen to thirty-two participants, assembled into a maximum of three "Forest" and three "Trees" teams of four to eight members each. The teams may vary in size, but there should be the same number of teams for each perspective (one Forest team and one Trees team, two Forest teams and two Trees teams, or three Forest teams and three Trees teams).

Time Required

One hour and twenty to forty minutes.

Materials

- A copy of The Forest vs. the Trees Theory Sheet for each participant.
- A copy of The Forest vs. the Trees Team-Selection Sheet for each participant.
- Several sheets of paper and a pencil for each participant.
- A clipboard or other portable writing surface for each participant.
- A flip chart and a felt-tipped marker for each team.
- A roll of masking tape for each team.

Physical Setting

A room large enough for the teams to work without disturbing one another. Movable chairs must be provided, and plenty of wall space must be available for posting newsprint.

Process

1. The facilitator introduces the goals of the activity.

2. The facilitator distributes copies of The Forest vs. the Trees Theory Sheet and discusses the content with the participants. (Five minutes.)

3. The facilitator distributes copies of The Forest vs. the Trees Team-Selection Sheet and instructs each participant to select a team—either Forest or Trees—based on the characteristics listed on this sheet. The "Forest" participants are asked to assemble in one end of the room and the "Trees" in the other. (Five minutes.)

4. The facilitator assembles the teams, making sure that there are as many Forest teams as Trees teams. The teams need not have (and probably will not have) the same numbers of members.

5. The participants are given paper, pencils, and clipboards or other portable writing surfaces. The members of each team are instructed to work individually to list what they perceive to be the behaviors of the opposite kind of team. (Forests generate perceptions of the behaviors of Trees; Trees generate perceptions of the behaviors of Forests.) (Five minutes.)

6. The facilitator gives each team a flip chart, a felt-tipped marker, and masking tape. The members of each team are asked to share their perceptions about behaviors while one member records these perceptions on the flip chart. The participants are encouraged to add any new ideas about behaviors that arise during this sharing. (Fifteen minutes.)

7. The facilitator instructs each team to choose a spokesperson to report the team's data, reassembles the entire group, and asks the spokespersons to take turns reporting. Each team's flip-chart paper is posted and stays in place so that all participants can see it during the next step. (Five to fifteen minutes; time varies depending on the number of teams reporting.)

8. The facilitator asks the teams to reassemble and to brainstorm what they want and need from the opposite kind of team when they are working together on problem-solving and planning tasks. (Forests generate wants and needs from Trees; Trees generate wants and needs from Forests).

The facilitator clarifies that each team is to appoint a recorder to write members' ideas on the flip chart. (Ten minutes.)

9. The members of each team are instructed to prioritize their top five wants and needs from the brainstormed list. (Ten minutes.)

10. The facilitator again instructs each team to choose a spokesperson to report the team's data, reassembles the entire group, and asks the spokespersons to take turns reporting. Each team's flip-chart paper is again posted and remains in place during the concluding discussion. (Five to fifteen minutes; time varies depending on the number of teams reporting.)

11. The facilitator leads a total-group discussion based on these questions:

■ What new insights do you have about the Forest perspective? About the Trees perspective?

■ How have the two perspectives and their associated behaviors led to conflict in group meetings that you have attended? How have the two perspectives and their behaviors contributed positively to group meetings?

■ How have your assumptions about the Forest perspective changed? How have your assumptions about the Trees perspective changed?

■ How will you use your new understanding of the two perspectives in future meetings? How can you share your understanding with others? What might you do differently to work better with people whose perspective is the opposite of yours?

(Twenty minutes.)

Variations

■ After step 7 the facilitator may encourage the Forest and Trees team members to ask for clarification of any perceptions of behavior that they do not understand.

■ This activity may be used with the *Myers-Briggs Type Indicator* or the Time-Management Personality Profile on page 149 in *The 1995 Annual: Volume 2, Consulting.*

■ The process described in this activity may be used for any dimension of the *Myers-Briggs Type Indicator* or another inventory on time management.

Submitted by Bonnie Jameson.

Bonnie Jameson, M.S., is a designer, trainer, and facilitator in all areas of human resource development and organization development. She is an associate professor at California State University at Hayward, California, where she teaches in the Nonprofit Management Program. Ms. Jameson consults with schools, nonprofit organizations, and businesses and has co-authored Inspiring Fabled Service *(Jossey-Bass/Pfeiffer, 1996) with Betsy Sanders. Her experiential activities have been published in the* Annual *since 1988.*

The Forest vs. the Trees Theory Sheet

Important issues can be looked at from two separate points of view: the "Forest" (or big-picture) perspective and the "Trees" (or detail) perspective. People with a Forest perspective are concerned with the future; they look at things with a wide-focus lens and generate global scenarios about what might happen. Those with a Trees perspective are concerned with immediate problems; they look at things with a narrow-focus lens and concentrate on specific details. Current research in the field of psychological type suggests that an individual generally has a strong preference for one perspective or the other and that his or her communication patterns are based on that preference.

Organizational leaders need to understand and be comfortable with both perspectives. For example, both perspectives are important in strategic planning. The visioning portion of strategic planning, which involves determining a future-oriented mission, values, and goals, requires the Forest or big-picture perspective. A team of policy makers must answer the global questions "why?" and "what?" in establishing the organization's purpose and the general means by which it will meet that purpose.

The operational portion of strategic planning, which involves determining the specific outcomes and action plans necessary to achieve the long-range goals, requires the Trees or detail perspective. The policy makers must figure out "what" tasks must be performed, "by when," and "who" is responsible for each task that contributes to achieving the long-term goals.

However, the Forest and Trees perspectives can clash and often do, leading to miscommunication, misunderstandings, interpersonal conflict, stress, ineffective meetings, and other negative results. It is important to realize that both perspectives are essential to organizational functioning and that neither is inherently superior to the other.

THE FOREST VS. THE TREES TEAM-SELECTION SHEET

Instructions: Please select the Forest perspective or the Trees perspective based on your preference for the characteristics listed below.

Trees Perspective	Forest Perspective
• Wants facts and details right away.	• Needs to understand the purpose (why something has to happen) before working on a solution.
• Prefers working on one aspect of a problem at a time.	• Needs an overview of the entire problem before discussing details.
• Prefers not to envision a possible future or scenario of the future.	• Needs to see and imagine possible scenarios for the future.
• Is bored with too much theory or abstraction.	• Wants theory to be verified.
• Wants to go directly to the action stage and implementation of a chosen solution.	• Prefers to envision how the situation will look at its best in the future before developing specific outcomes.

611. News Room:
A Group-Consensus Task

Goals

- To explore the communication processes that emerge in creating a collaborative product.

- To investigate the process of obtaining group consensus.

Group Size

A maximum of three groups with eight to ten participants per group.

Time Required

Fifty to fifty-five minutes.

Materials

- A pack of 3" x 5" index cards with "news" words written on each card for each group.

- A copy of News Room Suggested Word Options for the facilitator.

Physical Setting

A large open space. Tables and chairs for the groups are optional.

Process

1. The facilitator introduces the activity and divides the participants into groups, if need be.

2. The facilitator describes the activity: "You are the editors, writers, and producers for a news program (or news publication) and are under a strict deadline to write a fast-breaking news story on time. A news story typically

has multiple authors who must work together to produce one product. Using the information and resources available to you, you must, *as a group,* create a news story within a limited amount of time. The story will be broadcast (or goes to press) in fifteen minutes. As a group, you must select the words to be used and decide on their order of presentation within the news story." (Five minutes.)

3. Each group receives a pack of index cards with "news" words written on each card.

4. The facilitator says that the members of each group are to arrange the word cards to create the story. The group must reach consensus (at least some degree of agreement from each member) on the sequence of words in the story; it may not make decisions by majority rule or voting. Complete sentences are not necessary, but the "basics" of the story should be apparent. The group must use as many words as there are participants in the group. Words may not be used more than once. Each group is to select a spokesperson who will present its story for editorial approval at the end of the activity. The facilitator informs the group of the subject of the story and tells the members that no questions will be answered once the activity starts. (Ten minutes.)

5. As the groups work on the task, the facilitator gives time warnings. When the groups have completed the task or when the time is up, the facilitator asks for a spokesperson from each group to present its story, in turn. (Fifteen minutes plus five minutes per report).

6. The facilitator informs the groups that the producer (or editor-in-chief) says that because of new editorial priorities, the stories are too long. The groups have up to two minutes in which to eliminate three to five words from their stories.

7. When the time is up, the facilitator requests the spokespersons to present the groups' new stories. (Five minutes.)

8. The facilitator leads the group members in processing the activity. The following questions may be used:

- How did you feel as you went about this activity?
- Was it easy or difficult to reach consensus on the words in the story? Why or why not?
- What did you notice about the process as time pressures mounted? As changes had to be made?
- How does the process of a group creating a single product affect the members' communications?

- Are you currently involved in any situations in which there are multiple creators? What did this activity teach you that you could apply to those situations?

(Fifteen to twenty minutes.)

Variations

- An entire group or selected members may be designated as "mute" for the activity. To signify a mute person, tie a bandanna or scarf loosely around his or her neck or arm. Additional processing questions could include the following:

  - How was your communication impacted by being mute?

  - Were you able to contribute, or were you ignored?

  - How did you compensate for your limitations?

  - How did you have to think or act differently to communicate non-verbally?

- The words given may be pertinent to a story that is relevant to the group members, based on an issue that they are encountering.

- The re-editing task (steps 6 and 7) may be eliminated.

Submitted by Heidi Ann Campbell and Heather Jean Campbell.

Heidi Ann Campbell has worked as an experiential educator in youth camps and social-service settings. She also is a freelance writer/researcher whose work appears in publications such as Personnel Journal *and the 1997* Annual. *Her areas of research include youth values, cross-cultural communications, and generational issues.*

Heather Jean Campbell has worked as an outdoor-education instructor for a public school system and as an assistant youth-camp director, where she helped to develop and implement several environmental, adventure, and leadership-training programs. She also is a freelance researcher and writer in the areas of values, community, and communication studies.

NEWS ROOM SUGGESTED WORD OPTIONS

Earthquake: tremors, fire, buildings, collapse, shaking, people, warning, destruction, heat, bystanders, hidden, wreckage, rubble, emergency, fleeing, ambulance, broken, homeless, safety, help, no, crash, almost, forever, escape, near, around, call, above, sudden, preparation, evacuation

 Example of possible story: Tremors. No warning. Buildings collapse. People escape rubble. Bystanders help homeless. Emergency evacuation.

Search and Rescue Mission: climber, fate, snow, avalanche, helicopter, terrain, ground patrol, search, searchers, rope, leg, arm, hiking, lost, found, broken, fall, suspected, fright, delay, injuries, hope, unknown, almost, fears, continue, help, calculated, mishap, remote, planned, icy, nerves, need, ask, overnight, rescue

 Example of possible story: Climber lost overnight. Remote icy terrain. Ground patrol fears mishap. Suspected injuries. Helicopter search. Snow delays rescue. Unknown fears.

Election: opposition, winner, loser, parties, victory, unexpected, planned, votes, counted, narrow, incumbent, shakeup, recall, debate, careful, issues, results, avoided, clear, confused, challenge, victory, election, margin, defeat, decision, speech, rally, plans, announcement

 Example of possible story: Incumbent avoided debate. Issues confused. Votes counted. Opposition victory clear.

612. ENABLERS AND BARRIERS: ASSESSING YOUR TEAM

Goals

- To encourage a team to identify specific enablers and barriers that impact its effectiveness.

- To provide an opportunity for a team to recommend ways to increase its effectiveness.

Group Size

All members of a team, divided into subgroups of three to five participants each. If the team has fewer than six members, subgroups should not be formed.

Time Required

One and one-half to two and one-half hours. The time is dependent on the size of the team and the number of subgroups.

Materials

- A copy of the Enablers and Barriers Key-Factor Sheet for each participant.

- A copy of the Enablers and Barriers Force-Field Analysis Sheet for each participant.

- A pencil for each participant.

- An overhead transparency made from the Enablers and Barriers Key-Factor Sheet.

- An overhead transparency made from the Enablers and Barriers Force-Field Analysis Sheet.

- An overhead transparency made from the Enablers and Barriers Illustration of Forces.

- An overhead projector.

Physical Setting

A room large enough for the subgroups to work without disturbing one another. A table and chairs should be provided for each subgroup.

Process

1. After introducing the goals, the facilitator explains why the assessment is appropriate at this stage of the team's life:
   - If the team is just starting, the assessment will help members become aware of issues that need to be addressed.
   - If the team is mature, the assessment will help members become more effective.

   (Ten minutes.)

2. The facilitator provides an overview of the process.

3. The facilitator distributes copies of the Enablers and Barriers Key-Factor Sheet and pencils, displays the overhead transparency made from this sheet, defines the factors aloud, and answers any questions. (Five minutes.)

4. Participants are asked to select the key factor(s) they wish to examine. They may select all of them or one or more priority items. Unless the team has fewer than six members, the participants are asked to assemble into subgroups. Subgroups are assigned one or more of the key factors. (The number of factors examined by each subgroup is dependent on the number of subgroups and the number of factors selected by the group.) (Ten minutes.)

5. The facilitator distributes copies of the Enablers and Barriers Force-Field Analysis Sheet and displays the overhead transparency made from this sheet. The facilitator describes force-field analysis, explaining that, for each factor chosen, the subgroup members must identify both the forces working for the team (enablers) and those working against the team (barriers). The facilitator displays the Illustration of Forces transparency so that the participants can visualize the concept of the enablers and barriers that are pulling against each other. After ensuring that all participants understand the task, the facilitator asks the subgroups to begin. (Ten to fifteen minutes per key factor.)

6. Each subgroup brainstorms recommendations for action, building on the enablers and addressing the barriers they identified. (Five to ten minutes per key factor.)

The 1998 Annual: Volume 2, Consulting/© 1998 Jossey-Bass/Pfeiffer

7. The facilitator brings the group together and asks a spokesperson from each group to present its recommendations to the larger group. The large group is encouraged to add to the recommendations. (Up to one hour, depending on the size of the team, number of subgroups, and amount of discussion.)

8. After the final recommendations, the facilitator leads a concluding discussion by asking:

- How easy was it to identify enablers? Why?

- How easy was it to identify barriers? Why?

- Which recommendations are you most looking forward to implementing?

- How will you ensure that these recommendations will be implemented?

(Fifteen minutes.)

Variations

- The facilitator may wish to interview participants before the session begins (by telephone or face-to-face) to gather data about the enablers and barriers that impact the team's effectiveness. The data is categorized into the seven factors and provided to the subgroups.

- The activity may be continued by creating an action plan to prioritize, assign, and implement the recommendations.

- The activity may be used at the end of a team project to serve as an evaluation, identifying lessons learned.

Submitted by Karen Vander Linde.

Karen Vander Linde is the director of the Center of Excellence for Learning Systems at Coopers & Lybrand Consulting in Washington, D.C. She provides consulting services to organizations in the areas of learning systems management, assessment, design, development, delivery, and measurement. She also serves as senior facilitator for executive teams.

ENABLERS AND BARRIERS KEY-FACTOR SHEET

Following are the key factors that impact team effectiveness:

- *Communication:* Do the right people receive the right information at the right time? Do people with whom the team interacts receive information in a timely manner? Where do communication breakdowns or errors occur?

- *Common Direction/Goals:* Does the team have a clear mission? Do all team members agree on the desired outcome? Do specific tasks exist and are they completed in a timely way? Are roles and responsibilities clear?

- *Rewards and Recognition:* What are the incentives for being a member of the team? How are team members' contributions recognized? Who is rewarded? Who rewards?

- *Trust:* What trust issues or concerns exist among team members? How do team members demonstrate trust? How does the team build trust? Do nonmembers trust the team?

- *Decision Making:* How does the team make decisions? Are the right people involved in making decisions? Does the team have appropriate levels of decision-making authority?

- *Perceptions:* Does the team represent an appropriate diversity of viewpoints? What are the team members' perceptions of one another? What are nonmembers' perceptions of the team?

- *Conflict:* How does the team manage conflict? What conflicts currently exist in the team? How could conflict be managed more productively?

ENABLERS AND BARRIERS FORCE-FIELD ANALYSIS SHEET

Key Factor: _____

Forces Working For Us	Forces Working Against Us

613. System Review:
Preparing for Strategic Planning

Goals

- To provide participants with a simple framework for reviewing an organizational system in preparation for strategic planning.

- To encourage participants to examine both internal and external issues in reviewing their system.

Group Size

All members of an organization's strategic-planning team, divided into two subgroups of approximately equal size.

Time Required

One hour and fifteen minutes to one hour and twenty-five minutes.

Materials

- A copy of System Review Work Sheet A for each member of one subgroup.
- A copy of System Review Work Sheet B for each member of the other subgroup.
- A pencil for each participant.
- A flip chart and a felt-tipped marker for each subgroup.
- Masking tape for posting.

Physical Setting

A room in which the subgroups can work without disturbing one another. A table and chairs should be provided for each subgroup.

Process

1. The facilitator explains the goals of the activity.

2. The participants are instructed to form two subgroups of approximately equal size. The facilitator distributes copies of System Review Work Sheet A and pencils to one subgroup and then distributes copies of System Review Work Sheet B and pencils to the other subgroup. In addition, each subgroup receives a flip chart and a felt-tipped marker. The facilitator asks each subgroup to answer the questions on its work sheet and to choose one member who will be responsible for recording the answers on the flip chart and reporting later to the total group. After announcing that the subgroups have thirty minutes to complete their tasks, the facilitator tells them to begin. (Thirty-five minutes.)

3. After the subgroups have completed their work, the facilitator reconvenes the total group and asks the recorder for work sheet A to post his or her subgroup's flip-chart paper and present answers to the questions. After each answer the facilitator encourages questions and comments. (Ten to fifteen minutes.)

4. Step 3 is repeated with work sheet B. (Ten to fifteen minutes.)

5. The facilitator leads a discussion focusing on the following questions:

   ■ What kinds of issues did your group deal with—internal or external?

   ■ What similarities do you see between the responses from the two groups? What differences do you see?

   ■ What is working well in the organization? How can you perpetuate and capitalize on the organization's strengths?

   ■ What needs improvement? What process is currently in place for making these improvements?

   ■ What else do you need to do before you begin strategic planning? What additional information do you need? What tasks need to be completed? Who will do what and by when?

   As commitments are made, the facilitator asks a volunteer to record them for future reference. (Fifteen minutes.)

6. Before adjourning, the facilitator ensures that the participants set up a date and time to meet again for follow-up purposes.

Variations

- This activity may be used as part of a team-building intervention. In this case the system reviewed is the team rather than the entire organization.

- If the participants prefer to research answers to some of the questions so that they can work with more detailed information, the facilitator may conduct the activity in two sessions.

- The facilitator may give each participant both work sheets in advance, asking that they be completed and returned. Then the facilitator would prepare a handout listing verbatim answers for each work sheet. During the activity the participants would be asked to summarize the data and generate initial recommendations.

Submitted by Wayne Reschke.

Wayne Reschke is a consultant with nineteen years' of HRD experience as a trainer, a training director, a performance coach, and a designer of learning and performance systems. His areas of expertise include leadership development, career systems, performance management, and organizational assessment.

System Review Work Sheet A

Questions About Internal Issues*

1. What is the general level of employee skill/knowledge? Are our employees using "best practices" for their respective types of work? How productive are our employees?

2. How do our employees feel about their work? About the organization?

3. Do our organization's systems, procedures, and supporting technology work as intended? What are the shortcomings?

4. To what extent are costs managed effectively? Who is responsible for managing costs? What level of involvement do our nonmanagerial employees have in cost management?

---

*Based on *Productive Workplaces* by M.R. Weisbord, 1991, San Francisco: Jossey-Bass.

System Review Work Sheet B

Questions About External Issues*

1. How good are our organization's products/services from the customers' point of view?

2. How do our customers feel about working with and buying from our organization?

3. Do our customers perceive improvement in our products/services as a result of implementing better systems, procedures, and technology?

4. Are we generating adequate revenue?

---

*Based on *Productive Workplaces* by M.R. Weisbord, 1991, San Francisco: Jossey-Bass.

614. ETHICS IN ACTION: ALIGNING DECISIONS WITH ORGANIZATIONAL VALUES

Goals

- To emphasize the importance of aligning organizational decision making with organizational values.

- To offer participants an opportunity to practice making organizational decisions by testing them against organizational values.

Group Size

Eight to thirty managers from the same organization. Subgroups of four to six members each are formed.

Time Required

One and one-half to two hours.

Materials

- A copy of the Ethics in Action Work Sheet for each participant.
- A copy of the organization's vision statement for each participant.
- A copy of the organization's mission statement for each participant.
- A pencil for each participant.
- A flip chart and a felt-tipped marker for each subgroup.
- A flip chart and a felt-tipped marker for the facilitator's use.
- Masking tape for posting.

Physical Setting

A room large enough for subgroups to work without disturbing one another. A table and chairs should be provided for each subgroup.

Process

1. The facilitator announces the goals of the activity and distributes copies of the organization's vision and mission statements and pencils.

2. Subgroups of four to six members each are formed, and each subgroup is given a flip chart and a felt-tipped marker. Each subgroup is asked to identify the values (integrity, for example) expressed in the statements as well as any unwritten values that characterize the organization's culture. The facilitator instructs each subgroup to choose a spokesperson to record the values on the flip chart and later report them to the total group. (Fifteen minutes.)

3. After fifteen minutes, the facilitator asks the spokespersons to take turns reporting the identified values. All sheets of flip-chart paper are posted and remain so throughout the activity. (Five to fifteen minutes, depending on the number of subgroups.)

4. The facilitator leads a discussion about the recorded values. The purpose of this discussion is to have the participants reach general agreement—not necessarily consensus—about the organization's values so that they can proceed to the next step. Values that the participants decide are not characteristic of the organization are crossed off the posted flip-chart paper. (Ten minutes.)

5. The facilitator distributes copies of the Ethics in Action Work Sheet, reviews the instructions with the participants, and asks the subgroups to spend no more than thirty minutes completing the task. Each subgroup is again asked to choose a spokesperson who will report the results to the total group. (Thirty minutes.)

6. After all subgroups have completed the task, the spokespersons take turns reporting their subgroups' options, possible positive and negative results, and final decisions about Scenario 1. Then the facilitator leads a brief discussion about the various interpretations of the situation and applications of organizational values. The same pattern is used for Scenarios 2 through 4. (Twenty to thirty minutes.)

7. The facilitator then leads a concluding discussion based on the following questions:

   ■ What were your reactions to the final list of your organization's values? What surprised you?

   ■ What situations have you faced that are similar to the ones on the work sheet? How did you respond at the time? How would you respond now?

- What have you learned about the role of organizational values in decision making?

- What will you do differently in the future as a result of having participated in this activity?

(Fifteen minutes.)

Variations

- The facilitator may alter the scenarios for use with nonmanagerial employees as the decision makers. In this case the activity would be good for customer-service training and other purposes.

- The facilitator may create scenarios from actual situations in the organization's industry. Professional journals and the business sections of magazines and newspapers are good sources of such scenarios.

- The scenarios may be customized for a team and used as a team-building intervention. The team's particular values should be used in addition to the organization's.

Submitted by Jean G. Lamkin.

Jean G. Lamkin is the corporate training director for Landmark Communications, Inc., in Norfolk, Virginia. She is also an adjunct professor at The George Washington University, Hampton Roads Center, for the Human Resources Development graduate program. Her experience in training includes program and course design, evaluation, supervision, and leadership. She has worked with schools, government, quality programs, and professional groups.

ETHICS IN ACTION WORK SHEET

Instructions: Working as a group, you are to list three options for solving the problem in each scenario below and the potential positive and negative results of each of your options. Then decide which solution is *best aligned with your organization's values* and put a check mark by that solution to designate it as your choice.

Scenario 1

You manage your company's customer-service function. The company's products are delivered to customers' homes by contractors, all of whom have been given specific instructions about placing these items carefully on customers' doorsteps.

One of your customers is a continual problem to you and your people. He receives weekly deliveries and has called many times to complain about poor service, using abusive language every time.

Recently this customer demanded the replacement of his screen door, alleging that the contractor threw the package at the door and damaged it. You checked with the contractor, who assured you that the package was placed carefully on the doorstep, as always. You also sent one of your customer-service representatives to the customer's home, but could not find any damage. Nevertheless, you decided that the best option was to pay for a new screen door.

It has been two weeks since the screen-door incident, and the customer has called again. He is irate, claiming that the contractor broke his window. He threatens a lawsuit. You have checked with the contractor, who

	Options	Positive Results	Negative Results
1.			
2.			
3.			

says that no such thing happened. Again you send a customer-service representative to the customer's home; she sees no broken window. How should this customer be handled?

Scenario 2

One of your direct reports received a brochure for an advanced course on a new software program. There was no money in the budget for the course, but the employee convinced you that this training was essential for improving her skills and job performance. You reluctantly agreed to cut another budget category and use that money for the training.

When the employee returned from the course, she immediately gave two weeks' notice. Later you learned that the hiring employer had previously promised your employee a job if she completed the training you funded. You feel betrayed. Both the trained employee and the money used to train her are gone. How should you handle similar employee requests in the future?

Options	Positive Results	Negative Results
1.		
2.		
3.		

Scenario 3

Your weekend staff is faced with a dilemma: The computers are down and a critical deadline is four hours away. The company's contract for computer repair has a minimum charge of $1,000 to get the system back on line for a weekend emergency. Just last week you were humiliated by your boss's scathing criticism for going over budget; he lectured you about the fact that margins are thin and money is tight. Your boss is now out of town, and you feel reluctant to approve this new expenditure on your own.

An employee who is trying to be helpful suggests going around the service contractor by calling in his neighbor, who does the same work for another vendor, knows your computer system, will charge a lot less, and is available now. What should you do?

Options	Positive Results	Negative Results
1.		
2.		
3.		

Scenario 4

There is a growing conflict between two of your direct reports. It started about six months ago, and you are not sure what set it off.

At first the conflict did not seem to affect their work, but now they are undercutting each other's ability to get the job done. You have learned that they hide each other's papers and mail, refuse to take phone messages for each other, are rude to each other's customers and associates, and are dividing the office into two warring camps.

So far you have stayed out of this situation, hoping that it would resolve itself, but now your other employees are being distracted from their work. Some are even keeping score, awarding points to the combatants, and betting on the outcomes! What should you do?

Options	Positive Results	Negative Results
1.		
2.		
3.		

615. Sign Here:
Assessing an Appraisal System

Goals

- To give participants an opportunity to explore the characteristics of an effective performance-appraisal system.

- To assist participants in evaluating the strengths and weaknesses in their organization's current performance-appraisal system.

- To offer participants an opportunity to plan ways to improve the current performance-appraisal system.

Group Size

Up to twenty participants assembled into subgroups of three to five members each. (If there are fewer than six participants, subgroups need not be formed.) This activity is intended for managers at a level high enough to effect changes in their organization's performance-appraisal system.

Time Required

One hour and twenty minutes to two hours and twenty-five minutes, depending on whether subgroups are used and how many subgroups are formed.

Materials

- A copy of the Sign Here Theory Sheet for each participant.
- A copy of the Sign Here Work Sheet for each participant.
- A copy of the organization's current performance-appraisal form for each participant.
- A pencil for each participant.
- A flip chart and a felt-tipped marker for each subgroup.
- Masking tape for posting.

Physical Setting

A room large enough for the participants to sit comfortably while they view the subgroup presentations. Breakout rooms for the individual subgroup work are preferable but not essential; each subgroup can work at a separate table in the main room as long as the subgroups do not disturb one another. Plenty of wall space should be available for posting flip-chart paper.

Process

1. The facilitator introduces the activity by asking, "What is a performance-appraisal system supposed to do?" *Important Note:* If this question leads participants to voice negative feelings about the organization's current system, the facilitator should allow a few such comments, as they will "clear the air" and help the participants move on to the next steps. However, the facilitator should monitor the discussion carefully so that the participants do not become fixated on negativity and so that this step does not consume too much time. (Five to ten minutes.)

2. The facilitator distributes copies of the theory sheet and asks the participants to read it. After everyone has finished reading, the facilitator leads a brief discussion about the content. (Ten to fifteen minutes.)

3. The participants are assembled into three to five subgroups, and each subgroup is given a flip chart and a felt-tipped marker. Each participant receives a copy of the work sheet, a copy of the organization's current performance-appraisal form, and a pencil. The facilitator briefly reviews the work-sheet instructions with the participants. The subgroups are told that they have forty-five minutes to complete the task; they are advised to spend no more than twenty-five minutes on questions 1 through 7 and at least twenty minutes on question 8. Then the facilitator asks them to begin. (Five to ten minutes.)

4. While the subgroups work, the facilitator monitors their activity and offers assistance as needed. (Forty-five minutes.)

5. At the end of the work period, the facilitator reconvenes the total group and asks the spokespersons to take turns posting their flip-chart paper and making their presentations. After each presentation, the facilitator leads a brief discussion of reactions. At the conclusion of this step, all flip-chart paper is given to a volunteer to reproduce and distribute in handout form for future planning. (Five to ten minutes per subgroup.)

6. The facilitator leads a concluding discussion based on the following questions:

- What insights did you gain into your organization's use of performance appraisal?

- What was the most significant thing you learned about effective performance appraisal?

- What commitments will you make to improving your organization's appraisal form and performance-appraisal system?

(Ten to fifteen minutes.)

Variations

- After step 6 the facilitator may ask each subgroup to choose several improvement ideas and to do specific action planning, determining who will do what and by when.

- The facilitator may alter the work sheet to add questions that are specific to the organization.

- The activity may be combined with the creation of a set of organizational values, a vision statement, and a mission statement.

- The activity may be used with nonmanagerial employees to determine what changes they would like to see in the organization's performance-appraisal system. In this case the facilitator should ensure that their suggestions are given to their managers and that the managers are committed to giving feedback on the suggestions.

Submitted by Nancy Jackson.

Nancy Jackson, Ph.D., is an educator and a consultant specializing in communication. She teaches college courses in leadership; as a consultant she designs and delivers training in communication, teams, leadership, and problem solving. She is currently writing a book that focuses on skills that are essential for effectiveness in the workplace.

SIGN HERE THEORY SHEET

Manager: "Hey, good to see you."

Employee: "Nice to see you too."

Manager: "Sit down. Here's your appraisal. Any questions?"

Employee: (Shakes head "no," reading.)

Manager: "Good. I have a lot of these appraisals to do, and they're no picnic! Sign here. Thanks."

Employee: "Yeah, thanks. See you later."

Does this conversation sound like any of the performance appraisals that you have experienced in your career? This example may seem extreme, but similar scripts are played out in offices everywhere, once a year at evaluation time. This kind of appraisal is done hurriedly and without much thought, primarily to fulfill an obligation mandated by the organization.

Research on employee reactions to performance appraisal (Olson, 1981) shows that many employees have beliefs or feelings such as the following:

- Their managers do not preplan for appraisal interviews.

- Their work is not recognized.

- They are not given useful information about how they are performing or how they can improve.

- Data from appraisals are not collected in any systematic way, so their managers lack sufficient information to make good personnel decisions.

- There is no follow-up.

- Appraisals have no payoff for them.

However, this bleak picture is not universal. Many organizational leaders hold a belief that is critical to a good performance-appraisal system: People have the potential either to grow or to stagnate. Such leaders know that how the system is designed and used has a significant impact on the direction that employees take and how far they go.

An effective appraisal has these characteristics:

- It covers the scope of the job.

- It describes any standards that apply.

- It is based on accurate and sufficient data about performance.

- It addresses quality as well as quantity of work.

- It provides specific feedback.

- It offers guidance on how to improve.

- It includes an evaluation of interactions with other employees.

- It sets goals for the future.

- It affects the employee in terms of advancement or other results.

- It is done more than once a year.

After the initial appraisal, the manager should give feedback on a regular basis and should check on each employee's progress toward meeting goals. Eventually—after a predetermined number of months—another formal appraisal should be conducted. This pattern should continue, with the manager documenting each employee's performance and progress several times during the year, using the previous appraisal as a guideline. Using a performance appraisal in this way benefits everyone: The organization builds a stronger work force, managers build stronger teams and greater rapport with their employees, and employees reach more of their potential.

References

Olson, R. (1981). *Performance appraisal.* New York: John Wiley and Sons.

Sign Here Work Sheet

Instructions: Compare your organization's appraisal to the characteristics of an effective appraisal listed on the theory sheet. Then choose one member of your group to record the group's answers to the following questions on the flip chart and to report answers later to the total group. Although you and your fellow group members need to come to an agreement about answers to be recorded, you do not have to reach consensus.

1. What performance criteria are suggested or implied by your organization's values, vision, and/or mission statement? What criteria are currently used to evaluate employees? How do these two sets of criteria compare?

2. What performance factors are the most important to your organization's success? How are they measured?

3 What difficulties are associated with evaluating performance in your organization?

4. What are the strengths of the current *appraisal form?*

5. What are the strengths of the current *performance-appraisal system* (the way in which the form is used)?

6. What are the weaknesses of the current *appraisal form?*

7. What are the weaknesses of the current *performance-appraisal system?*

8. Given your organization's circumstances, what specific changes can you make to the appraisal form and the performance-appraisal system?

616. Managerial Perceptions: What Do Employees Really Want?

Goals

- To check the perceptions of managers and/or supervisors about what employees want from their jobs.
- To learn the results of research about what employees want from their jobs.
- To make plans to apply what has been learned.

Group Size

Five or six groups of four to six supervisors or managers each.

Time Required

One hour to an hour and ten minutes.

Materials

- One copy of the Managerial Perceptions Work Sheet for each participant.
- One copy of the Managerial Perceptions Discussion Questions Sheet for each participant.
- One copy of the Managerial Perceptions Research Summary Sheet for each participant.
- A clipboard or portable writing surface for each participant or tables.
- Pens or pencils for participants.
- A flip chart and markers or a whiteboard and markers.

Physical Setting

A room large enough so that subgroups will not disturb one another. Each group should be able to be seated face-to-face.

Process

1. The facilitator reviews the goals of the activity, explaining that it is based on research in business and industry by Kovach (1995) that spans over fifty years. The facilitator says that a handout of the research results will be given out later.

2. The facilitator divides the participants into subgroups of four to six each and asks them to be seated so that they face each other.

3. Each participant is given one copy of the Managerial Perceptions Work Sheet and is instructed to read the Job Factors in the left-hand column and to individually rank order these factors in Column A, with 1 being what they think is most important and 10 being what they think is least important. (Five to ten minutes.)

4. While the participants are working, the facilitator makes a copy of the work sheet on a newsprint sheet or whiteboard.

5. When participants have finished, the facilitator fills in Column B with the job factors as rank ordered by managers from Kovach's research. They are as follows, in order of importance:

   - good pay
   - job security
   - promotion and growth
   - good working conditions
   - interesting work
   - help with personal problems
   - loyalty to employees
   - full appreciation of work done
   - tactful discipline
   - feelings of being in on things

6. The facilitator provides participants copies of the Managerial Perceptions Discussion Questions Sheet and instructs groups to discuss the first question among themselves. (Five to ten minutes.)

7. The facilitator now fills in Column C, the rankings of what, according to Kovach, employees really want from their jobs, as follows, in order of importance:

   - interesting work
   - full appreciation of work done

- feelings of being in on things
- job security
- good pay
- promotion and growth
- good working conditions
- loyalty to employees
- tactful discipline
- help with personal problems

(Five minutes.)

8. The facilitator tells participants to calculate the numbers for Columns D and E on their work sheets (differences between A and C, and B and C), eliminating minus signs so that the results are positive numbers. They are told to total each column and calculate the average individual score in their group by adding all Column D scores together and dividing by the number of people in the group. (Five minutes.)

9. The facilitator asks participants to discuss questions 2 through 5 from the Managerial Perceptions Discussion Questions Sheet in their groups. (Twenty minutes.)

10. The facilitator distributes copies of the Managerial Perceptions Research Summary Sheet to participants and gives them ten minutes to read and discuss the research in their groups, with emphasis on any surprises and back-home applications. (Ten minutes.)

11. The facilitator then leads a discussion of the activity, using the following questions:

- What surprised you about the activity?
- What insights did you gain about what employees want from their jobs?
- What insights did you gain about managerial perceptions of what employees want from their jobs?
- What learnings can you apply in your work setting? How will you go about it?
- What is one thing you will do differently as a result of this activity?

(Ten minutes.)

Variations

- A column can be added to the Managerial Perceptions Work Sheet for group rankings of the job factors. Participants should be advised to avoid bargaining, voting, or averaging while reaching consensus on the ranking. In this case, the Managerial Perceptions Interpretation Matrix can be used to record changes from individual to group scores.

■ If a goal of the activity is to reach consensus, the Managerial Perceptions Interpretation Matrix Sheet can be posted on a flip chart or whiteboard while discussing how well each group worked together in arriving at a consensus. The "gain" score can be calculated by subtracting the group score from the group's average individual score. If the average individual score is higher than the group score, then the gain score is positive. If the group score is higher than the average individual score, then the gain score is negative. The lower the score, the better. If there are participants whose individual scores are equal to or better than the group score, then these individuals may have had information that could have been beneficial to the group reaching consensus. Groups should discuss how the group process worked. (Ten minutes.)

■ Subgroups may be composed of managers and supervisors together or they can be grouped separately by role or by function (e.g.,marketing, administration, operations).

■ If there are time constraints, the calculations and individual averages can be skipped.

■ A survey can be done prior to the training session to validate the research for what managers believe employees want and what employees really want in the organization.

Reference

Kovach, K. (1995). Employee motivation: Addressing a crucial factor in your organization's performance. *Employment Relations Today, 22*(2), 93–107.

Submitted by John Sample.

John Sample, Ph.D., is principal in the human resource development and consulting firm of Sample & Associates. His firm specializes in the assessment, development, and evaluation of human resources. He also provides case analysis and preparation assistance and testimony for attorneys in legal matters relating to negligent training and supervision. Dr. Sample is a past scholarly reviewer for the Human Resource Development Quarterly, *and he has published over fifty articles on training and development.*

MANAGERIAL PERCEPTIONS WORK SHEET*

Instructions: Think for a few moments about what you believe employees want from their jobs. Working alone, rank order the ten factors in Column A, with 1 being most important and 10 being least important.

When your facilitator gives you the actual rankings for Columns B and C, write them on your sheet.

When instructed by the facilitator, calculate Columns D and E by subtracting the smaller number from the larger in each case so that your answers are positive numbers. Then total the numbers in each column and write the total at the bottom of each column.

	A Individual	B Managers Believe	C Really Want	D Difference A–C	E Difference B–C
Feelings of Being in on Things					
Full Appreciation of Work Done					
Good Pay					
Good Working Conditions					
Help with Personal Problems					
Interesting Work					
Job Security					
Loyalty to Employees					
Promotion and Growth					
Tactful Discipline					
Total					

*Kovach, K. (1995). Employee motivation: Addressing a crucial factor in your organization's performance. *Employment Relations Today, 22*(2), 93–108.

MANAGERIAL PERCEPTIONS DISCUSSION QUESTIONS SHEET

1. Review your top three rankings of what managers think employees want from their jobs. Are your rankings (Column A) consistent with the top three factors according to other managers (Column B)? How had you determined your rankings?

2. Review the rankings of what employees really want from their jobs, according to Kovach's research (Column C). Are your rankings (Column A) consistent with the top three factors in Column C? What about the average individual rankings? What are the organizational costs associated with satisfying the top three factors? What are the costs if they are not met? Take turns sharing with others in your group.

3. Are the top three factors in Column B consistent with what you as a manager want most from your job? If not, what factors are most important to you? Are other unlisted factors important to you? Are you receiving what you want from your own manager? Share with others.

4. Do your perceptions of what your employees want from their jobs impact how you treat them? Are your perceptions a factor in how they treat one another? How they react to you? How they treat customers and clients? Share with others.

5. Now that you have more insight into what employees in your organization may want from their jobs, how will you use it in the workplace? Is there a way to verify that your employees would agree with the rank ordering that Kovach reported?

MANAGERIAL PERCEPTIONS RESEARCH SUMMARY SHEET

Kovach (1995) has been researching trends in employee motivation for many years. He compared data gathered in 1946 with data gathered from employee and manager groups in 1981 and 1994. His chief finding is well worth noting:

- Over the fifty-year period, supervisors continued to believe that employees placed high wages above other job rewards, whereas employees consistently ranked wages in fifth place out of the ten factors.

- Employee rankings have remained relatively stable over the fifty-year period, and there were no changes in the rankings of the top five factors between 1981 and 1994.

- Managers rank rewards as they would want them for themselves and assume that their employees desire the same rewards.

- It is much easier for management to pay more or to make work cleaner and safer than it is for them to make certain types of work more interesting (telemarketing, data input, etc.).

- Women put "full appreciation of work" in first place, whereas men ranked it second. Kovach theorized that female employees may place greater importance on interpersonal relations and communication than do male employees, a difference that should be noted by managers.

MANAGERIAL PERCEPTIONS INTERPRETATION MATRIX SHEET

(Optional for Use with a Consensus Activity)

	Group 1	Group 2	Group 3	Group n
Average individual scores				
Group score				
Group gain score				
Number of group members equal to or better than group score				

Introduction
to the Inventories, Questionnaires, and Surveys Section

Inventories, questionnaires, and surveys are feedback tools that help respondents understand how a particular theory applies to their own lives. Understanding the theories involved in the dynamics of their own group situations increases respondents' involvement. Instruments allow the facilitator of a small group to focus the energies and time of the respondents on the most appropriate material and also to direct, to some extent, the matters that are dealt with in the session. In this way, the facilitator can ensure that the issues worked on are crucial, existing ones, rather than the less important ones that the members may introduce to avoid grappling with the more uncomfortable issues.

The contents of the Inventories, Questionnaires, and Surveys Section are provided for training and development purposes. These instruments are not intended for in-depth personal growth, psychodiagnostic, or therapeutic work. Instead, they are intended for use in training groups; for demonstration purposes; to generate data for training or organization development sessions; and for other group applications in which the trainer, consultant, or facilitator helps respondents to use the data generated by an instrument for achieving some form of progress.

Each instrument includes the theory necessary for understanding, presenting, and using it. All interpretive information, scales or inventory forms, and scoring sheets are also provided for each instrument. In addition, we include all of the reliability and validity data contributed by the authors of instruments; if readers want additional information on reliability and validity, they are encouraged to contact the instrument authors directly. (Authors' addresses and telephone numbers appear in the Contributors list, found near the end of this book.)

Other assessment tools that address certain goals (and experiential learning activities and presentation/discussion resources to accompany them) can be located using our comprehensive *Reference Guide to Handbooks and Annuals*. This book, which is updated regularly, indexes all the *Annuals* and all the *Handbooks of Structured Experiences* that we have published to date. With each revision, the *Reference Guide* becomes a complete, up-to-date, and easy-to-use resource for selecting appropriate materials from all the *Annuals* and *Handbooks*.

The 1998 Annual: Volume 2, Consulting includes three assessment tools in the following categories:

Individual Development

Mentoring Skills Assessment by Michael Lee Smith

Groups and Teams

Innovation Capability Audit by Dave Francis

Consulting and Facilitating

Strategic Target Actions Review by Robert C. Preziosi and Patrick J. Ward

Mentoring Skills Assessment

Michael Lee Smith

Abstract: Before the Industrial Revolution, apprenticeship programs played an important role in career development. However, circumstances changed, and the programs were all but lost outside of trade unions. Similarly, informal mentoring was more common earlier this century, when job positions were less competitive. It seems that society has come full circle. We are experiencing major changes in how business is conducted, so we need a system that will support and foster the growth of the workforce. Well-designed mentoring programs can fill this need.

Mentoring programs can increase an employee's chances to progress in an organization. Having a mentor enables one to build on strengths and shore up weaknesses within the context of a relationship that supports success. Mentoring also complements both teams and learning organizations.

The Mentoring Skills Assessment identifies fifteen actions around which mentors and mentees can establish expectations and negotiate actions to allow the mentoring process to be as positive in results as it is in promises.

Mentoring itself is not new. In Greek mythology, Mentor was the friend and adviser of Odysseus and teacher of his son, Telemachus. The word mentor since has come to mean a trusted counselor or guide.

Mentoring Programs

Mentoring programs are found in many settings, including education, small and large businesses and the military (Gunn, 1995; Loeb, 1995; Rothman, 1993; Sullivan, 1992). Mentoring has always been present in the business environment, usually to help new employees learn about their organizations and for all employees to learn new skills (Silver, 1996; Smith, 1994). These programs are even more necessary when new skills are needed to cope with the modern workplace. This is especially true today, because one can expect the skills one has to be obsolete in three to five years (Nocera, 1996). In addition, mentoring is needed as an alternative to the security and care taking that is no longer part of organizational life (Gunn, 1995).

Mentoring programs may be formal (with corporate sponsorship) or informal (spontaneous or with few guidelines). Either can be effective, although most sources suggest that formal programs are more effective (Gaskill, 1993; Rubow & Jansen, 1990; Wright & Werther, 1991). Regardless of the program's formality, it is possible that mentoring can make the difference in an individual's success or failure in an organization.

A survey of 1,250 prominent men and women conducted by the consulting firm of Heidrick and Struggles found that one of the factors contributing to the respondent's success was being involved in a mentoring relationship. Nearly two-thirds of the respondents reported having had a mentor (Murray, 1991).

Regardless of the program's formality, many benefits can derive from mentoring, such as the following (Alleman, 1989; Bloch, 1993; Geiger-Dumond & Boyle, 1995; Howe, 1995; Loeb, 1995; Murray, 1991; Wright & Werther, 1991):

- Helping newly hired or promoted employees become fully productive and understand the organization's expectations, policies, and resources in a compressed time frame
- Career guidance.

- Low-cost transfer of skills.
- Decreased turnover.
- Creation of future leaders.
- Greater job satisfaction.
- Increased learning for the mentor and mentee.
- Improved organizational climate.
- Positive affirmative action results.
- Increased productivity.
- Improved recruitment efforts.
- Increased ability to manage relationships more effectively.

Three good sources of guidance on designing mentoring programs are Kram (1985), Murray (1991), and Phillips-Jones (1993a).

The Mentoring Relationship

The essence of mentoring is the relationship between mentor and mentee. For most participants, this relationship is different from any others they have within their organizations. It is a helping relationship, with learning and growth as the expected outcomes for the mentee. Often, the mentor experiences these same benefits, which is why the mentor should not usually be the mentee's supervisor. Mentor and mentee must be able to negotiate roles, communicate effectively, set goals, actively listen, manage conflict, and more.

In addition to the interpersonal skills mentioned previously, the mentoring relationship also requires mutual trust, openness, and a willingness to attempt new behaviors. Such behaviors are often new to the mentoring pair, but the relationship is crucial for success. The role each will play as the relationship develops must be clear. To allow it to develop without guidance will put the mentoring relationship in jeopardy. According to Zachary (1994), "the preparation of the relationship by both partners together is critical for development of naturally satisfying relationships."

THE ASSESSMENT

The mentor and mentee versions of the assessment are designed to facilitate the development of an effective mentoring relationship. Each consists of fifteen actions or behaviors that are expected to take place during any successful mentoring relationship. The mentor/mentee is asked to indicate if each of the mentoring actions should take place (yes or no), how often it should occur (occasionally, regularly, or often) and how important each is to the mentoring relationship (hardly needed, somewhat needed, needed, highly needed, essential).

The mentors and mentees complete their respective assessments prior to their first meeting or before a mentoring program orientation. In this way, their expectations are not influenced by the orientation session (e.g., in terms of what should occur, who should do what, and the importance of each event or behavior). Their individual feelings about "what," "how often," and "importance" are captured before they meet as a mentoring pair. The individual responses then are the source for negotiating expectations as mentor and mentee.

Validity and Reliability

No statistical validity and reliability data are available on the mentoring assessments. However, they have face validity, because their purpose is to prepare for the first meeting between mentor and mentee.

Administering and Scoring the Instrument

Begin by distributing the appropriate versions of the Mentoring Skills Assessments to mentors and mentees. If an orientation session is scheduled, copies of the completed assessments should be sent to the session facilitator in advance. If no orientation session is scheduled, mentors and mentees should set a time to meet and mutually acceptable deadlines for completing the assessments.

Interpretation of Results Prior to Program

When the mentoring assessments are prepared prior to the orientation session for a formal mentoring program, the facilitator "scores" the assessments by simply adding and averaging the mentor and mentee responses independently for each item.

The sample results reported here are from a session of twenty-five mentors and mentees. The facilitator should look at the mentoring actions for which there is agreement between mentors and mentees and for which there are differences. Agreement indicates mutual expectations and, therefore, the actions are likely to happen. Disagreement, on the other hand, indicates items for which negotiation needs to take place early in the relationship. Without negotiation, the differences between mentor and mentee present potential problems for the development of the relationship.

The facilitator's analysis serves as an example of what the mentors and mentees should do when they first meet and compare their individual responses.

In the absence of an orientation session, a letter should accompany the assessments that describes the mentoring process, the program goals, the role of the mentoring coordinator, and whatever resources are available for use, such as self-awareness questionnaires, books, tapes, and so on.

Part One

First, the facilitator should review the percentage of mentors and mentees who responded "yes" to each item. The items in the sample that are marked with an asterisk are the ones that should be noted and discussed.

	Mentor		Mentee
	92 percent	A	100 percent
	100 percent	B	92 percent
	92 percent	C	100 percent
	92 percent	D	92 percent
	100 percent	E	92 percent
*	80 percent	F	100 percent
*	100 percent	G	75 percent
	100 percent	H	100 percent
	100 percent	I	92 percent
	100 percent	J	100 percent
*	67 percent	K	67 percent
	92 percent	L	83 percent
	92 percent	M	83 percent
	100 percent	N	92 percent
	100 percent	O	100 percent

In this example, there is general agreement that most of the actions should take place. Any action with 15 percent or greater disagreement between mentors and mentees or an action with less than 80 percent "yes" responses from either group should be highlighted and discussed. In this example, items F, G, and K would be highlighted and discussed, as follows.

F. Discuss company politics: 80 percent mentors vs. 100 percent mentees. Mentees uniformly expect to discuss "politics" within the organization. Twenty percent of the mentors do not agree. The mentors can be very helpful to the mentees regarding who has power and who does not, what the organization really considers to be important, and other aspects of the organization that the mentee can benefit from, instead of making "political" mistakes.

G. Discuss/share information about detailed job tasks: 100 percent mentors vs. 75 percent mentees. The mentors all agree they should give detailed information (advice) about the mentee's job. Mentees apparently are less willing to have mentors go into detail. Level of detail aside, mentoring in the work environment should have the job as a prime area for attention, not just personal goals or interpersonal skills. This area will have to be discussed carefully so that each is comfortable with just how involved in job details the mentor should become. Mentors are not usually expected to tell mentees exactly how to do their jobs, but asking questions about objectives, plans, and progress is expected. Mentors are expected to coach mentees, but the level of detail is something for negotiation. (If the mentor does not know the mentee's specific job or discipline, he or she is expected to find sources in the organization for such information when the mentee needs it.)

K. Ask for feedback on how others view me: 76 percent mentors vs. 67 percent mentees. Many mentors and mentees do not expect the mentors to ask mentees about how they (the mentors) are perceived in the organization. One could decide not to do this. However, one of the benefits for the mentor is to receive feedback from the mentee that he or she is not likely to obtain any other way.

Part Two

The second analysis is of the differences and similarities between mentor and mentee responses regarding how often the actions should take place and how important they are to the mentoring relationship. The results for the sample are shown below with plus signs (+) where there is basic agreement and minus signs (-) where there is disagreement. The items with an asterisk are the ones that are different enough to discuss. (Of course, the areas of similarity should receive some mention also to show how much agreement exists, which is a positive indicator of a successful mentoring relationship).

Frequency				Importance		
	Mentor	Mentee		Mentor	Mentee	
(+)	2.1	2.2	A	3.7	3.8	(+)
(+)	1.6	2.0	B	3.3	3.4	(+)
(+)	1.6	1.6	C	3.3	3.8	(-)
(+)	2.1	2.0	D	4.1	3.9	(+)
(+)	2.0	2.2	E	3.5	3.8	(+)
(+)	1.3	1.5	F	2.2	2.7	(-)
(+)	2.0	2.3	G	3.6	3.9	(+)
(-)	1.8	2.3	*H	3.9	3.9	(+)
(+)	2.1	2.0	I	3.4	3.1	(+)
(-)	1.9	2.4	*J*	3.6	4.3	(-)
(+)	1.2	1.4	K	2.3	2.0	(+)
(+)	2.0	2.2	L	3.4	3.6	(+)
(-)	1.2	2.4	*M*	2.5	3.9	(-)
(+)	1.9	2.3	N	3.1	3.5	(+)
(+)	1.8	1.9	O	3.6	3.7	(+)

Any response difference of .5 or more in frequency and .7 or more in importance should be noted for discussion. In this sample, J and M have "significant" differences in both frequency and importance. Action H has a difference in frequency only. The discussion might take the following form:

H. Explore mentee's strengths and weaknesses.

- Frequency: mentors 1.8, mentees 2.3
- Importance: mentors 3.9, mentees 3.9

Mentors and mentees agree that this is one of the most important actions for mentors during mentoring. However, mentors do not think it should happen as often as do the mentees. This may indicate a reluctance by mentors to talk about weaknesses. Few people have trouble talking about strengths or receiving feedback about them. The mentoring relationship is one in which it should be safe to talk about weaknesses. The lack of feedback and consequent lack of development in areas of one's weaknesses, whether job skills, interpersonal skills, or non-technical skills, should be the subject of mentoring meetings. Having an opportunity to explore areas that need development or that could interfere with job or career success is the purpose of mentoring.

J. Give feedback that is positive and negative regarding mentee's jobs plans, progress, and performance.

- Frequency: mentors 1.9, mentees 2.4
- Importance: mentors 3.6, mentees 4.3

This mentor action is similar to H but is specific to giving feedback about job plans, progress, and performance. Both mentors and mentees believe that it is important. In fact, it is the most important action (at 4.3) for the mentees. Mentors see it as taking place less often then mentees. Again, this may reflect a reluctance by mentors to give specific feedback (although it is regarded as needed during mentoring). Mentors should be prepared to give such feedback, and mentees will need to show their willingness to receive the feedback by asking for it. It may feel awkward at first, but mentees must speak up if they want the feedback. Mentors will not find such willing recipients of coaching in their normal job interactions.

M. Meet at least once a month.

- Frequency: mentors 1.2, mentees 2.4
- Importance; mentors 2.6, mentees 3.9

The responses to this item reflect a busy workplace. Commitment is needed by both parties to meet frequently enough for a mentoring relationship to develop and continue. Mentees think it is very important to meet at least once a month. Mentors are less certain about the need, as evidenced by their responses at 2.5 importance and 1.2 frequency. The program will not work without regular meetings. In fact, mentors and mentees will probably need to meet more frequently at the beginning. After getting to know each other, once a month may be sufficient. The frequency of meetings will, of course, depend on each mentoring pair's negotiation, but a time commitment must be made. In fact, that is why it is best for the mentee to handle the agenda setting and meeting arrangements, as he or she is usually more interested in the relationship.

Part Three

All actions for which either mentors or mentees rate importance below "3" should also be discussed, if they have not been discussed previously. In the example, all of the actions for which mentor or mentee rated importance below "3" (F, K, M) were noted for discussion, because it is assumed that most mentoring relationships will include all fifteen actions on the Mentoring Skills Assessment. Once the mentor and mentee negotiate their relationship, they can decide whether and how often any of the actions should take place. None of the actions, however, should be rejected too easily (which could happen if both parties scored an item below "3" and just ignored it).

References

Alleman, E. (1989, Winter). Two planned mentoring programs that worked. *Mentoring International, 3*(1), 7.

Bloch, S. (1993). The mentor as counselor. *Employee Counseling Today, 5*(3), 10.

Gaskill, L.R. (1993, Winter). A conceptual framework for the development, implementation, and evaluation of formal mentoring programs. *Journal of Career Development, 20*(2), 148–155.

Geiger-Dumond, A., & Boyle, S. (1995, March). Mentoring: A practitioner's guide. *Training & Development, 49*(3), 54.

Gunn, E. (1995, August). Mentoring: The democratic version. *Training, 32*(6), 64–67.

Howe, E.S. (1995, February). The benefits of mentoring. *Pennsylvania CPA Journal, 2,* 16.

Kram, K.E. (1985). *Mentoring at work.* Glenview IL: Scott, Foresman.

Loeb, M. (1995, June). The new mentoring. *Fortune, X*(11), 213.

Murray, M. (1991). *Beyond the myths and magic of mentoring.* San Francisco, CA: Jossey-Bass.

Nocera, J. (1996, April 6). Living with layoffs. *Fortune, 6,* 73.

Phillips-Jones, L. (1993a). *Mentoring program coordinator's guide.* Grass Valley, CA: Coalition of Counseling Centers.

Phillips-Jones, L. (1993b). *The mentors and proteges.* Grass Valley, CA: Coalition of Counseling Centers.

Rothman, H. (1993). The boss as mentor. *Nation's Business, 81*(4), 66–67.

Rubow, R., & Jansen, S. (1990, July). A corporate survival guide for the baby bust. *Management Review, 79*(7), 52.

Silver, S. (1996, March 24). Flatter organizations require new skills. *The Star-Ledger,* p. 55.

Smith, M.L. (1994, March/April). Creating business-development talent through mentoring. *Journal of Management in Engineering, 10*(2), 44–47.

Sullivan, C.G. (1992). *How to mentor in the midst of change.* Alexandria, VA: Association for Supervision and Curriculum Development.

Wright, R.G., & Werther, Jr., W.B. (1991). Mentors at work. In R.B. Frantreb (Ed.), *Training and Development Yearbook 1992/1993.* Englewood Cliffs, NJ: Prentice-Hall.

Zachary, L. (1994, October). Mentoring relationships: Tools for partner participation. *Mentor, 6*(4), 6.

Michael Lee Smith, SPHR, *is presently consulting in the areas of human resources and training. He has twenty-eight years' experience as a manager of human resources and a director of training for engineering and telecommunications companies. He has published thirty-five articles, including a time-management role play in the 1993* Annual.

Mentoring Skills Assessment: Mentee Version

Michael Lee Smith

Name: _____ Location: _____

(Check One): Newly hired or promoted _____ Current employee _____

Instructions: For each of the items that follow, you will need to decide the answer to the following three questions and place check marks in the appropriate columns:

1. Should this activity take place? (Yes or No)

2. How often should this activity take place? (Occasionally, Regularly, or Often)

3. How important is this activity? (Hardly Needed, Somewhat Needed, Needed, Highly Needed, Essential)

| Take Place? | | Frequency | | | Item | Importance | | | | |
Yes	No	Occasionally (1 point)	Regularly (2 points)	Often (3 points)		Hardly Needed (1 point)	Somewhat Needed (2 points)	Needed (3 points)	Highly Needed (4 points)	Essential (5 points)
___	___	1	2	3	A. A mentor gives information on the roles and responsibilities of being an employee here.	1	2	3	4	5
___	___	1	2	3	B. A mentor shares his or her experiences of making transitions or of being new here.	1	2	3	4	5

Take Place?		Frequency				Importance				
Yes	No	Occasionally (1 point)	Regularly (2 points)	Often (3 points)		Hardly Needed (1 point)	Somewhat Needed (2 points)	Needed (3 points)	Highly Needed (4 points)	Essential (5 points)
___	___	1	2	3	C. A mentor discusses careers at this company.	1	2	3	4	5
___	___	1	2	3	D. A mentor discusses my personal career goals.	1	2	3	4	5
___	___	1	2	3	E. A mentor discusses/shares information about job problems and solutions.	1	2	3	4	5
___	___	1	2	3	F. A mentor discusses company politics.	1	2	3	4	5
___	___	1	2	3	G. A mentor discusses/shares information about detailed job tasks.	1	2	3	4	5
___	___	1	2	3	H. A mentor explores my strengths and weaknesses.	1	2	3	4	5
___	___	1	2	3	I. A mentor acts as a sounding board for my issues and concerns.	1	2	3	4	5
___	___	1	2	3	J. A mentor gives feedback that is positive or negative regarding my job plans, progress, and performance.	1	2	3	4	5

The 1998 Annual: Volume 2, Consulting/© 1998 Jossey-Bass/Pfeiffer

Take Place?		Frequency				Importance				
Yes	No	Occasionally (1 point)	Regularly (2 points)	Often (3 points)		Hardly Needed (1 point)	Somewhat Needed (2 points)	Needed (3 points)	Highly Needed (4 points)	Essential (5 points)
—	—	1	2	3	K. A mentor asks me how others perceive him or her.	1	2	3	4	5
—	—	1	2	3	L. A mentor meets with me at least once a month.	1	2	3	4	5
—	—	1	2	3	M. A mentor takes me to meetings, job sites, negotiations, or sales calls.	1	2	3	4	5
—	—	1	2	3	N. A mentor encourages me to speak up, take initiative, and not be satisfied with the status quo.	1	2	3	4	5
—	—	1	2	3	O. A mentor periodically evaluates the mentoring relationship.	1	2	3	4	5

MENTORING SKILLS ASSESSMENT: MENTOR VERSION

Michael Lee Smith

Name: _____ Location: _____

(Check One): Newly hired or promoted _____ Current employee _____

Instructions: For each of the items that follow, you will need to decide the answer to the following three questions and place check marks in the appropriate columns:

1. Should this activity take place? (Yes or No)

2. How often should this activity take place? (Occasionally, Regularly, or Often)

3. How important is this activity? (Hardly Needed, Somewhat Needed, Needed, Highly Needed, Essential)

| Take Place? | | Frequency | | | Item | Importance | | | | |
Yes	No	Occasionally (1 point)	Regularly (2 points)	Often (3 points)		Hardly Needed (1 point)	Somewhat Needed (2 points)	Needed (3 points)	Highly Needed (4 points)	Essential (5 points)
___	___	1	2	3	A. A mentor gives information on the roles and responsibilities of being an employee here.	1	2	3	4	5
___	___	1	2	3	B. A mentor shares his or her experiences of making transitions or of being new here.	1	2	3	4	5

Take Place?		Frequency				Importance				
Yes	No	Occasionally (1 point)	Regularly (2 points)	Often (3 points)		Hardly Needed (1 point)	Somewhat Needed (2 points)	Needed (3 points)	Highly Needed (4 points)	Essential (5 points)
—	—	1	2	3	C. A mentor discusses careers at this company.	1	2	3	4	5
—	—	1	2	3	D. A mentor discusses the mentee's personal career goals.	1	2	3	4	5
—	—	1	2	3	E. A mentor discusses/shares information about job problems and solutions.	1	2	3	4	5
—	—	1	2	3	F. A mentor discusses company politics.	1	2	3	4	5
—	—	1	2	3	G. A mentor discusses/shares information about detailed job tasks.	1	2	3	4	5
—	—	1	2	3	H. A mentor explores the mentee's strengths and weaknesses.	1	2	3	4	5
—	—	1	2	3	I. A mentor acts as a sounding board for the mentee's issues and concerns.	1	2	3	4	5
—	—	1	2	3	J. A mentor gives feedback that is positive and negative regarding the mentee's job plans, progress, and performance.	1	2	3	4	5

| Take Place? | | Frequency | | | | Importance | | | | |
Yes	No	Occasionally (1 point)	Regularly (2 points)	Often (3 points)		Hardly Needed (1 point)	Somewhat Needed (2 points)	Needed (3 points)	Highly Needed (4 points)	Essential (5 points)
		1	2	3	K. A mentor asks the mentee how others perceive the mentor.	1	2	3	4	5
		1	2	3	L. A mentor meets with the mentee at least once a month.	1	2	3	4	5
		1	2	3	M. A mentor takes the mentee to meetings, job sites, negotiations, or sales calls.	1	2	3	4	5
		1	2	3	N. A mentor encourages the mentee to speak up, take initiative, and not be satisfied with the status quo.	1	2	3	4	5
		1	2	3	O. A mentor periodically evaluates the mentoring relationship.	1	2	3	4	5

The 1998 Annual: Volume 2, Consulting/© 1998 Jossey-Bass/Pfeiffer

INNOVATION CAPABILITY AUDIT

Dave Francis

Abstract: The successful management of innovation requires that unique answers be found to the following three key questions:

1. Are we sufficiently innovative?

2. Are we innovative in the "right" ways?

3. If the answer to question 1 or 2 is "no," what needs to be done?

The Innovation Capability Audit assesses an organization's capacity for innovation. The Audit can be used for training or as an organizational survey instrument. It provides a straightforward method for a group to explore the organizational dimensions of innovation and initiate a process of organization development to strengthen innovative prowess. The audit is based on extensive research conducted by the author at the Centre for Research in Innovation Management at the University of Brighton, United Kingdom.

The management of innovation is an important topic. Virtually every management journal regularly has pertinent articles. Organizations that innovate have superior profit and growth performance (Miles & Snow, 1978). Few doubt that there is much innovation to be done: As innovation specialist Professor John Bessant says, "It has been estimated that up to 80 percent of the new products that we will be buying in ten years' time have yet to be invented" (Bessant, 1991).

However, not all innovation adds value. It must be managed to promote functional, not dysfunctional, innovation. Functional innovation is considered to be the application of concepts, ideas, or techniques that enhance the competitive capability of the organization. Dysfunctional innovation, on the other hand, is the investment of resources in costly, unproductive, or distracting initiatives.

Innovation processes are directed toward one or more of four domains—Paradigm, Process, Position, and Product—as shown in Figure 1:

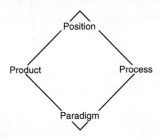

Figure 1. Domains of Innovation

- Innovation can be strategic—redefining the *positioning* of the organization. For example, a chemical company may seek to offer differentiated rather than commodity products. In this case, innovation in product and service must be managed to deliver the new competitive strategy.

- Innovation can be cultural—redefining the dominant *paradigm* of the organization. In this context, a paradigm may be defined as the system of beliefs, mind-sets, values, and practices that define collective thinking processes. For example, a local theater may change its role from being a deliverer of high culture to a center for participative education in the performing arts. In this case, innovation must re-align the beliefs, mind-sets, values, and practices of the entire staff.

- Innovation can introduce or improve *products* in ways that add value for customers and enable the organization's products to be equivalent (preferably superior) to the offers of competing organizations.

- Innovation can introduce or improve *processes* that reduce costs, improve quality, or increase agility.

As an organization innovates, its capacity to learn, adapt, and thrive improves. Further advantage can be gained by mastering fluid forces of change.

DESCRIPTION OF THE AUDIT

The Innovation Capability Audit is designed as an organization-wide survey. Its fifty-four items assess an organization's capacity for innovation as measured by eighteen different "innovation drivers." Each item is scored on a six-point scale that describes the extent to which each item is perceived as true.

Validity

The items in this audit are drawn from research and case studies that address the preconditions for organizational innovation. At present, no one universally agreed-on model of innovative capacity exists. However, the Innovation Capacity Audit is designed to be an action-research tool rather than a rigorous data-gathering instrument. Used in this manner, the items are hypotheses that have high levels of face validity.

Administration

The total time required to administer, score, and interpret the Innovation Capability Audit is approximately ninety minutes. Each participant will need a copy of each of the elements of the audit: Innovation Capability Audit, Innovation Capability Audit Scoring Sheet, Innovation Capability Audit Interpretation Sheet, and Innovation Capability Audit Work Sheet. To best facilitate this session, human resource professionals should review leading works on the organizational aspects of innovation (Coyne, 1996; Drucker, 1994; Kanter, 1983; Millson, Raj, & Wilemon, 1992; and Utterback, 1994).

1. *Introduce the session* by saying that innovation is a vital attribute of today's organizations, and the group will examine the extent to which their own organization supports or blocks innovation. This introduction can be illustrated with examples from your own experience.

2. *Distribute the Innovation Capability Audit* and ask each participant to complete it. If necessary, define the organization or part of the organization (for example, a unit or department) being assessed and ensure that participants share a common understanding.

3. *Present a brief lecturette* on the attributes of the innovative organization. The content for this lecturette may be drawn from material in the Innovation Capability Audit Interpretation Sheet.

4. *Distribute the Innovation Capability Audit Scoring Sheet, the Innovation Capability Audit Interpretation Sheet, and the Innovation Capability Work Sheet,* and review their instructions. Ask participants to form subgroups of two to five people, with members of the same organization working together. Ask subgroups to complete the analysis of the audit results.

5. *Invite each subgroup to share at least one insight* gained from the session. These insights should be recorded and posted on a newsprint flip chart.

References

Bessant, J. (1991). *Managing advanced manufacturing technology: The challenge of the fifth wave.* Oxford/ Manchester: NCC-Blackwell.

Coyne, D.W.E. (1996). *Building a tradition of innovation.* Paper presented at the UK Innovation Lecture, London. Published by DTI, London.

Drucker, P.F. (1994). *Innovation and entrepreneurship.* Oxford: Butterworth-Heinemann Ltd.

Kanter, R.M. (1983). *The change masters.* New York: Simon & Schuster.

Miles, R.E., & Snow, C.C. (1978). *Organizational strategy, structure, and process.* New York: McGraw-Hill.

Millson, M.R., Raj, S.P., & Wilemon, D. (1992). A survey of major approaches for accelerating new product development. *The Journal of Product Innovation Management, 9,* 53–69.

Utterback, J.M. (1994). *Mastering the dynamics of innovation.* Boston, MA: HBS.

Dave Francis, D. Litt., is leader of the Innovation Consulting Group at the Centre for Research in Innovation Management, based at the University of Brighton in the United Kingdom. He is a behavioral scientist, specializing in developing productive innovation in organizations. He has written or co-authored twenty-seven books, including Improving Work Groups *(Jossey-Bass/Pfeiffer, 1992) and* Step-by-Step Competitive Strategy *(Routledge, 1994).*

INNOVATION CAPABILITY AUDIT

Dave Francis

Instructions: Innovation is a vital skill, and this audit will help to provide information needed to strengthen innovation in your organization. Please answer each item with care and honesty; the intention is to benefit everyone. Individual results are strictly confidential and will never be identified by name.

The facilitator will define the organization or part of the organization that is the target for review. Please refer to this target as you respond to each item. You may feel that you do not have sufficient knowledge to be objective, but please respond to each statement, even if you give a subjective opinion.

Choose your response based on the following scale:

This statement is true:　1 To little or no extent　　3 To a moderate extent　5 To a very great extent
　　　　　　　　　　　2 To a slight extent　　　　4 To a great extent　　　6 Totally

1. Top managers take innovation very seriously.	1	2	3	4	5	6
2. This organization's record of innovation gives it real advantage over competitors.	1	2	3	4	5	6
3. If needed, radical changes will be quickly implemented.	1	2	3	4	5	6
4. Creative individuals are well-rewarded.						
5. The organization is an early adopter of state-of-the-art technology.	1	2	3	4	5	6
6. This organization is good at getting things done.	1	2	3	4	5	6
7. Employees are empowered to take significant initiative.	1	2	3	4	5	6
8. It is expected that staff at all levels will innovate.	1	2	3	4	5	6
9. Most people here welcome change.	1	2	3	4	5	6
10. Significant resources are invested in developing people.	1	2	3	4	5	6
11. Technical experts are influential in decision making.	1	2	3	4	5	6

This statement is true: 1 To little or no extent 3 To a moderate extent 5 To a very great extent
  2 To a slight extent 4 To a great extent 6 Totally

12. Customers are actively involved in the development of new products.

    1 2 3 4 5 6

13. Extensive collaboration occurs between teams and departments.

    1 2 3 4 5 6

14. People can obtain management's support to implement well-considered initiatives.

    1 2 3 4 5 6

15. Top priority is given to developing new products and processes.

    1 2 3 4 5 6

16. Managers strive to understand new ideas in great depth before making a change.

    1 2 3 4 5 6

17. Decisions about launching new products are taken after very careful analysis.

    1 2 3 4 5 6

18. New ideas are fully driven through, despite setbacks or difficulties.

    1 2 3 4 5 6

19. Senior managers inspire people to be innovative.

    1 2 3 4 5 6

20. Everything we do is part of a strategy to gain competitive advantage.

    1 2 3 4 5 6

21. Top managers give careful thought before making a radical decision.

    1 2 3 4 5 6

22. Outstanding individuals are highly valued.

    1 2 3 4 5 6

23. Our technological strengths and weaknesses have been carefully analyzed.

    1 2 3 4 5 6

24. Once a decision is made, initiatives are implemented rapidly.

    1 2 3 4 5 6

25. Employees speak up even when challenging important people.

    1 2 3 4 5 6

26. Managers and staff identify developing new ideas as a key objective.

    1 2 3 4 5 6

27. Almost everyone is 100 percent in support of management's plans.

    1 2 3 4 5 6

28. There is a constant search for new ways to define problems.

    1 2 3 4 5 6

This statement is true: 1 To little or no extent   3 To a moderate extent   5 To a very great extent
2 To a slight extent   4 To a great extent   6 Totally

29. Technical specialists share their knowledge widely.   1 2 3 4 5 6

30. We frequently benchmark how we compare with other organizations.   1 2 3 4 5 6

31. Things get done; there is no unnecessary bureaucracy.   1 2 3 4 5 6

32. People who drive through changes are recognized as heros.   1 2 3 4 5 6

33. The organization can take an idea and quickly turn it into a product that people want to buy.   1 2 3 4 5 6

34. Those leading a change process can fully describe the advantages and disadvantages.   1 2 3 4 5 6

35. Decisions to support or kill an initiative are taken by managers who really understand the issues.   1 2 3 4 5 6

36. Management insists that only a limited number of initiatives are undertaken at once, to prevent overstretching the organization.   1 2 3 4 5 6

37. The organization's leader is tough on those who seek to block change.   1 2 3 4 5 6

38. New products (or services) really give the customer superior value.   1 2 3 4 5 6

39. Senior management has a recent history of making bold decisions.   1 2 3 4 5 6

40. Exceptional individuals are able to fit into the organization.   1 2 3 4 5 6

41. The organization is investing to develop all the capabilities needed to win in the future.   1 2 3 4 5 6

42. Projects are managed effectively.   1 2 3 4 5 6

43. Personal initiatives are supported, providing people work within guidelines.   1 2 3 4 5 6

44. People are appraised based on their success in being innovative.   1 2 3 4 5 6

This statement is true:	1 To little or no extent	3 To a moderate extent	5 To a very great extent
	2 To a slight extent	4 To a great extent	6 Totally

45. Everyone is keen to help someone with a creative suggestion.　　　1　2　3　4　5　6

46. We rarely make the same mistake twice.　　　1　2　3　4　5　6

47. Those with deep technical skills are highly respected.　　　1　2　3　4　5　6

48. We learn through strong links with partners, industry associations, universities, and consultants.　　　1　2　3　4　5　6

49. The way the organization is structured helps not hinders innovation.　　　1　2　3　4　5　6

50. People with ideas can win the resources they need.　　　1　2　3　4　5　6

51. Departments involved in developing new products or processes work closely together.　　　1　2　3　4　5　6

52. This organization is striving to be truly world class in every aspect of performance.　　　1　2　3　4　5　6

53. When it is important, decisions are made quickly.　　　1　2　3　4　5　6

54. Top managers take personal responsibility for major initiatives.　　　1　2　3　4　5　6

INNOVATION CAPABILITY AUDIT SCORING SHEET

Instructions: Transfer your responses for each item on the Innovation Capability Audit to the answer grid that follows. Add the scores in each horizontal column and enter them in the "Total" column.

Topic	Item Score			Total
Ia. Innovating Leadership	1	19	37	
Ib. Provides Strategic Advantage	2	20	38	
Ic. Prudent Radicalism	3	21	39	
IIa. Exceptional Individuals	4	22	40	
IIb. Full Competencies Portfolio	5	23	41	
IIc. Capable Implementation	6	24	42	
IIIa. Selective Empowerment	7	25	43	
IIIb. Innovation Demanded	8	26	44	
IIIc. High Enrollment	9	27	45	
IVa. Continuous Learning	10	28	46	
IVb. Respect for Mastery	11	29	47	
IVc. Fruitful Linkages	12	30	48	
Va. Apt Organizational Form	13	31	49	
Vb. Supported Champions	14	32	50	
Vc. High-Performing New Product/Process Development	15	33	51	
VIa. Guiding Mental Maps	16	34	52	
VIb. Sound Decision Processes	17	35	53	
VIc. Resourced Initiatives	18	36	54	

Innovation Capability Audit Interpretation Sheet

Unblocking Innovation in Your Organization

Developing innovation capability in an organization is complex and challenging. Eighteen dimensions of innovation capability can be identified, as shown on the wheel diagram (Figure 2) and defined in the sections that follow. Each dimension can serve as a driver or as a blockage (that is, a cleared blockage becomes a driver). Each organization has to find ways of overcoming blockages and transforming them into drivers.

Figure 2. Drivers of Organizational Innovation

Interpretation Guidelines

Begin by reading the descriptions that follow about the eighteen innovation drivers. Share your scores from the Innovation Capability Audit with the other members of your subgroup. In particular, identify low-scoring dimensions and assess their importance to your organization, using the Innovation Capability Audit Work Sheet. Then plan what you need to do to confirm the diagnosis and work on innovation blockages.

Dimensions of Innovation Capability

Ia. *Innovating Leadership.* The organization is led assertively by top managers who share a driving vision of the organization's future and create a context within which innovation thrives. The key characteristics of organizations in which leaders promote innovation include the following:

- Senior managers take innovation very seriously.
- Top managers inspire people to be innovative.
- The organization's leaders are tough on those who seek to block change.

Ib. *Provides Strategic Advantage.* The organization has a well-developed strategy that identifies the capabilities, technologies, products, services, and processes necessary for continued competitive advantage. Organizations in which innovation promotes competitive advantage demonstrate the following characteristics:

- The organization's record of innovation is superior to its competitors.
- Innovation is directed to achieving competitive advantage.
- New products (or services) provide the customer with superior value.

Ic. *Prudent Radicalism.* Bold and far-reaching changes will be made but only after great thought. Organizations that combine radicalness and prudence are identified by the following traits:

- Radical changes can be quickly implemented.
- Top managers give careful thought before making a radical decision.
- Senior management has a recent history of making bold decisions.

IIa. *Exceptional Individuals.* Exceptional individuals are recruited, rewarded, respected, and retained. The following are key characteristics of organizations that recruit, retain, and motivate exceptional individuals:

- Creative individuals are well rewarded.

- Outstanding individuals are highly valued.

- Exceptional individuals fit into the organization.

IIb. *Full Competencies Portfolio.* The organization continuously develops the capabilities needed to support a stream of innovation. The key characteristics of organizations that have a full portfolio of competencies include the following:

- The organization is an early adopter of state-of-the-art technologies.

- Technological strengths and weaknesses have been carefully analyzed.

- The organization is investing to develop all of the capabilities needed to win in the future.

IIc. *Capable Implementation.* Innovative ideas can be quickly and effectively implemented. Organizations that can put new ideas into action share traits such as the following:

- The organization is good at getting things done.

- Once a decision is made, initiatives are implemented rapidly.

- Projects are managed effectively.

IIIa. *Selective Empowerment.* The management philosophy of the organization supports able individuals to take initiatives. The following are key characteristics of organizations that encourage empowerment without losing control:

- Employees are empowered to take significant initiatives.

- Employees speak up even when important people are challenged.

- Personal initiatives are supported, providing people work within guidelines.

IIIb. *Innovation Demanded.* Everyone is expected to innovate. Organizations that expect innovation can be identified by the following indicators:

- It is expected that staff at all levels will innovate.

- Managers and staff have key objectives to develop new ideas.

- People are appraised based on their success in being innovative.

IIIc. *High Enrollment.* People actively support innovation initiatives. The organizations that enroll staff in innovation demonstrate the following characteristics:

- People welcome change.
- Almost everyone supports management's plans.
- Employees help people with creative ideas.

IVa. *Continuous Learning.* Challenge and learning are continuous processes. The key traits of organizations that learn continuously include the following:

- Significant resources are invested in developing people.
- There is a constant search for new ways to define problems.
- The organization rarely makes the same mistake twice.

IVb. *Respect for Mastery.* Those who have in-depth specialist knowledge help to guide the organization forward. A respect for mastery in organizations is demonstrated by the following characteristics:

- Technical experts are influential in decision making.
- Technical specialists share their knowledge widely.
- Those with in-depth technical skills are highly respected.

IVc. *Fruitful Linkages.* The organization is outward looking. Cooperative links are maintained with the outside world (including customers, consultancies, trade associations, standards organizations, suppliers, universities, joint-venture partners, and so on). These are win-win collaborations. When organizations construct fruitful linkages, they show the following traits:

- The organization actively involves customers in the development of new products.
- The organization frequently benchmarks how it compares with other organizations.
- The organization learns through strong links with partners, industry associations, universities, consultants, and so on.

Va. *Apt Organizational Form.* The structure and form of the organization helps not hinders the innovation process. Organizations that are structured for innovation demonstrate the following tendencies:

- There is a extensive collaboration between teams and departments.
- Things get done; there is no unnecessary bureaucracy.
- The way the organization is structured helps not hinders innovation.

Vb. *Supported Champions.* Those who can make things happen are enabled and supported. The key characteristics of organizations that support champions include the following:

- People obtain management's support for well-considered initiatives.
- People who drive through changes are recognized as heroes.
- People with ideas can win the resources they need.

Vc. *High-Performing New Product/Process Development.* There are effective processes for managing new product/process development. Organizations that have effective processes for developing new products and processes share the following traits:

- Top priority is given to developing new products and processes.
- The organization takes ideas and quickly produces products that people want to buy.
- Efforts are concentrated on launching new products that really attract customers.

VIa. *Guiding Mental Maps.* Innovations are directed by a theory of what needs to change and how. Effective conceptual maps for planning change are demonstrated by the following characteristics:

- Managers strive to understand new ideas in great depth before making a change.
- Those leading a change process can fully describe the advantages and disadvantages.
- The organization is striving to be truly world class in every aspect of performance.

VIb. *Sound Decision Processes.* Timely and wise decisions are taken about initiatives. The key characteristics of organizations that have effective decision-making processes include the following:

- Decisions about launching new products are taken after very careful analysis.
- Decisions to support or kill an initiative are taken by managers who really understand the issues.
- When it is important, decisions are made quickly.

VIc. *Resourced Initiatives.* Innovation projects are owned by senior managers and driven through. Organizations that provide initiatives with the necessary resources show the following indicators:

- New ideas are fully driven through, despite setbacks or difficulties.
- Management insists that only a limited number of initiatives are undertaken at once, to prevent overstretching the organization.
- Top managers take personal responsibility for major initiatives.

INNOVATION CAPABILITY AUDIT WORK SHEET

Instructions: Determine the three *lowest* topic scores for yourself and for your subgroup's average. To determine your subgroup's average, combine individual totals for each topic and divide by the number of members in the subgroup, as follows:

Topic	My Score	Scores of Other Subgroup Members (List)	Total of Subgroup Scores (My Score + Scores of Other Subgroup Members	Average Score (Total ÷ Number of Subgroup Members)
Ia. Innovating Leadership				
Ib. Provides Strategic Advantage				
Ic. Prudent Radicalism				
IIa. Exceptional Individuals				
IIb. Full Competencies Portfolio				
IIc. Capable Implementation				
IIIa. Selective Empowerment				
IIIb. Innovation Demanded				
IIIc. High Enrollment				
IVa. Continuous Learning				
IVb. Respect for Mastery				
IVc. Fruitful Linkages				
Va. Apt Organizational Form				
Vb. Supported Champions				
Vc. High-Performing New Product/ Process Development				
VIa. Guiding Mental Maps				
VIb. Sound Decision Processes				
VIc. Resourced Initiatives				

My lowest scores:	
Topic	Score
Topic	Score
Topic	Score

My subgroup's lowest scores:	
Topic	Score
Topic	Score
Topic	Score

The innovation blockages (those with the lowest scores) are probably the major issues your organization has to face. These results need to be verified by discussion and further evaluation. In your subgroup, select *one* probable blockage to discuss. Look back in the explanation section at the characteristics of organizations that do not have that blockage and discuss the following questions:

1. Is this a real blockage for us?

2. Is it important? Why or why not?

3. Why does the blockage occur?

4. What can we do to unblock this indicator within the next ninety days?

Strategic Target Actions Review

Robert C. Preziosi and Patrick J. Ward

Abstract: The Strategic Target Actions Review (STAR) is a diagnostic questionnaire that helps an organization determine its level of long-term effectiveness. It can be used by internal or external consultants to assess levels of organizational functioning in the following areas: continuous learning, customer focus, organizational purpose, process improvement, strength of culture, systems support, values-based leadership, and work team development. By assessing itself in each of these areas, an organization can focus on areas for improvement while celebrating areas of strength. The results of the questionnaire provide an important baseline by which to quantify organizational variables for objective measurement on an ongoing basis.

$\mathbf{F}$or the last two decades, companies throughout the world have faced unparalleled changes and accompanying challenges. Faced with these developments, some have faltered, swept away in changing seas. Others thrive in spite of economic cycles, leadership changes, and market variability. Successful companies somehow manage to chart courses that, while leading them into unavoidable squalls, have kept them from going under or ending up aground.

Companies that do prosper are not immune from the storms and rough seas. Why are some companies able to sustain themselves while others end up on the rocks? Perhaps they have found that certain strategic business practices and principles lead to continuous prosperity and sustainability. In their commitment to these practices and principles, they are able to take more accurate readings and realistically assess their condition and direction. Guided by these developed skills, they are able to react early enough to avoid the brunt of storms and avoid being tossed about. They have consciously built an institution that endures because it is able to analyze its course and respond to changing conditions. The ability to critically assess the needs of ship and crew allows some companies to utilize resources in ways that other companies have not even imagined.

THE STAR MODEL

Organizational leaders must develop a systemic view to ensure vigilance in providing needed direction. The Strategic Target Actions Review (STAR) is intended to provide just such a comprehensive model to assist organizations in establishing this vigilance to improve organizational coordination and to assist in the achievement of common goals.

In particular, the STAR represents a *model of target actions* necessary for companies to flourish, as well as a *system of measurement* by which organizations can take readings and adjust their courses in order to continue to flourish.

Elements of the Model

The STAR model contains eight elements of organizational strategic sustainability. These model categories are based on research into the organizational variables essential to effectiveness and longevity (Collins & Porras,

1994; Preziosi, 1980, 1994; Ward, 1993; Ward & Preziosi, 1994). While the model incorporates previous research, it also builds on it by the inclusion of an additional element: *customer focus* (both internal and external.)

The target elements are depicted in Figure 1, and their definitions are as follows:

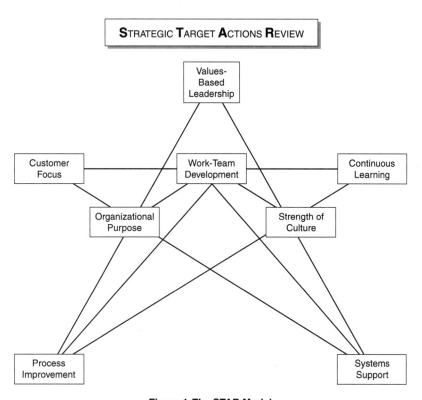

Figure 1. The STAR Model

Values-Based Leadership

Acts of leadership throughout the organization are based on an enduring and consistent set of values. Such leadership provides the consistency necessary for a greater sense of employee security. Employees feel more comfortable and assured of their roles and of the parameters in meeting internal and external customer needs.

Organizational Purpose

The organization has a clear vision of its strategies, goals, and objectives. Leadership in the organization acts in ways consistent with the purpose. Managers and supervisors work to assist employees in carrying out identified goals and to provide feedback and training regarding performance and customer reactions and expectations.

Strength of Culture

Norms, expectations, and behaviors are deep rooted and accepted by all who work in the organization. There is a sense of pride in membership in the organization, with intrinsic and extrinsic rewards for members who show commitment. Organizational leadership fosters a sense of membership among employees.

Work-Team Development

Leadership provides clear direction as to the goals of the organization and respective work groups. Members emphasize cooperative behavior in carrying out individual and group tasks. Organization members are able to utilize and resolve conflict. Input from all team members is expected and reinforced by members and management.

Process Improvement

There are measurements and feedback mechanisms to monitor individual and work-group procedures and outputs. Employees are encouraged and feel safe to identify problems, and their observations receive responses. Mistakes are investigated for contributing factors and are used as learning aids to improve work processes and outputs.

Systems Support

Materials, methods of technology, assistance, and sufficient staffing support the needs of the work groups for efficiency.

Customer Focus

Individuals and work groups are aware of the identities and needs of internal and external customers. Feedback mechanisms are in place, including feedback from direct-line employees, which is encouraged and used in training and development for product/service development. Individuals and work groups understand the importance of responding to internal and external customer needs.

Continuous Learning

The organization provides time and support for employee training and monitors new development and changes in its industry or field. It shows commitment to developing and advancing employees and to allowing them to utilize newly acquired skills. The organization is open to admitting its own mistakes and using the information to drive needed change.

USING THE STAR IN ORGANIZATIONS

Validity and Reliability

Content validity for the STAR is based on the research previously mentioned and was confirmed by an expert panel. Statistically, internal reliability has been assessed using coefficient alpha. Questions within each category scored in the .80 range, with the exception of "Values-Based Leadership," which scored in the upper ranges of .70. Language and wording can be ambiguous because of group and regional differences; therefore, it is important that the questionnaire be reviewed by a representative sampling of the intended population to ensure common understanding of the terminology. Although the rendered quotient is of value, it is further recommended that the questionnaire be used as part of a multiple-methods strategy that incorporates employee interviews and feedback of results for validation and discussion.

Questionnaire Administration

The questionnaire is intended to be used in an entire organization. Although administration in an individual work unit would certainly yield valuable data, sustainability is more appropriately an organization-wide concept. For best results, the questionnaire is best administered by an internal or external consultant.

The STAR is composed of forty-eight items, representing six statements for each of the eight scales. Respondents are asked to indicate their opinions via Likert scales that range from 1 to 6. This is a *forced-choice* inventory. Although respondents may indicate mild agreement or mild disagreement, the scale precludes *neutral* responses. Respondents indicate their choices for each statement, then transfer their answers to the STAR Scoring Sheet.

Scoring

Scores for each of the scales can be obtained for an individual by averaging the respective questions for that scale (the total of the responses, divided by 6). Responses from desired subsets (by department, location, management, and so on) can also be obtained by combining individual scores for members of those subsets and averaging them to yield a group average score. (See Footnote 1 for more detailed statistical analysis options.)[1]

Interpretation

Results from the STAR questionnaire can be used to compare people's perceptions in any number of ways:

- Management and employees

- Department to department

- Product (or service) to product (or service)

- Territory to territory

Results may also be used to compare individual items or categories across respective groups. In this way, specific issues affecting the organization may be identified, localized, and then further investigated by means of interviews. Brainstorming and other group techniques may then be incorporated to identify planned interventions.

Results of the STAR establish important baselines. Organizational variables are quantified for more objective measurement. Future applications may then be used to help measure the efficacy of organizational interventions and remediation efforts.

---

[1]Resultant scores can also be rescaled for direct comparison vis-à-vis a force-field analysis chart. To do this, the lower (positive) scores are subtracted from the upper limit of the highest (negative) score. (The upper limit would be 6.999 but for practical purposes 7 can be used). In this way, a positive score of 1 could be directly compared with the relative impact of a negative score of 6. The positive score of 1 would be subtracted from the upper limit of the negative score, yielding a score of 6 (7–1), which would be placed in the positive column of the force-field chart for a direct comparison. All results of the force-field chart can also be magnified by a common number for easier comparative analysis.

References and Bibliography

Collins, J.C., & Porras, J.I. (1994). *Built to last.* New York: HarperCollins.

Preziosi, R.C. (1980). The organizational diagnosis questionnaire. In Pfeiffer, J.W., & Jones, J.E. (Eds.), *The 1980 annual handbook for group facilitators* (pp. 115–120). San Francisco, CA: Jossey-Bass/Pfeiffer.

Preziosi, R.C. (1994). Determining leader behavior types through value cue-action leadership. *Journal of Leadership Studies, I*(3), 50–56.

Ward, P.J. (1993). *A study of organizational variables affecting worker empowerment.* Doctoral Dissertation. Miami, FL: University of Miami.

Ward, P.J., & Preziosi, R.C. (1994). Fostering the effectiveness of groups at work. In Pfeiffer, J.W., (Ed.), *The 1994 annual: Developing human resources* (pp. 213–226). San Francisco, CA: Jossey-Bass/Pfeiffer.

Robert C. Preziosi, D.P.A., is a professor of management education in the School of Business and Entrepreneurship at Nova Southeastern University in Fort Lauderdale, Florida. He is also the president of Management Associates, a consulting firm. He has worked as a human resources director, a line manager, and a leadership-training administrator and has consulted with all levels of management in many organizations, including American Express, the Department of Health and Human Services, Lennar, Siemens, and many hospitals and banks. Dr. Preziosi has been training trainers since the 1970s; his areas of interest include leadership, adult learning, and all aspects of management and executive development. In 1984 he was given the Outstanding Contribution to HRD Award by ASTD; in 1996 he received the Torch Award, the highest leadership award that ASTD gives, for the second time. He is the only person ever so honored.

Patrick J. Ward, Ph.D., is the principal of Organization Analysis & Development, an industrial and organizational consulting firm. He has provided consultation services in the United States and the Caribbean for over ten years. He previously served as Vice President of Organization Development and HR for the Avanti Case-Hoyt Corporation, a national marketing communications company. Dr. Ward also maintains a private clinical practice with Neuropsychology and Counseling Services of Mount Dora, Florida. He has published articles on the topics of group development in organizations, employee and management development, conflict resolution, therapeutic counseling practices, and addiction. Dr. Ward is a member of ASTD and the American Psychological Association.

STRATEGIC TARGET ACTIONS REVIEW

Robert C. Preziosi and Patrick J. Ward

Instructions: This questionnaire is designed to allow you to register your opinions regarding your organization. Please review each of the following statements, and place an "x" in the box that corresponds to your opinion.

1 = Strongly Agree	3 = Mildly Agree	5 = Disagree
2 = Agree	4 = Mildly Disagree	6 = Strongly Disagree

	1	2	3	4	5	6
1. The formal values and beliefs of this organization are well known to all employees.	☐	☐	☐	☐	☐	☐
2. My fellow employees are open to critical feedback in order to improve performance.	☐	☐	☐	☐	☐	☐
3. I have access to the technology and support that I need to get my job done quickly.	☐	☐	☐	☐	☐	☐
4. My organization has a formal vision statement or statement of purpose that is made available and is known by employees.	☐	☐	☐	☐	☐	☐
5. This organization rewards people for cooperation and working well in teams.	☐	☐	☐	☐	☐	☐
6. This organization has identified heroes who are respected by all employees.	☐	☐	☐	☐	☐	☐
7. My work group is aware of our customers (internal and external).	☐	☐	☐	☐	☐	☐
8. Training and education are made available to anyone who wants to upgrade his or her individual skills.	☐	☐	☐	☐	☐	☐
9. The actions of the leaders of this organization are consistent with the formal or public values they stress.	☐	☐	☐	☐	☐	☐
10. There are measurements in place that allow employees of this company to track and monitor their work.	☐	☐	☐	☐	☐	☐

1 = Strongly Agree	3 = Mildly Agree		5 = Disagree		
2 = Agree	4 = Mildly Disagree		6 = Strongly Disagree		

	1	2	3	4	5	6
11. The company provides training and information on new techniques and procedures.	☐	☐	☐	☐	☐	☐
12. Management works with employees to carry out the identified goals of the organization.	☐	☐	☐	☐	☐	☐
13. Departments and work groups are cooperative and supportive of one another.	☐	☐	☐	☐	☐	☐
14. There is a sense of community or a pride of membership in this organization.	☐	☐	☐	☐	☐	☐
15. Feedback from customers (internal and external) is used in planning and designing work.	☐	☐	☐	☐	☐	☐
16. This organization provides opportunities for employees to use newly acquired skills.	☐	☐	☐	☐	☐	☐
17. The leaders of this organization are interested and supportive concerning the efforts of employees.	☐	☐	☐	☐	☐	☐
18. Employees are encouraged to point out problems with this company's work procedures.	☐	☐	☐	☐	☐	☐
19. I am able to obtain quickly the materials and information that I need to perform tasks.	☐	☐	☐	☐	☐	☐
20. Management practices in this organization are consistent with the goals and objectives that have been identified.	☐	☐	☐	☐	☐	☐
21. This organization's leadership provides clear direction to the goals of my work group.	☐	☐	☐	☐	☐	☐
22. There are rewards and recognition for employees who show commitment to this organization.	☐	☐	☐	☐	☐	☐
23. Responding to customer needs (internal or external) is stressed as important within my immediate work group.	☐	☐	☐	☐	☐	☐

	1 = Strongly Agree	3 = Mildly Agree	5 = Disagree
	2 = Agree	4 = Mildly Disagree	6 = Strongly Disagree

	1	2	3	4	5	6
24. This organization is open to admitting its own mistakes and to using this information to inspire needed changes.	☐	☐	☐	☐	☐	☐
25. Leaders and managers of this organization take responsibility for their decisions and stand behind them.	☐	☐	☐	☐	☐	☐
26. Recommendations and suggestions of employees are heard and taken into consideration.	☐	☐	☐	☐	☐	☐
27. Other departments respond quickly when help or assistance is needed.	☐	☐	☐	☐	☐	☐
28. I know exactly how the work that I perform contributes to the goals of the organization (for example, how my work fits to the overall picture).	☐	☐	☐	☐	☐	☐
29. There is little unresolved conflict, and people deal with disagreements or problems openly.	☐	☐	☐	☐	☐	☐
30. Management and supervisors strive to make employees feel part of this organization.	☐	☐	☐	☐	☐	☐
31. Employees are given the support and freedom necessary to meet customer needs.	☐	☐	☐	☐	☐	☐
32. This organization provides time and support for employee training.	☐	☐	☐	☐	☐	☐
33. People's interactions with one another reflect the important values identified in this organization.	☐	☐	☐	☐	☐	☐
34. Employee mistakes are used for identifying training and process-improvement needs.	☐	☐	☐	☐	☐	☐
35. Our department has adequate staffing to respond to the needs of our internal/ external customers.	☐	☐	☐	☐	☐	☐
36. Rewards and recognition encourage employees to support the goals of the organization.	☐	☐	☐	☐	☐	☐

1 = Strongly Agree		3 = Mildly Agree		5 = Disagree	
2 = Agree		4 = Mildly Disagree		6 = Strongly Disagree	

	1	2	3	4	5	6
37. My supervisor/manager encourages input from members of my work group.	☐	☐	☐	☐	☐	☐
38. This organization makes it clear about what values are important regarding work and customers.	☐	☐	☐	☐	☐	☐
39. Feedback from direct-line employees is encouraged and used in training and development for service or product development.	☐	☐	☐	☐	☐	☐
40. This organization is aware of developments and changes in its field and stays on the forefront.	☐	☐	☐	☐	☐	☐
41. Employee interactions with customers reflect the values identified as important in this organization.	☐	☐	☐	☐	☐	☐
42. My work group receives regular feedback from the people (internal or external customers) who receive our work.	☐	☐	☐	☐	☐	☐
43. The efficiency of our work group is recognized and rewarded.	☐	☐	☐	☐	☐	☐
44. This organization provides orientation and training for employees regarding its purposes and goals.	☐	☐	☐	☐	☐	☐
45. Members of my work group are able to resolve efficiently problems that arise in our work.	☐	☐	☐	☐	☐	☐
46. Company expectations of employee behavior are accepted and supported by employees.	☐	☐	☐	☐	☐	☐
47. Direct-line employees are seen as important and are supported in this organization.	☐	☐	☐	☐	☐	☐
48. This organization seeks to develop and advance its employees.	☐	☐	☐	☐	☐	☐

STAR Scoring Sheet

Instructions: Transfer the scores from the questionnaire to the respective question blanks below. Add each column, and then divide the total by six. This will yield comparable scores for each of the eight scales.

Values-Based Leadership	Systems Support	Work-Team Development
1. _____	3. _____	5. _____
9. _____	11. _____	13. _____
17. _____	19. _____	21. _____
25. _____	27. _____	29. _____
33. _____	35. _____	37. _____
41. _____	43. _____	45. _____
Total _____	Total _____	Total _____
Average _____	Average _____	Average _____

Process Improvement	Organizational Purpose	Strength of Culture
2. _____	4. _____	6. _____
10. _____	12. _____	14. _____
18. _____	20. _____	22. _____
26. _____	28. _____	30. _____
34. _____	36. _____	38. _____
42. _____	44. _____	46. _____
Total _____	Total _____	Total _____
Average _____	Average _____	Average _____

Customer Focus

7. _____

15. _____

23. _____

31. _____

39. _____

47. _____

Total _____

Average _____

Continuous Learning

8. _____

16. _____

24. _____

32. _____

40. _____

48. _____

Total _____

Average _____

Overall Rating

Values-Based Leadership _____

Process Improvement _____

Systems Support _____

Organizational Purpose _____

Work-Team Development _____

Strength of Culture _____

Customer Focus _____

Continuous Learning _____

Total _____

Average _____

Introduction
to the Presentation and Discussion Resources Section

Every facilitator needs to develop a repertoire of theory and background that can be used in a variety of situations. Learning based on direct experience is not the only kind of learning appropriate to human-interaction training. A practical combination of theory and research with experiential learning generally enriches training and may be essential in many types of cognitive and skill development. Affective and cognitive data support, alter, validate, extend, and complement each other.

The 1998 Annual: Volume 2, Consulting includes ten articles, in the following categories:

Individual Development: Personal Growth

Conventional Human Resource Development and the Gestalt Alternative by H.B. Karp

Problem Solving: Change and Change Agents

Developing an Innovative Organizational Culture: Dimensions, Assessments, and a Change Process by Markus Hauser

Diversity and Organizational Change by Ginger Lapid-Bogda

Making the Deal Work: Managing the People Side of Mergers and Acquisitions by Timothy Galpin

Groups and Teams: Team Building and Team Development

Three Team Traps by Sara Pope

Consulting: Consulting Strategies and Techniques

The A^2D^4 Process for Designing and Improving Organizational Processes by Neil J. Simon

Creating the Dynamic Enterprise: Strategic Tools for HRD Practitioners by Lisa Friedman and Hermann Gyr

A New Way of Guiding Large-Scale Organizational Change
by Laura Hauser

Consulting: Interface with Clients

Collaborative Contracting: A Key to Consulting Success
by Homer H. Johnson and Sander J. Smiles

Leadership: Top Management Issues

Informal Rewards As a Performance-Management Tool
by Bob Nelson

As with previous *Annuals,* this volume covers a wide variety of topics. The range of articles presented should encourage a good deal of thought-provoking, serious discussion about the present and future of HRD. Other articles on specific subjects can be located by using our comprehensive *Reference Guide to Handbooks and Annuals.* This book, which is updated regularly, indexes the contents of all the *Annuals* and the *Handbooks of Structured Experiences.* With each revision, the *Reference Guide* becomes a complete, up-to-date, and easy-to-use resource for selecting appropriate materials from the *Annuals* and *Handbooks.*

Here and in the *Reference Guide,* we have done our best to categorize the articles for easy reference; however, many of the articles encompass a range of topics, disciplines, and applications. If you do not find what you are looking for under one category, we encourage you to look under a related category. Also, in attempting to balance the contents of both volumes of the *Annual,* we may place an article in the "Training" *Annual* that also has implications for "Consulting," and vice versa. As the field of HRD becomes more sophisticated, what is done in a training context is based on the needs of, and affects, the organization. Likewise, from a systemic viewpoint, anything that affects individuals in an organization has repercussions throughout the organization, and vice versa. We encourage you not to be limited by the categorization system that we have developed, but to explore all the contents of both volumes of the *Annual* in order to realize the full potential for learning and development that each offers.

Conventional Human Resource Development and the Gestalt Alternative

H.B. Karp

Abstract: The Gestalt approach to individual and organizational improvement can be differentiated from conventional human resource/organization development (CHRD) in several ways. This article first discusses general differences between the approaches and refers to Herman's (1974) ten specific distinctions. It then adds eleven more distinctions between CHRD and the Gestalt approach: emphasis on change vs. emphasis on experiencing the present; breaking down resistance vs. honoring resistance; external vs. internal standards; informed choice vs. conscious choice; focus on the individual's interactions with others vs. focus on how individuals interact with all aspects of the work environment; shared responsibility vs. individual responsibility; normative shoulds vs. valuing "what is"; valuing similarities vs. valuing differences; protecting others vs. protecting self; impulsivity vs. spontaneity; and empowering others vs. empowering self.

O rganizations are undergoing change at an increasingly rapid rate, as are the values that support these changes. The last decades focused primarily on management by objectives; Situational Leadership®; individual growth and accountability; the formation of teams and group structures; and total quality management. The emphasis today is on larger, system-wide interventions, e.g., "rightsizing," reengineering, and self-directed work teams, with the result that less emphasis is placed on increasing individual strength and accountability.

Although organizations have changed and continue to evolve in an attempt to respond to current conditions, the one element that has stayed fairly constant is the importance of the individual worker and the need to keep some focus on the specific interfaces between the worker and the work, the worker and other people in the organization, and the worker and the organization itself.

According to Bennis and Mische (1995), "70 to 80 percent of all reengineering efforts end in failure—failure in the sense that the effort did not produce the intended result or that the experience was extremely negative." This is a costly and discouraging statistic; a failed or aborted change effort can be considerably worse than no change at all. The major problem seems to be not with the current "engineering" approach to the field of organizational improvement but, rather, with the fact that we simply refuse to learn from our experience. Once a new approach or philosophy has been accepted, it seems that all previous lessons are discarded.

The present trend toward large, system-wide structural change is certainly responsive to current economic and social conditions. What is essential to increasing the probability of a program's success, however, is to maintain the awareness that the necessary (but not sufficient) condition for success is the maximizing of each individual's strengths and accountability.

The body of knowledge and technology that sees organization development and effectiveness most in individual terms is the Gestalt theory base. The Gestalt approach to organization development and its reverence for individuality first emerged as a force in the mid-1970s from the work and writings of Stan Herman. As the field began emphasizing the growing need for group processes, Herman made the point that, paradoxically, it is the strength of each individual that is the key to building the most effective team.

Other writers maintained this perspective (Karp, 1995, 1996; Maurer, 1995; Nevis, 1987): that it is the individual's choice and how each choice is made that is the basic stuff of organizational change.

Herman's 1974 article, "The Shadow of Organization Development," is as relevant today as it was the day it was published. In it, he draws ten distinctions between the conventional human relations approach to group process and the Gestalt approach. Interestingly, the term "human relations" is the only one that might seem antiquated today. The terms "team values" and "group norms" are just as relevant in today's organizations.

This article presents eleven additional distinctions and invites the reader to look at the differences between the two compared systems and to choose whatever makes the most sense to him or her.

GENERAL CONTRASTS BETWEEN CONVENTIONAL HUMAN RESOURCE DEVELOPMENT AND GESTALT APPROACHES

Conventional human resource development advocates a normative set of values as the "one best way" to be or to proceed, and is characterized by several assumptions:

- Human behavior is subject to certain "laws" or specific directions;

- These laws and/or directions are better than others and are particularly better than those going in the opposite direction;

- Because of these assumptions about how people exist, it is possible, if not desirable, to clearly define and categorize individuals and to deal with them by lumping them into groups; and

- Individuals and organizations that do not conform to the normative values are not maximizing their full potential and, therefore, are subject to training and consultative work that is specifically geared to getting them "on board."

The Gestalt (G) approach is also characterized by certain assumptions about the individual and the organization, and these are quite different from those of CHRD.

1. There is no "one best way" to be. Specifically, there is no human characteristic that is, in and of itself, bad or undesirable.

2. Human effectiveness is the natural state; people have been taught how to disempower themselves.

3. The most effective organizations are those whose norms, values, and approaches reflect those of its members, rather than the other way around.

4. The effectiveness of the individual and the organization are determined wholly by the situation to which they are responding.

5. Individuals and organizations are infinitely more different than they are similar; any attempt to categorize them with a view toward dealing with them more effectively will produce the opposite effect. This reduced effectiveness will be caused by focusing on the very few similarities that group members may have in common, thereby ignoring the vast wealth of differences.

As an example, there may be some accuracy in saying that master sergeants, as a group, are similar to one another in that they are quite different from elementary-school teachers. However, just below the surface, each sergeant (or teacher, for that matter) is as different from a counterpart as he or she is different from any member of any other group.

SPECIFIC CONTRASTS BETWEEN CONVENTIONAL HUMAN RESOURCE DEVELOPMENT AND GESTALT APPROACHES

Emphasis on Change vs. Emphasis on Experiencing the Present

CHRD: Emphasis is on constant change in reaction to external, past, and future conditions.

G: Emphasis is on experiencing fully what is occurring at the moment.

The observation that most CHRD consultants refer to themselves as "change agents" illustrates the heavy value that this approach places on constant movement. The underlying value is that, if the organization stays in motion, it will be able to respond more appropriately to internal and external pressures, much as a boxer maintains a dancing movement, rather than standing flat footed. Although flexibility is a desirable attribute, the extension of this value is that the organization will find itself mostly in a reactive stance.

Being in service to change is no more functional than being in service to no change. The Gestalt-oriented consultant, in contrast, can be described as a "what's happening agent." By focusing on each event as it is happening and by maintaining an awareness of the parameters of the present situation, one is clearer about whether or not a change is dictated. The extension of this approach is that the organization will find itself in a reactive, proactive, or even a nonactive stance, depending on which is the way to get what is needed or wanted in a given situation.

Breaking Down Resistance vs. Honoring Resistance

CHRD: Emphasis is on avoiding, breaking down, or reducing resistance.

G: Emphasis is on surfacing and legitimizing resistance.

Reducing resistance, particularly to change, is one of the key values of CHRD. Beginning as early as the Harwood studies and continuing through today, the primary thrust of the OD practitioner has focused on facilitating change and placing specific emphasis on ways and means of reducing resistance to it. Theories and approaches, such as force-field analysis and participative management, and earlier approaches, such as marathons and T-groups, have been geared specifically to diminishing resistance.

The Gestalt perspective is quite different. In the first place, there is no assumption that change, in and of itself, is necessarily good. Secondly, there is a clear Gestalt value that people have an absolute right—if not an obligation—to protect themselves. Third, and most important of all, people are going to protect themselves anyway, whether or not they are given permission to do so.

In viewing resistance as a neutral or even positive factor, rather than a negative one, the consultant is in a better position to work with it creatively. By simply honoring the individual's right to resist and by encouraging the right to state that resistance openly, the consultant may prompt several of the following things to occur:

1. Information may surface that suggests that the change may not be for the good;

2. Upon hearing out loud the statement of his or her resistance, the individual may be in a better position to choose either to continue or to stop the resistance; and

3. The clear resistance (real objections) may be separated from the pseudo resistance ("You can't make me"; "I don't feel like thinking about it"; "Sez you!").

From the Gestalt view, anything that is done that reinforces the "other's" sense of self-worth and dignity will facilitate clearer and more effective contact between two or more people. This is most certainly true when it reinforces the message: "I don't have to want what you want." Once the clear resistance surfaces and is honored, there is a greater probability that it can be dealt with more effectively, for the following reasons:

1. Something may emerge out of the interaction that will legitimately reduce the "other's" resistance.

2. Energy usually reserved for protecting one's right to resist is now released for other work.

3. If the decision is to go ahead anyway, despite the resistance, doing so from a stance of "agreeing to disagree" is more productive than doing so from a stance of "see what you are making me do."

If the consultant chooses to approach resistance from the stance of honoring it, two elements must be present at all times. First, there has to be a clear and explicit understanding that there will be no attempt to persuade, sell, or coerce the other person in an attempt to reduce the resistance. Second, the consultant never probes the other individual in terms of "why" the resistance, only in terms of what or how the individual is resisting. "Why" probes frequently produce an immediate reaction of justification and unnecessary defensiveness, e.g., "I'm in trouble for not agreeing immediately" or "Who do I think I am disagreeing like this?" Whereas, the "what" or "how" probe, e.g., "What is your objection?" or "How is this a problem for you?" has a greater tendency to produce increased awareness. It is from this stance of increased awareness that the consultant can often assist the individual in making more effective choices that will result in getting the individual and the organization more of what is wanted.

External vs. Internal Standards

CHRD: Reliance is on external standards for appropriate behavior.

G: Reliance is on "self" as the final arbiter for appropriate behavior.

A natural fallout from CHRD's focus on interpersonal interaction and process is the strong tendency to focus on group norms, goals, and values that surface as the result of an OD effort. As the norms emerge from group interaction, they frequently become the standard for future appropriate behavior. Once these norms are established, the individual now has a clear set of external guidelines by which to guide his or her internal actions, and as long as an individual acts within this framework of group norms, group support will probably be forthcoming. If he or she does not conform, rejection or censure by the group can be expected until conformance occurs (Janus, 1973).

An example of this occurred several years ago. During a weekend encounter group, a norm arose very early on that an individual was not having an authentic experience unless tears were a part of the process. The group would remain focused on an individual until tears appeared. This sort of thing occurs in different forms in today's groups.

The Gestalt perspective is quite different. Perls (1969) defined maturity as ". . .relying on internal, rather than external resources." This implies that the individual is the foremost authority on himself or herself and is, therefore, the best one to determine what is appropriate in any given situation. The process includes the following:

1. The individual becoming clear about what he or she wants;

2. Becoming clear about what it is others want; and, then,

3. Making a decision about what is appropriate by taking all these factors into consideration, in terms of what is available in the ongoing situation.

Informed Choice vs. Conscious Choice

CHRD: Emphasizes extensive data gathering and analysis prior to session or meeting.

G: Emphasizes "hot" data.

Most CHRD technology places high emphasis on data gathering and categorizing prior to the problem-solving or team-building session or staff meeting. This is particularly true for the "action research" approach to organization development.

There are two primary problems that many practitioners have discovered when pursuing this approach. First, the data, although highly relevant at the time of collection, has in whole or in part, gone "cold"—no longer relevant—by the time the meetings or consulting sessions are held. Second, sometimes information that is disclosed openly to a consultant, who is neutral, is not owned by anyone when it is disclosed as "group information." Thus, a sensitive and sometimes key issue is made public and, frequently, no one will deal with it. This tends to block a group's work, rather than facilitate it. It is much like saying, "OK, who threw the dead fish on the floor?"; if no one answers, the consultant gets to pick it up.

The Gestalt view is that everybody knows at all times what they want/don't want, like/don't like, and how they are stopping themselves from dealing more effectively with individual and organizational issues. By simply asking the participants to address themselves to the salient organizational issues and using the first part of the meeting/session to surface them, a higher degree of relevance, at a lower level of threat, is probable. One of the better techniques is simply, at the beginning of the session, to ask each participant to publicly respond in terms of "What is the best possible outcome that could occur for you in this session?" and, then, "What is the worst possible outcome?" This approach tends to, first, demand more relevance, particularly in terms of the individual's perspective; and, second, to ensure that the level of disclosure will be safe for each individual in attendance, i.e., no dead fish will be thrown.

The difference between the two approaches to choice is that CHRD emphasizes the word "informed," which suggests a cognitive or objective approach, and the "what," i.e., what is the information that we have available on which to base the choice. The Gestalt approach emphasizes the word "conscious" and the "how"—how the choice is made. The focus is on the responsibility of the choice and having it be all right for an individual to want whatever he or she wants, even though it may be contrary to the wants of others and/or the organization itself.

The consultant has a greater probability of surfacing issues and agendas that are relevant, at the time, to the individual's perspective, by pulling "hot" data in the meeting than by structuring the session based on an instrument that was responded to some time prior to the session, and that was formulated in terms of what the consultant or team leader thinks is relevant.

Since all decisions are subjective at the point of choice, e.g., "I want. . .," the subjectivity of the choice and its ensuing responsibility needs to be surfaced and legitimized as much as the subjective information that contributed to it. Then the group is free to note conflict, consequences, and commitment—all of which may surface new wants, resistances, and a new choice.

This distinction does not discount the need for, or the appropriateness of, data being collected prior to an event. There are times when this is exactly the approach to take, e.g., a system-wide attitude survey. The point is that, quite often, collecting massive amounts of data prior to an event is not necessary or relevant, and one would be better off using hot data. For each situation, there is a choice.

Focus on the Individual's Interactions with Others vs. Focus on How Individuals Interact with All Aspects of the Work Environment

CHRD: Emphasis is on interpersonal competence and communications.

G: Emphasis is on an individual's ability to make and maintain effective contact with things as well as people.

One of the earliest and strongest underlying assumptions of CHRD is that good work is the result of good working relationships (Schein, 1969). The approach that results devotes a large part of organizational resources to human relations training, team building, and other technologies that are designed to facilitate working together in a more supportive, trusting, and growthful environment. The assumption is that as people find better ways to work together, the work will improve.

The Gestalt view is just the opposite: that good working relationships come out of doing good work together. The primary thrust is on performance, and, from this perspective, it becomes important that the individual's energy be centrally focused on the task at hand. The issue of *what* is being done becomes as important—if not more so—as who it is being done with. In fact, the nature and quality of the work relationship is of secondary importance as long as the parties involved can work together productively. Once the parties are free to not like each other, each can take the huge amounts of energy invested artificially in maintaining a "warm" relationship and put that energy into producing and accomplishing better work.

As in most Gestalt interventions, there is a paradox here: I am free to be who I am, and you are free not to like it. Conversely, you are just as free to be who you are, and I am equally free not to like that. Suppose that we manage to accomplish something well together, because the job or situation simply demands it—something that we, individually, take pride in. It is from this stance that we are in the best position to authentically start liking each other a little more.

This distinction between the two approaches is less than it was a few years ago. The effects of massive downsizing have changed the social contract between the employee and the organization. In his "new paradigm," Noer (1993) suggests that there is no social obligation between the employee and the organization past the work being performed and paid for. Still the issue is worth keeping in mind, as not all organizations are adopting this new set of values.

Shared Responsibility vs. Individual Responsibility

CHRD: Responsibility is viewed in terms of group effort.

G: Responsibility is viewed in terms of individual effort.

In cases where there is a strong emphasis on interdependent work, responsibility frequently falls to the group for effective performance. In the CHRD mode, many important issues are cast and discussed in terms of "we," e.g., "we have a problem here"; "we aren't communicating well"; "what we need is more team action." When organizational issues are perceived and discussed, they initially are put into a "we" frame of reference; there is a blurring of the boundaries among individuals. This approach may be used intentionally to provide a sense of purpose, harmony, and ownership around the current issue. But even to the extent that this approach is successful, it simultaneously carries a very heavy price in the further loss of individual awareness, tunnel vision, and a reduction of needed individual accountability.

Take, for example, the time-worn axiom "You can't delegate responsibility." This statement strongly suggests that, although the task can be delegated, the responsibility for the subordinate's behavior is still maintained by the superior.

This makes the superior a potential victim, as he or she is held fully accountable for the subordinate's behavior. To be functional, I suggest that the axiom be restated to read: "If authority is delegated, it is imperative that the associated responsibility also be delegated." That is, you can't "weasel" out of the responsibility for your own behavior. It is the accountability that cannot be delegated, not the responsibility. For example, if I lend my car to my son, and he causes an accident, he is responsible for the accident, and I am accountable for the damages. This is an important distinction. The police can't pull my license, and I can't say, "Sue him."

The Gestalt approach suggests that whether the individual is operating as a team member or working alone, the greatest probability for effective contribution arises from constant awareness of how that individual is unique and separate from everything and everyone else. Having an "I" orientation rather than a "we" orientation increases the probability that individual resources will emerge more quickly and that individual accountability for needed action will more readily and clearly be assigned.

Take, for example, a unit dealing with a newly arisen problem. The CHRD approach would be something like this: "Ladies and gentlemen, we have a problem. . .and I'd like some suggestions on how we can best deal with it." The G approach would be something like this: "Ladies and gentlemen, in my view the unit is faced with a problem. . . . I would like each of you to respond in terms of (1) Is this a problem for you?, (2) How is it a problem?, and (3) If it is a problem, what can you do to deal with it?"

In the Gestalt approach, each individual is encouraged to view the situation from his or her perspective, and to judge, from this perspective, how much of it will affect him or her. Once the individuals can identify the elements that, authentically, are problems, each person's resources can be focused on the specific area in which he or she can best contribute.

Again, paradoxically, even when the specific problem has very little or no impact on a particular individual, that person is in the best possible position to offer creative support to others, as his or her position then becomes more clearly defined as one of pure support. By initially focusing on the individual perspective, one lays the groundwork for obtaining the most productive collaborative effort.

Normative Shoulds vs. Valuing "What Is"

CHRD: Emphasis is on how things should be within the organization.

G: Emphasis is on dealing with the legitimacy and reality of the ever-changing "what is"—the present situation.

In the 1950s, the major thrust of CHRD was (and, to some extent, still is) based on the normative values of the "ideal" organization. Classic approaches to OD, such as McGregor's "Theory Y," Likert's "System 4," and Blake and Mouton's "9'9," illustrate the central concern for finding and defining the human characteristics that describe the human condition at its best. Once this was accomplished, it was reasoned, organizations could be developed consistent with these characteristics in order to provide more growthful and productive environments for their employees at all levels.

Although growth and increased productivity are also the aims of the Gestalt approach, the way to achieve them is quite different. In contrast to the CHRD view of the "ideal," Gestalt holds that each person is perfect as is, and there is no human characteristic that does not hold equal availability for effectiveness and ineffectiveness, i.e., there is no "bad" way to be. By encouraging people to be more fully who they are right now, one increases the possibility of their attaining greater clarity, awareness, and appreciation of the self. From this position, the individual can more readily choose the appropriate response to each unique situation.

Valuing Similarities vs. Valuing Differences

CHRD: Teamwork, based on a normative perspective, is the value.

G: Working in team combinations is a situational alternative.

The heart of the CHRD approach to team building is that it is built around established normative concepts such as Theory Y, consensus decision making, and a collaborative approach to conflict resolution. The assumption is that all groups can perform more effectively when structured along the CHRD value of team building, from a normative perspective. In this situation, the consultant enters the system, educates the group members in the CHRD values and techniques, and then assists them in realigning according to the new way of doing things. Figure 1 illustrates the entry conditions.

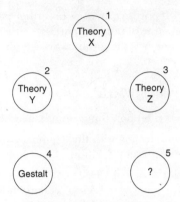

Figure 1. Entry Conditions

The team leader, #1, is a little "Theory X-ish," member #2 is a little "Theory Y-ish," #3 is a strong advocate of Theory Z, #4 is Gestalt based, and #5 is a little confused about the whole thing. The CHRD consultant enters and starts working with the group boundary from a normative (for example, Theory Y) frame of reference. The goal is that all group members will eventually begin pushing in the same direction, from a common theory base and set of values (Figure 2).

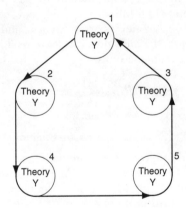

Figure 2. CHRD Goal

The Gestalt practitioner places the value on how individuals are different. The underlying assumption is that each individual can make the best contribution to group results from a position that is clearly his or her own. Furthermore, there is the assumption that each individual knows best what that position is for himself or herself.

In contrast to the CHRD approach, the Gestalt-oriented consultant begins by working with individual boundaries, assisting each individual within the work group to become clearer about and more appreciative of how different—rather than similar—each individual is from the others. The "X-ish" member will become clearer about and more comfortable with his "Xness," the "Y" member with her "Yness," and so on. Even the confused individual is encouraged to increase, rather than decrease, the present confusion in order that it may be experienced more fully, which may then lead to discovery of what it is all about.

Once the individual group members are clearly differentiated, team construction occurs through developing linkages among the members from their respective positions. All things considered, a team composed of strong, differentiated individuals has a higher probability for task effectiveness than does one composed of people who are trying to see things the same way. In contrast to the CHRD approach, the G approach illustrated in Figure 3 creates "snap-away" linkages that allow individuals to work in isolation or in different configurations or in smaller groups, depending on which is appropriate to the task at hand.

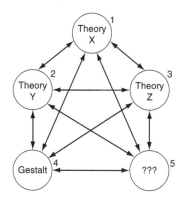

Figure 3. Gestalt Approach

This creates another Gestalt paradox: Because there is a higher toleration for individual differences, no normative values must be mouthed, and teamwork is considered a situational alternative, there is a higher probability of a more authentic team spirit developing.

Protecting Others vs. Protecting Self

CHRD: The primary focus is on the welfare of the group.

G: The primary focus is on people protecting themselves.

It is important to point out that these two orientations are not seen as mutually exclusive either by the CHRD or the Gestalt approaches. The main difference is the priority placed on each.

From the CHRD perspective, the welfare of the group/client system is of paramount importance. In some cases, this is even to the exclusion of the consultant's welfare. Frequently, the consultant will respond supportively to a stressed individual when feeling nonsupportive or will take on a direct confrontation when feeling battered or threatened simply because a confrontation appears to be conducive to group effectiveness.

The Gestalt-oriented consultant, on the other hand, contributes to group effectiveness by taking care of himself or herself first. Although this may sound self-serving, just the opposite is true. Herein lies yet another Gestalt paradox: I am best as a resource to others only when I take care of myself first. In an extreme example, if I happen to be your sole means of support in a given situation, I am serving you best by guarding your prime means of support.

A major Gestalt value is to have people take care of themselves, whenever possible, rather than to have them depend on or look unnecessarily to others. The Gestalt consultant, therefore, has an obligation, not only to maintain his or her own credibility and welfare by operating congruently with this value, but also to use his or her own reactions as a barometer to assess what is going on within the group, rather than relying solely on observations and the reactions of others.

For example, in an unstructured team-building session, a consultant said to the group, "I don't feel safe here." Various members of the group checked out their own feelings of safety, and several concurred with her observation. The result was that the group members spent some necessary time looking more closely at how they were dealing with one another and, subsequently, made some adjustments that allowed them to proceed more productively.

The phenomenon of massive downsizing has created a new and painful organizational reality, referred to earlier in this article. With productive and valued people being laid off, the team cannot take care of its members even if it wants to. The stronger and more self-reliant each team member is, the higher the probability that downsizing will have a less debilitating effect on the members who are left.

Impulsivity vs. Spontaneity

CHRD: The value is saying it as it happens.

G: The value is saying it through choice.

CHRD emphasizes disclosing exactly what is felt, when it is felt, and letting "the chips fall where they may." Although this frequently may be productive, it also often results in needless hassles and blocking of group movement.

An example is a situation that occurred during a recent OD program. At the end of the first day's session, when the participants were asked if there was any unfinished business for the day, a unit manager turned to his administrative assistant and said, "This may sound crazy, but last week I overheard several employees saying some pretty bad things about you. Do something to straighten this situation out!" It took over two hours to get the group members back to a point where they were willing to continue work the next day. The immediate response of the assistant was severe indignation, which became increasingly heightened when the manager would not give her some direction, the sources, or a suggested plan of action. The balance of the group members closed ranks behind the administrative assistant and all but permanently isolated the manger.

The Gestalt approach advocates spontaneity, as opposed to impulsivity. The distinction is that the focus is on the result rather than on the process. The Gestalt theory lists four stages of contact:

1. Block: No awareness of feeling

2. Inhibition: Awareness of feeling but no disclosure

3. Impulsivity: Awareness of feeling and simultaneous disclosure

4. Spontaneity: Awareness of feeling and disclosures based on conscious choice

Spontaneity is the end result of internal awareness (all that is being felt and thought) and external awareness (the uniqueness of the present situation). This combined awareness and the conscious choice either to disclose or not to, as opposed to the "random blurt," results in higher quality contact. Implicit in spontaneity is the individual's recognition of the fact that there is both a potential gain and a potential risk involved in either choice.

In the case cited above, it probably would have been more productive had the manager chosen not to disclose until he was really clear about what he wanted and about the appropriateness of disclosing in that particular setting.

Empowering Others vs. Empowering Self

CHRD: Management empowers the workforce.

G: Power is a purely personal phenomenon.

One of best-intentioned and totally erroneous concepts to emerge from CHRD's move to broad-based structural interventions is the notion that management (or anyone, for that matter) can empower someone else. In the first place, it is the height of arrogance to assume that I can magically "lay hands" on you, and you will grow strong. In the second place, it is impossible, because empowerment is a purely intrapsychic phenomenon. Management can take every opportunity to encourage every employee to participate fully in every decision. Regardless of this, if the employee resists making a choice, fears the consequences of his or her participation, would prefer the boss's or team member's approval to his or her own, or refuses to take direct responsibility for his or her actions, that employee is powerless, and there is little that management can do about it.

There are things that management can do, from the Gestalt perspective, that will assist an employee in regaining the power that he or she has given away or lost. A few of them are as follows:

1. Provide honest and clear feedback.

2. Hold the employee accountable for work done well or not well.

3. Value the employee for his or her uniqueness.

4. Assist the employee in creating options and encouraging conscious choice among them.

5. Honor and encourage the employee's resistance.

Conclusion

When viewed as a single configuration (or Gestalt, if you will), the eleven differences discussed in this article emphasize the uniqueness of the Gestalt approach, contrasted to conventional human resource development.

The main thrust of the Gestalt theory base is that the individual is perfect as is. Removing the blocks to the expression of this perfection is what good consulting, therapy, or human resource management is all about.

A second major Gestalt thrust is on interactive contact, that is, that the individual must make effective contact not only with people but with things, as well. The inability of a person to make good contact with an idea, goal, piece of equipment, etc., can have as great a negative side effect on the next personal interaction as can a poor interpersonal confrontation. Both can negatively affect work behavior. Today's consultants and managers must begin to place as much emphasis on the nonhuman contact points, specifically results orientation, as they place on the interpersonal ones.

The use of paradox is unique to the Gestalt theory base. Whereas CHRD is generally based on linear (cause and effect) thinking, Gestalt theory frequently views and deals with cause and effect as being one and the same thing. For example, CHRD advocates the facilitation of change, whereas Gestalt sees the increased awareness of what is occurring at the moment as a change in and of itself. Thus the paradox, "We change by not changing" (Beiser, 1970). The implication is that, as the rate of change continues to increase, the consultant/manager will function best from a stance of increasing situational awareness.

As the theory base and applications of organization development continue to expand and diversify, it is essential to maintain the perspective that it is still the individual's effectiveness and well-being that remains at the core of all OD work. Paradoxically, maintaining this sharp, unvarying focus on the individual will help even more appropriate and complex organizational structures to evolve and to meet the needs of the times.

References

Beiser, A.R. (1970). The paradoxical theory of change. In J. Fagan & I.L. Shepherd (Eds.), *Gestalt therapy now*. Palo Alto, CA: Science and Behavior Books.

Bennis, W., & Mische, M. (1995). *The 21st century organization: Reinventing through reengineering*. San Francisco, CA: Jossey-Bass.

Herman, S. (1974). The shadow of organization development. In J.W. Pfeiffer & J.E. Jones (Eds.), *The 1974 annual handbook for group facilitators*. San Francisco, CA: Jossey-Bass/Pfeiffer.

Janus, R. (1973, October). Dangers of group thinking. *International Management, 28.*

Karp, H.B. (1995). *Personal power: An unorthodox guide to success*. Lake Worth, FL: Gardner.

Karp, H.B. (1996). *The change leader: Using a Gestalt approach with work groups*. San Francisco, CA: Jossey-Bass/Pfeiffer.

Maurer, R. (1995). *Beyond the wall of resistance: Unconventional strategies that build support for change*. Austin, TX: Bard Books.

Nevis, E.C. (1987). *Organizational consulting: A Gestalt approach*. Cleveland, OH: GIC Press.

Noer, D. (1993). *Healing the wounds: Overcoming the trauma of layoffs and revitalizing downsized organizations*. San Francisco, CA: Jossey-Bass.

Perls, F.S. (1969). *In and out the garbage pail*. Moab, UT: Real People Press.

Schein, E.H. (1969). *Process consultation: Its role in organization development*. Reading, MA: Addison-Wesley.

H.B. Karp, Ph.D., is presently on the faculty of management of Christopher Newport University in Newport News, Virginia. He also is the owner of Personal Growth Systems, a management-consulting firm in Chesapeake, Virginia. He consults with a variety of Fortune 500 and governmental organizations in the areas of leadership development, team building, conflict management, and executive coaching. He specializes in applying Gestalt theory to issues of individual growth and organizational effectiveness. He is the author of many articles, of Personal Power: An Unorthodox Guide to Success, *and of* The Change Leader: Using a Gestalt Approach with Work Groups.

Developing an Innovative Organizational Culture: Dimensions, Assessments, and a Change Process

Markus Hauser

Abstract: The degree of innovativeness in an organization is highly dependent on the organizational culture. However, this dependence has not received appropriate attention within the organizational behavior literature and in the management of innovation projects. This article identifies three critical dimensions of organizational culture: content, structure, and strength. Based on these dimensions, an optimal model for an innovative culture is presented, along with recommendations for the development and management of an innovative organizational culture. A questionnaire and an analysis tool are included that can help to assess the current organizational culture with respect to innovation processes and aid in the practical application of the knowledge gained about the organization.

I am very grateful to Ms. Natasha Gordon for her valuable comments on this paper.

THE INNOVATION PROCESSES

Innovation is a highly repetitive process, beginning with the search for problems that have the potential to be transformed into profitable products or competitive advantages. Once a problem is identified (e.g., by a research and development specialist, a marketing or finance manager, or a multifunctional committee) an individual or team begins to search for possible solutions to the problem. The next step in the innovation process ends with the acceptance of one or several solutions to the problem based on necessary technical (e.g., feasibility studies) and financial criteria (e.g., the amount of investment necessary, market potential, estimated prices) as well as on the probability of the success of the project. The few ideas left after this evaluation stage (Booz-Allen & Hamilton, 1982) are developed further and eventually implemented (e.g., put on the market). Different kinds of organizational or group cultures are advantageous in different phases of the innovation process.

ORGANIZATIONAL CULTURE AND THE INNOVATION PROCESS

Culture is defined as the commonly shared values, norms, and knowledge within a group or an organization (Keller, 1990; Schein, 1993b). As the term culture is highly ambiguous and often misunderstood, it is helpful to define an optimal cultural pattern for innovation into three dimensions. This separation clarifies the concept of culture and identifies different intervention points. The three dimensions of a culture within an organization or group are: content, strength, and structure. The combination of these determines the function of the culture within the innovation process (see Figure 1).

A two-year project conducted by the author analyzed these conceptual aspects of organizational culture. The project entailed the introduction and evaluation of a "Picture Archiving and Communication System" in a major hospital. Because of the considerable amount of money invested, many institutions were involved, each with its own expectations in respect to the ideas, orientation, and priorities of the innovation project. Different cultural contents—values, norms, and knowledge—of the diverse groups (subcultures) collided in workshops and discussions. Despite the diversity of the participating groups, the understanding of the team members and their values and goals were not ranked high on the agenda, resulting in a partly inefficient innovation process. When the case was analyzed later, it was apparent that some central elements of culture were at odds with the innovation process.

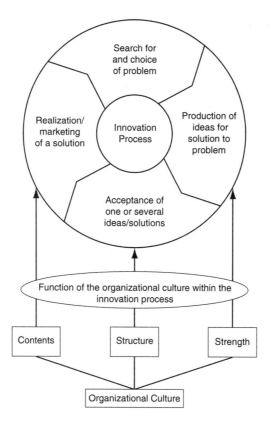

**Figure 1. Organizational Culture Within
the Innovation Process**

Based on this finding, an optimal cultural pattern was delineated (see Table 1). This pattern later proved its practical importance as an analytical and development tool for two industrial firms that wanted to improve their innovativeness.

The following examines the individual dimensions of organizational culture and the effects of culture on different stages of the innovation process, under the assumption that all other factors are constant.

Table 1. Summary of Findings Concerning Culture and Innovation (Hauser, 1997)

Dimensions of Culture	Search for and Choice of Problem	Production of Ideas for Solution to Problem	Acceptance of One or Several Ideas/ Solutions	Realization/ Marketing of a Solution	Remarks
Content of Culture					
Willingness to Communicate	+	+	+	+	
Functional Conflict Resolution	+	+	+	+	
High Power	– (+)	– (+)	– (+)	– (+)	Depends on the possibility of resistance (high position of innovative individual in an otherwise conservative organization)
Trust	+	+	+	+	
Technological Orientation	+	+	n.a.	+	Depends on orientation toward spe-cific technolo-gies or gen-eral functions
Structure of Culture					
Relation Between Subcultures					Irrelevant if innovation projects are limited to a single sub-culture

Table 1. (continued)

Conflicting	+/–	+/–	–	–	Depends on process of communication (are mutual understanding and shared goals possible?)
Neutral	n.a.	n.a.	n.a.	n.a.	
Complementary	+	+	+	+	
Relations Between Culture and Subculture					
Multiple Culture					
• with Conflicting Subcultures	+	+/–	–	–	Depends on communication process
• Neutral Subcultures	n.a.	n.a.	n.a.	n.a.	
• Complementary Subcultures	+	+	+	+	Depends on common understanding
Chaos Culture	n.a.	n.a.	n.a.	n.a.	Unsystematic influence
Monoculture	–	–	+	+	
Integrated Multiple Culture	+	+	+	+	
Strength of Culture	+/–	+/–	+/–	+/–	Negative tendencies depend on contents

n.a. = no systematic effect

The Dimension of Content

The first dimension is the content of the organizational culture. The most important values and norms for successful (technological) innovation projects are:

- willingness to communicate,
- functional conflict resolution (accepting conflict as a part of innovation and dealing with them in an rational way instead of emotionally),
- trust within the organization (between different hierarchical levels and functional areas), and
- technological orientation (in a general sense, not restricted to specific technologies).

Power has an ambiguous influence on the innovation process (Schein, 1993a). It is negative for the outcome of the project when used in a personalized way by a nonexpert (McClelland, 1980). If a person uses his or her power in a socialized way (in a way that is not purely motivated by self-interest) and if he or she is an innovation-oriented, creative person in an otherwise conservative firm as well as an expert in the field, positive effects can be expected concerning the time needed for the project and the project's budget.

The Dimension of Structure

The second dimension is structure. Generally, there are a lot of subcultures in organizations, because of socialization, professional background, and so on (Trice & Beyer, 1993). The relations between the subcultures may be conflicting, neutral, or complementary (Keller & Treichler, 1993). Assuming that there is a strong market-oriented culture in the marketing department and an equally strong technologically oriented culture in the R&D department, there are different possibilities regarding how these two groups get along with each other. They can be in constant conflict, interfere very little in one another's affairs (neutral), or work together harmoniously in the realization that each group has special skills, values, and norms that are of advantage in the context of innovation (complementary).

Conflicting Subcultures

Conflicting subcultures cause severe negative impacts in times when consensus is necessary. Moreover, when the acceptance of solutions and their subsequent realization and marketization is the primary goal, conflicting subcultures are a source of inefficient work.

Contrary effects are expected in the early stages of innovation. Given the assumption that members of different subcultures are able to communicate reasonably well with one another, conflict can enable different perspectives on and diverse solutions to a problem to emerge and an environment of creativity to develop. If this assumption (efficient communication) does not hold true, it is highly unlikely that the creative potential of diverse task-group members can be exploited (Ebadi & Utterback, 1984).

Neutral Subcultures

Neutral subcultures do not have systematic effects on the innovation process because of the lack of productive interaction between the members of the subcultures.

Complementary Subcultures

Complementary subcultures are the basis for the generation of a broad, encompassing perspective on a problem as well as the basis of diverse and numerous ideas, because of their different perceptions regarding what is true and important.

The advantages of open conflict do not readily occur between complementary subcultures as they do between conflicting subcultures, because the values and norms of the cultures do not contradict one another. However, conflict can be positive when the process of mutual understanding, mutual exchange, and adoption of a proposition from members of the subcultures leads to reaching a consensus on how problems are to be solved and to focusing work toward bringing the product to the marketplace. Particularly in the last stage of the innovation process, the diverse knowledge of the different subcultures can be used to full advantage.

Combinations of Subcultures and Overall Culture

The following is evident concerning the relationship between the overall culture and the subcultures: When an organization lacks a strong, cohesive, overall culture but its subcultures have developed strongly over time (multiple cultures), the relationships between the subcultures have varying and often diametrically opposed effects on the innovation process. If, for example, the marketing and R&D cultures have conflicting viewpoints and approaches, positive effects may result in the first two phases of the innovation process. This would be attributable to the environment giving rise to discussion characterized by a multiplicity of viewpoints and multilateral thinking caused by the different perceptions and priorities of the groups. This certainly holds true when the members of the two groups are able to discuss their opinions in a rational, factual manner. If this is not the case, no benefit can be gained from the interaction of different subcultures, and the results are negative. Strong complementary subcultures in combination with a strong overall culture result in effective innovation processes. No specific effects can be seen from the interaction of neutral subcultures.

A cohesive, strongly developed, overall culture combined with weakly delineated subcultures (monoculture) is the basis for a strong, integrative force leading to a positive outcome in the later phase of the innovation process. At the same time, this situation does not foster creativity and diversity in the approach to solving the problem. This means that the early stages of the innovation process are not likely to be as efficient as they were in the previous scenario.

A culture with no significant values at all (chaos culture) does not show any consistent effects on the innovativeness of an organization and is therefore not relevant to this analysis.

When an organization exhibits strong overall values and norms as well as strong subcultures (integrated multiple culture), positive effects in all stages of the innovation process will be observed, owing to a diverse base of perceptions, ideas, and priorities that spurs creativity (Amabile, Hennesey, & Grossman, 1986; Sternberg, 1988). In such an organization, the integration of the different subcultures is guaranteed in the later stages of the process, when consensus is needed.

The Dimension of Strength

The strength of a culture—measured by the extent to which people within the organization believe in and perpetuate the values of the culture—directly affects how significant the indicated effects of the different cultural patterns will be on the innovation process. Weak cultures, therefore, will cause less significant effects than will strong cultures. In general, the effect of the strength of a culture is dependent on the content dimension.

COMBINED EFFECTS OF THE THREE DIMENSIONS ON INNOVATION PROCESSES

We can analyze the interaction among the three dimensions of culture and the expected effects on the innovation process. Different cultural patterns can be characterized along the three dimensions and judged in terms of their compatibility with the strategic goals of innovation.

Table 2. Combined Effects of Content, Structure, and Strength on Innovation Processes

Content	Structure	Strength	Effect on Innovation Processes
Innovation oriented	Integrated multiple	Strong	++++
Innovation oriented	Integrated multiple	Weak	+++
Innovation oriented	Multiple	Strong	++
Innovation oriented	Multiple	Weak	+
Innovation oriented	Mono	Strong	+/-
Innovation oriented	Mono	Weak	+/-
Noninnovation oriented	Multiple	Weak	+/-
Noninnovation oriented	Multiple	Strong	−
Noninnovation oriented	Integrated multiple	Weak	− −
Noninnovation oriented	Integrated multiple	Strong	− − −
Noninnovation oriented	Mono	Weak	− − − −
Noninnovation oriented	Mono	Strong	− − − − −

With the help of Table 2, organizations can analyze their cultural appropriateness with respect to pursuing a strategy of innovation. Analysis can be based on interviews, document analysis, participating observation in multifunctional group meetings, and questionnaires.

Members of different functional areas and hierarchical levels can be asked the questions in the instrument that is included in this article, in order to analyze the organization's culture with respect to its effects on innovation. (The full questionnaire, together with its scales and a tool for analyzing deviations from the optimal, innovation-oriented culture, appears at the end of this article.) The following are some general questions, based on those in the instrument:

- Is there effective and timely communication between members of the organization? (Do channels of communication flow both vertically and horizontally within the hierarchy of the firm, as well as between different functional departments?)

- Are conflicts solved in a rational, factual manner?

- Is the power to make and enact decisions based on rank or on expertise?

- Is there a high level of trust between superiors and subordinates and between members of different functional departments?

- Are people, in general, trained to utilize technologies? Do people in the organization concentrate on specific technologies or are they oriented toward using special functions that diverse technologies can supply?

- Are there subcultures within the organization (functional, professional, hierarchical)?

- Are the relations between these subcultures conflicting, neutral, or complementary?

- Is the organizational culture strong or weak? Are the subcultures strong or weak? What culture/subculture relationship can be deduced from this analysis?

After having analyzed the cultural dimensions with these tools, it is possible to get an idea of where the organization stands compared to the optimal pattern of an innovative culture. The question, of course, is what to do when this analysis results in an unfavorable outcome.

Management Tools: Changing the Culture to Innovativeness

The members of the organization first must be shown what the optimal pattern of an innovative culture is. This will enable individuals to analyze their own positions using Table 2 and will give them an indication of what needs to be changed and developed with respect to the organizational culture. This information also affords a certain amount of motivation to change people's values and norms. However, because of the considerable resistance expected in any cultural-change process, additional procedures must be carried out. Based on the information shown in Table 2 and the literature on attitude change (Fiol, Harris, & House, 1992), the following factors should be taken into account when deciding how to change an organization's culture:

- Before the values and norms can be changed, it is necessary to reduce the strength and influence of the noninnovation-oriented culture.

- In order to change the content, strength, and structural dimensions, it is necessary to change the attitudes and behaviors of top management as well as the assumptions and practices that underlie recruitment and incentive policies. For fast results, one can alter the structural dimension by carefully selecting the participating members of the innovation team.

Changing Noninnovation-Oriented Values and Norms

The strength of noninnovative cultures can be reduced through altering recruitment policies. The employment of innovative and creative people with good communication skills and knowledge of up-to-date technologies is the first step. This communicates to the members of the organization that innovation is valued. Moreover, the newly hired people will be the pioneers of the change in attitudes within the organization. Their behaviors and approaches will challenge the old values and undermine the strength of the noninnovation-oriented culture.

An organization also can recruit stakeholders outside the immediate business, such as customers and suppliers, to be on the innovation team. This will further develop the team's values in the right direction.

Supporting Value Change

Innovation-oriented values should be stressed in the vision or mission statement of the organization. These values should be reflected in the behaviors of the top managers in order to illustrate their commitment to innovation. Behaviors include evidencing trust and confidence in those who display innovation, communicating regularly in support of creativity and innovation, and learning and using new methods of conflict resolution. The commitment to innovation should have a cascading effect within the organization as subordinates imitate the behaviors of managers.

Incentive systems should be adapted to be more oriented toward group performance in innovation settings (as most innovation processes are conducted by groups). This will create a greater willingness among individuals to communicate and exchange ideas and information.

Personnel-development programs should stress the importance of effective communication skills in efficient team work and the importance of up-to-date technological know-how to technological innovation. The organization should provide the necessary practical training to reinforce this. Such steps will allow new cultural values to be infused, a stronger overall culture to be created, and the relationships between subcultures and overall cultural values to be managed.

These propositions are primarily long-term oriented, and the problem of insufficient innovation in an organization is usually urgent, so there is a strong need for a short-term solution as well. This can be achieved by changing the structure of the innovation team.

Changing the Team Structure

The innovation team should be changed according to the stage of the innovation process that the team is currently in. It is best to have more heterogenous groups in the beginning of the innovation process and more homogeneous groups in the acceptance and realization/marketization phase. This can be done by changing group members (Hoffman & Maier, 1961; Triandis, Hall, & Evans, 1965). This will subsequently alter the culture-subculture(s) as well as the subculture-subculture relationships. The values of the heterogenous group members should be complementary, not contradictory. If that is not possible, team members should be chosen who have at least neutral opinions of the members of the other subculture(s). Thorough and careful selection of the members of the innovation team is important to ensure that the cultures are complementary rather than conflicting and, hence, optimal to the facilitation of effective innovation.

THE INNOVATIVE CULTURE QUESTIONNAIRE

The following is a questionnaire designed to assess the innovation orientation in an organization. The questionnaire has been applied successfully in an industrial setting. A broad study encompassing all departments and hierarchical levels was conducted with the questionnaire.

Administration

The respondent is asked to fill out the questionnaire with respect to his or her department and hierarchical level and to indicate the scale number that reflects his or her opinion concerning frequency, importance, or strength of each questionnaire item. The first thirteen items reveal the dimension of content; items fourteen through nineteen reveal the dimensions of structure and strength. The time necessary to complete the questionnaire is approximately twenty minutes.

Scoring

The results of the respondents are summed and averaged for each question. An analysis tool is presented to provide a better understanding of the organizational culture.

Note that the higher the differences between different hierarchical levels and functional areas, the higher the expectancy of heterogeneous subcultures. Also, the more interaction between different subcultures, the higher the expectance of complementary subcultures, given that conflicts between subcultures are infrequent. Low interactive activity indicates neutral subcultures.

The instrument scales are as follows:

Strength (1: very strong; 2: strong; 3: neither strong nor weak; 4: weak; 5: very weak)

Importance (1: very important; 2: important; 3: neither important nor unimportant; 4: unimportant; 5: very unimportant)

Frequency (1: always; 2: often; 3: occasionally; 4: seldom; 5: never)

INNOVATIVE CULTURE QUESTIONNAIRE

Instructions: This questionnaire is very important in obtaining a picture of our organization's ability to innovate. Please fill in the name of your department and your hierarchical level. Then respond to each item by marking the scale number that most accurately indicates your perception of the organization. The scale indicates the strength, importance, or frequency of the content of the item, as follows:

1 = Very strong/very important/always
2 = Strong/important/often
3 = Neither strong nor weak/neither important nor unimportant/occasionally
4 = Weak/unimportant/seldom
5 = Very weak/very unimportant/never

Department: _____

Hierarchical Level: _____

Items	Strength, Importance, or Frequency				
1. Do you perceive communication to be effective within the organization?	1	2	3	4	5
2. Do managers often share information with you?	1	2	3	4	5
3. Have you often experienced cross-functional communication?	1	2	3	4	5
4. Have you often experienced communication across hierarchical levels?	1	2	3	4	5
5. Are conflicts generally resolved in a rational manner?	1	2	3	4	5
6. How often do you experience influence by managers that is based solely on position power rather than expert power?	1	2	3	4	5
7. How often do you think managers use their power for personal, rather than organizational, goals?	1	2	3	4	5

1 = Very strong/very important/always
2 = Strong/important/often
3 = Neither strong nor weak/neither important nor unimportant/occasionally
4 = Weak/unimportant/seldom
5 = Very weak/very unimportant/never

Items	**Strength, Importance, or Frequency**				
8. How strong do you perceive the trust between you and your superior to be?	1	2	3	4	5
9. How strong do you perceive the trust to be between you and other functional areas?	1	2	3	4	5
10. In general, do employees of other functional areas do what they promise to do?	1	2	3	4	5
11. How important do you perceive technology to be for your job?	1	2	3	4	5
12. How often do you read publications that present the newest technological developments in your job area?	1	2	3	4	5
13. How often do you read technological publications that are *not* directly concerned with the organization's applied technology?	1	2	3	4	5
14. Are there a lot of distinct cliques in your organization?	1	2	3	4	5
15. How strong do you perceive these separate groups to be?	1	2	3	4	5
16. Is there a lot of conflict between these cliques?	1	2	3	4	5
17. Is there a lot of interaction between these cliques?	1	2	3	4	5
18. Do these cliques have different opinions, values, and norms?	1	2	3	4	5
19. Do you think there are strong, overall values in the organization?	1	2	3	4	5

Relationship of Items to Scales

1. Willingness to communicate; strength scale
2. Willingness to communicate; frequency scale
3. Willingness to communicate; frequency scale
4. Willingness to communicate; frequency scale
5. Mode of conflict resolution; frequency scale
6. Power; frequency scale
7. Specific application of power; frequency scale
8. Trust; strength scale
9. Trust; strength scale
10. Trust; frequency scale
11. Technology orientation; importance scale
12. Technology orientation; frequency scale
13. Technology orientation; frequency scale
14. Subcultures; frequency scale
15. Subcultures; strength scale
16. Relations between subcultures; frequency scale
17. Neutral/not neutral subcultures; frequency scale
18. Relations between subcultures; strength scale
19. Overall culture; strength scale

Deviation Analysis: The Optimal Cultural Pattern

Calculate the average of all responses for every item and scale. Fill in the results in the table that follows. The numbers in the first row reflect the continuum in which the average of all respondents lie. Fill in the averages in the approximate positions where they belong on this continuum. The numbers in the first column indicate the referred items from the questionnaire. With this tool, deviation from the optimal pattern can be identified and the adaption of the culture with the help of the management tools presented in this article can begin.

It must be taken into consideration that this is a cultural model that is optimal only when all dimensions are as indicated. Strong deviation in one

Table 4. Deviation Analysis: The Optimal Cultural Pattern

Question	1	2	3	4	5
1.	x				
2.	x				
3.	x				
4.	x				
5.	x				
6.					x
7.					x
8.	x				
9.	x				
10.	x				
11.	x				
12.	x				
13.	x				
14.	x				
15.	x				
16.					x
17.	x				
18.	x				
19.	x				

item (especially for the structural and strength dimensions) may change the effect of the cultural pattern from positive to negative. Of course, the data can be used for more complex statistical procedures, but this deviation analysis often proves to be sufficient.

Conclusion

Organizational culture has a large effect on the innovativeness of an organization. The three dimensions of culture (content, structure, and strength) have specific positive or negative influences on the different stages of innovation. The interaction of these three dimensions reveals an optimal cultural pattern for the purpose of innovation: an overall culture with strong innovation-oriented values combined with complementary subcultures. With knowledge of the three dimensions, an instrument to analyze the organization's culture, analysis of the pattern revealed, and careful management, organizational innovativeness can be developed.

References

Amabile, T. M., Hennesey, B.A., & Grossman, B.S. (1986). Social influences on creativity: The effect of contracted-for reward. *Journal of Personality and Social Psychology 50,* 14–23.

Booz-Allen & Hamilton. (1982). *New product management for the 1980s.* New York: Author.

Ebadi, Y.M., & Utterback, J.M. (1984). The effects of communication on technological innovation. *Management Science, 30,* 572–585.

Fiol, C.M., Harris, D., & House, R.J. (1992). *Charismatic leadership: Strategies for effecting social change.* Working paper of the Reginald Jones Center, Wharton School, Philadelphia, PA.

Hauser, M. (1997). *Innovativeness of firms and organizational culture—An integrative view.* 18th National Business Conference Proceedings on Highly Effective Organizations Through People, Technology, and Innovation, Hamilton, Ontario, Canada.

Hauser, M. (in press). Organizational culture and innovativeness of firms—An integrative view. *International Journal of Technology Management.*

Hoffman, L.R., & Maier, N.R. (1961). Quality and acceptance of problem solutions by members of culturally homogeneous and heterogeneous groups. *Journal of Abnormal Psychology, 6,* 401–407.

Keller, A. (1990). *Die rolle der unternehmungskultur im rahmen der differenzierung und integration der unternehmung* [The role of organizational culture in differentiation and integration of the organization]. Bern/Stuttgart: Paul Haupt.

Keller, A., & Treichler, C. (1993). Unternehmungskulturstrategien im zürcher ansatz [Management of corporate culture within the framework of the Zurich management model]. *Die Unternehmung, 47,* 55–66.

McClelland, D.C. (1980). Individual motivation and organizational behavior: The two faces of power. *Journal of International Affairs, 24,* 59–72.

Schein, E.H. (1993a). Innovative cultures and organizations. In T.J. Allen & Scott Morton (Eds.), *Information technology and the corporation of the 1990s* (pp. 125–146). New York: Oxford University Press.

Schein, E.H. (1993b). On dialogue, culture, and organizational learning. *Organization Dynamics, 22,* 40–51.

Sternberg, R.J. (1988). *The nature of creativity.* Cambridge, MA: Cambridge University Press.

Triandis, H., Hall, E., & Evans, R. (1965). Member heterogeneity and dyadic creativity. *Human Relations, 18,* 33–55.

Trice, H.M., & Beyer, J.M. (1993). *The culture of work organizations.* Englewood Cliffs, NJ: Prentice-Hall.

Markus Hauser, Lic. Oec. Publ., *works at the Institute for Research in Business Administration in the Department of Strategic Management and Leadership at the University of Zurich, Switzerland. He is also a partner at Max & Hansen Consulting. He has consulted with industrial firms, the hotel industry, and hospitals in the areas of organizational change management, product innovation, organizational culture, and leadership.*

DIVERSITY AND ORGANIZATIONAL CHANGE

Ginger Lapid-Bogda

Abstract: Diversity is often viewed as a *training program,* limited to a human resources initiative focused on race and gender and separate from organizational change efforts. However, as the article describes, the definition of diversity is much broader, encompassing primary, secondary, and tertiary dimensions that go beyond race and gender.

The aim of diversity is to allow all individuals to contribute fully to the success of the organization. Thus, integrating diversity and organizational change efforts can enhance the success of most types of organizational change. Organization development theory and principles can also add significantly to the outcomes of diversity initiatives through the effective use of contracts, assessments, action research methodology, and other critical components.

In the current competitive world, diversity and organization development must be partners in successful organizational change efforts.

Many consultants (as well as most managers) view diversity as an initiative of human resources, separate from organizational change efforts. This dichotomous thinking negatively impacts the effectiveness of any organizational change initiatives, whether the focus for the change is diversity or other types of organizational change, such as quality, organizational redesign, team building, or coaching. Where does this polarized thinking come from?

Misunderstanding diversity as an issue of race and gender, a repackaging of affirmative action in 1990s clothing, leads to this narrow view. From this perspective, diversity means raising the organization's numbers of white women as well as men and women from a variety of ethnic/racial backgrounds. It may also mean adding a few differently-abled people in "behind the scenes" jobs. This limited definition of diversity ignites political dynamite on two fronts:

- White men see reverse discrimination;

- Many men and women of color, as well as white women, live with the organizational perception that they came into the organization (or other institutions) under the affirmative action umbrella, not as a result of their own merit.

A DEFINITION OF DIVERSITY

Diversity, however, breaks the affirmative action framework and goes beyond race and gender (Thomas, 1990). In fact, the new diversity paradigm defines it as the process of creating and maintaining an environment that naturally enables all participants to contribute to their full potential in the pursuit of organizational objectives (Thomas, 1993).

Figure 1 can be helpful to more fully understand what it means to enable all persons to contribute their full potential to their organizations.

Primary Dimensions

The *inner circle* shows the primary dimensions of diversity—those that are fundamental to a person's self-concept or core self. These dimensions, though not necessarily visible, are unchangeable in that they are not a matter of

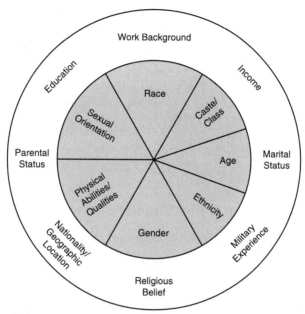

From Loden and Rosener, *Workforce America! Managing Employee Diversity as a Vital Resource.* Burr Ridge, IL: Irwin, 1991. Used with permission.

Figure 1. Dimensions of Diversity

choice. They form the basis on which people make instantaneous judgments about one another, often through the process of stereotyping.

Secondary Dimensions

The *outer circle* consists of secondary dimensions of diversity. These are aspects of a person's identity that are important to a definition of self, but are not as fundamental as the primary dimensions.

Tertiary Dimensions

In addition, it would be possible to add a *third circle* that consists of the tertiary dimensions of diversity, such as learning style, personality, and professional orientation.

All three categories (primary, secondary, and tertiary) contribute to the formation of a person's unique life experiences, perspectives, and skill sets. An effective organization can learn to recognize, understand, appreciate, respect, and utilize these multiple aspects of a person in the pursuit of its mission and objectives.

This broadened definition of diversity sheds light on another reason for misunderstanding the connections between diversity and organizational change. Diversity is often perceived as a *program*, not a significant and complex organizational change process. Defined in this way, diversity frequently is dealt with as a training program for employees (usually managers only). Training programs by themselves, however, rarely have the muscle to change the organization's culture. A diversity effort that focuses primarily on training is, therefore, not likely to achieve long-term or long-lasting results.

THE CONTRIBUTION OF DIVERSITY TO ORGANIZATIONAL CHANGE

Integrating diversity and organizational change efforts can enhance the success of most types of organizational change. All major organizational change involves a cultural change, and a diversity effort is cultural change at its core. It requires an organization to search its collective soul and focus on essential aspects of its culture: seminal values; organizational demands for conformity in thought, interpersonal style, and action; power structure and power dynamics; employee participation; and inclusion/exclusion issues, to name a few.

Cultural Differences

In addition, most organizational changes involve diversity components. An organizational redesign, for example, may combine functions that have previously been separate, such as marketing and manufacturing. Certainly, marketing and manufacturing have two distinct "cultures," and a successful redesign needs to pay attention to those cultural issues involved. Diversity offers both the perspective and the technology to deal with these intercultural issues, whether they are triggered by redesigns, mergers, or global expansions.

When an organization is redesigned, some of its subsystems discover they have to transact a new form of "business" with new, unfamiliar "partners." Naturally, they assume that their established styles of doing business, their traditional practices, priorities, values, and methods, will be perfectly acceptable, perfectly functional. Thus, marketing is surprised when this assumption turns out to be invalid for manufacturing. Marketing assumes that its new partner, manufacturing, simply has not appreciated the benefits of changing and adapting to *marketing's* traditional way of doing business.

Thus, organizational redesign invariably leads to organizational conflict. A diversity perspective adds insight to the identification of and techniques for the management of such issues. Conflict, by definition, means that differences exist. These differences may be based on style, role, values, priorities, power, mental models and patterns of thinking, or culture. The diversity perspective of *valuing and utilizing differences* offers a *positive* framework from which to manage conflict.

Team Effectiveness

Team effectiveness has even clearer diversity connections. For a team to develop and be effective, its members must find productive ways to both elicit and manage individual and subgroup differences. In any group development model, there is always some version of a "storming" stage fairly early in a group's development. The group must navigate this troublesome phase successfully to evolve toward more productive phases of development. Successful navigation cannot occur if differences are submerged or conformity is forced upon diverse members. To be effective means to acknowledge differences and to utilize them creatively to gain the team's objectives.

Organizational Cultural Shift

In the case of a complex organizational change (for example, going from a production-driven to a marketing-driven focus or moving toward Total Quality), a fundamental shift in organizational culture must occur. A cultural change of this magnitude and complexity poses a major challenge for most organizations because of the *ambiguity* involved and the *enormity* of the task. An understanding of diversity enables organizations to find ways *not* to insist on conformity in a major change process, but to encourage employees to contribute, to take a fresh look, and to continuously evolve.

THE CONTRIBUTION OF ORGANIZATION DEVELOPMENT TO DIVERSITY

A Clear Contract

From the opposite perspective, the question is how organizational change theory and organization development strategies and methods can assist in diversity change efforts. Unfortunately, many organizations—as well as many diversity consultants—view diversity as a human resource issue. In relegating diversity to this HRD context, they charter the HR department to roll out diversity programs without utilizing effective change technology.

For example, OD's action research method illuminates the steps that must be taken for effective change to occur. There must be a contract for the diversity effort that defines the goals, roles, expectations, resources, and scope of the intended change. Many diversity initiatives violate this principle by starting with a focus that is too narrow to be effective (i.e., a mentoring program only) or too broad to accomplish and too vague to measure ("change the work environment"). Other diversity change efforts begin without serious consideration of the required resources. Are the organization's leaders truly committed to the effort? Do they have proficiency in the skill-sets they need to support the implementation of this effort? Do they have the authority to spend the time and money necessary for what they are trying to achieve? Contracting helps resolve the above issues at the front end.

Needs Assessment

A systemic organizational assessment is just as essential to a successful diversity effort as to any organizational change initiative. Without an assessment, how can an organization know what issues exist and what their various underlying root causes might be? The organization's decision makers cannot know where to put their time and resources. Perhaps a training program is needed—but what type, by what time, and for whom? On the other hand, training may not be the most effective approach. For example, holding senior managers accountable for achieving diversity goals, as well as for changing organizational practices, may result in more diversity success, in less time, and at a lower cost than a program.

Also, it will be difficult for the organization to know whether diversity-related progress has been made over time unless there is a baseline against which to compare the change. An effective assessment process will address these concerns.

Data Feedback

Action research methodology also offers techniques and processes dealing with data feedback and intervention. Without feedback for key people in the organization, the energy to plan and take effective action is greatly depleted. Thoughtful consideration must be given to who will benefit from the data, what information is most relevant for people to know, how the feedback should be delivered, and what the best timing is.

Selecting Appropriate Interventions

In the area of intervention, OD offers insight from a strategic and systems perspective. What is the range of possible interventions? What types of interventions is the organization ready for? What interventions will have the greatest impact and stimulate changes in other parts of the organization? How should the organization deal with the inevitable resistance that occurs with any organizational change, but especially a diversity change?

Measurement and Evaluation

The action research emphasis and technology related to evaluation and renewal are particularly important in the area of diversity. Organizations frequently find diversity difficult to measure for two reasons. First, diversity changes generally do not occur quickly, and consequently sponsors must be patient because success can only be measured over time.

Second, many diversity outcomes (except numeric outcomes such as hiring or retention statistics) are more *qualitative* than quantitative. The variety of evaluation tools supplied by the behavioral sciences can be extremely useful here. In the area of renewal (continuously reassessing the change effort), successful diversity initiatives require that the organization constantly take stock of how it is doing and be flexible enough to shift paradigms and change direction as needed. There are some "best practices" when it comes to diversity (Morrison, 1992), but there is no clear template that any organization can follow in every situation. No organization is like any other organization.

Critical Components of an Organizational Change Effort

A successful diversity initiative, like any other organizational change effort, requires several critical components as specified by organizational change theory. A diversity vision, clear, compelling, and communicated, must be put in place. Next, a strategy must be designed to achieve that vision. Third, goals (or objectives) need to be developed. Fourth, accountabilities for achieving established goals must be established for every involved person. Fifth, if the change process is to be sustainable, a change infrastructure must be created. A diversity change infrastructure may not exactly parallel the infrastructure of other change initiatives; for example, it may include employee networks or advocacy groups and, always, a diversity council or steering committee. But every change requires a commitment to ongoing support structures to oversee and maintain the change.

Finally, as for any successful change, the organization must adjust its performance evaluation and reward systems. In any organization, what you get is what you inspect and reward, not necessarily what you expect. The organization must clearly and consistently reward actions that support diversity and sanction those behaviors that create or perpetuate barriers to its success.

SENIOR MANAGEMENT COMMITMENT

The last (and probably most important) lesson diversity initiatives can learn from organizational change theory and practice involves senior management commitment. A diversity effort without the active, visible, sustained involvement and support of senior leadership will have a short life (Morrison, 1992). Senior managers' awareness of the personal implications of diversity and the potential consequences of management's backstage and public behavior is critical. Coaching managers to perform the specific public roles required of them can make or break the diversity effort.

The partnership between diversity and organizational change efforts is necessary to the optimum success of either. In the current competitive and global environment, each organization must ask itself a two-part question: What core principles are so fundamental to the integrity and success of the organization that everyone must adhere to them? And what are the dimensions that support these principles and that depend on the expression, display, and application of people's differences?

References

Loden, M., & Rosener, J.B. (1991). *Workforce America! Managing employee diversity as a vital resource.* Burr Ridge, IL: Irwin.

Morrison, A. (1992). *The new leaders: Guidelines on leadership diversity in America.* San Francisco, CA: Jossey-Bass.

Thomas, R.R., Jr. (1990, March/April). From affirmative action to affirming diversity. *Harvard Business Review,* pp. 107–117.

Thomas, R.R., Jr. (1993). Utilizing the talents of the new work force. In A. Cohen (Ed.), *The portable MBA in management: Insights from the experts at the best business schools.* New York: Wiley.

Ginger Lapid-Bogda, Ph.D., *is an organization development consultant with Bogda & Associates in Los Angeles, California. She has taken advanced training in Gestalt and OD and is a certified Enneagram instructor. Currently, she consults with Fortune 500 companies on topics including the strategic management of change, diversity strategy, and leadership coaching. Dr. Lapid-Bogda is an award-winning speaker and author in the areas of managing change and resistance, diversity, and politics and power.*

MAKING THE DEAL WORK: MANAGING THE PEOPLE SIDE OF MERGERS AND ACQUISITIONS

Timothy J. Galpin

Abstract: Most mergers and acquisitions never realize their intended financial and strategic impact because of their "people" aspects. The change dynamics created by a merger heighten people's resistance to making the integration of two companies successful. In addition, many key people voluntarily exit the merging organizations.

The article identifies the key change-management dynamics encountered during a merger or acquisition. Understanding the causes of resistance and managing the resistance are addressed using a "resistance-pyramid" model. A re-recruitment strategy is also necessary to maintain the key human capital of merging companies. A "re-recruitment strategy matrix" is provided to address this critical issue. Finally, the organization development (OD) professional's role in merger-integration management is discussed.

First, the Bad News

Throughout the 1990s, mergers and acquisitions have been viewed by business executives as the easiest ways to become bigger faster—at least on paper. Merger activity during 1996, at over $500 billion, was more than the record set in the previous year. However, given the dismal rate of success for most mergers, it is astonishing that companies still pursue such endeavors. The failure statistics should be enough to scare most rational managers away from even considering a merger or acquisition. When it announces an acquisition, a company's stock price rises only 30 percent of the time; just 23 percent of all acquisitions earn what they cost in capital; and, on average, managers grade the financial performance of their alliances as "C minus" (Growing Your Company, 1996).

Unlike the 1980s, when mergers and acquisitions were the main financial transactions as companies were bought for their hard assets and later broken apart and sold piece by piece because the parts were worth more than the whole, mergers in the 1990s were designed to exploit a close strategic fit between two organizations. Even though the focus of mergers today is mainly on bringing together similar companies within the same industry in order to make an operational leap and gain market share by taking advantage of the "four Cs" (synergies in customers, competencies, channels of distribution, and organizational content), the job of integrating two companies (no matter how similar) is an enormous challenge. The fact that an alliance appears to be a good fit often increases the pressure on management to deliver on strategic promises faster, thereby increasing the risk.

The means of overcoming this formidable task is to regard the integration process as nothing less than a comprehensive change-management effort. Not many corporate initiatives change the structure, systems, operations, or environment of a company more dramatically than a merger or acquisition. All the complexities found in any change effort occur during the merger of two organizations. Moreover, the change dynamics are even more excessive because they must be addressed in both organizations. Table 1 illustrates the change-management dynamics that are brought on by a merger or acquisition.

Table 1. Change-Management Dynamics Brought About by a Merger

Aggressive financial targets	How to grow
Short time lines	Restructuring
Intense public scrutiny	Reengineering
Culture clashes	Where to downsize
Politics and positioning	Personnel-retention problems
Communications issues	Employee-motivation difficulties

MERGERS CREATE RESISTANCE

On hearing about a merger or acquisition, the first things that run through managers and employees minds are their personal issues. They begin asking questions, such as "Will I lose my job?" "Will my pay and benefits be changed?" "To whom will I report?" and "Will I have to move?" These questions and the anxiety engendered by them creates an enormous amount of resistance in an organization to a merger. Before people become focused on expanded market share or begin to integrate systems, data bases, and operational procedures, they consider the impact of the merger or acquisition on themselves. The resistance created can destroy even the best-planned mergers.

This sentiment is supported throughout the writings on strategic organizational change. For example, Clemons, Thatcher, and Row (1995) conducted a study of why major change efforts have failed in large companies across various industries. Their research revealed that the failures were unrelated to the technical aspects of organizations. Generally, companies have the skill, or can hire it, to implement the technical aspects of change efforts. Clemons et al. found that a major reason for failure is what they term "political risk." They describe political risk as the risk that changes will not be completed because of organizational resistance or because of the progressive fading of commitment to an effort. They contended that when resistance is substantial, organizations will falter at both change-project development and implementation. Peck (1995) also presented the results of a study of major change projects. He identified "organizational resistance" as being the major barrier to success. Peck found that organizational resistance to change was identified by 92 percent of his respondents as being the main problem they encountered.

This finding was supported by Longo (1996) in her presentation of the difficulty of change efforts. She noted, "The number one source of difficulty with implementation [of change] is the disregard for, or misunderstanding of, the resistance to change" (p. 69). Moreover, in a *Financial Times* (Mastering Management, 1996) article about creating "high performance workplaces," resistance to change is reported to be a major obstacle to success. The *Financial Times* states, "Institutional obstacles, resistance to change, unsupportive cultures, and incoherent strategies . . . explain why high performance workplaces have not diffused more widely" (p. 3). Last, within a World Wide Web site entitled *Frequently Asked Questions About Organizational Change: Answers to Questions Often Asked by Heads of Companies* (World Wide Web, 1996), the first two questions listed were (1) "How do I obtain commitment to our plans from my organization?" and (2) "How do I minimize resistance from middle management in implementing this change?" (p. 1).

OVERCOMING RESISTANCE TO MERGERS AND ACQUISITIONS

The lack of understanding of resistance to mergers and acquisitions is common within organizations, even among managers at all levels. This may be attributed to the education and training that most managers receive, in combination with their practical experiences. Many M.B.A. programs and management-training courses focus much more on the "hard" aspects of business (the technical, operational, and financial aspects) and deal in a very cursory way with the subject of organizational change. Management education does a poor job of addressing how to manage the resistance encountered during change efforts such as mergers and acquisitions.

Moreover, the practical experience of managers regarding merger or acquisitions planning reinforces their training and education. Often, managers concentrate only on the technical, operational, and financial aspects of the merger. Understanding more about the "hard" (technical, operational, and financial) aspects of the deal, while lacking a sound understanding of people's potential resistance to the alliance in both organizations, creates a focus for most managers on the "hard" aspects and away from managing their people's resistance to change. In order to successfully integrate two companies, managers must be able to manage resistance to change.

Figure 1 presents a three-level "resistance pyramid" that helps to explain the reasons for people's resistance to change during mergers.

Each of the levels of the pyramid indicates a progressive hierarchy of reasons for resistance to change during merger integration. At the first level,

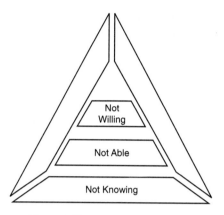

Figure 1. The Resistance Pyramid[1]

"not knowing" refers to people who lack knowledge and information about the integration effort. At the second level, "not able" represents people's lack of ability and skill to perform the changes necessitated by the merger. At the top of the pyramid, "not willing" refers to the personal reluctance to make an effort to change.

Managing Each Level of Resistance

Not Knowing

Each level of the resistance pyramid can be managed with tangible actions. Figure 2 identifies these actions. First, to manage "not knowing" requires that people be kept informed about the integration effort. Communication and free exchange of information play an important role in reducing people's resistance at this level.

This is supported by the literature on reducing resistance to change. For example, May and Kettelhut (1996) assert, "Open communication and collaboration are essential [to effect change]. Open communications clarify expectations and reduce ambiguity" (p. 9). Haslett (1995) emphasizes communication as being a key first step during any change effort. The World Wide Web (1996) site previously mentioned advises that companies need to make sure that people "are kept well-informed," as an answer to the question, "How do I minimize resistance from middle management in implementing this

---

[1]Adapted from Galpin (1996).

change?" (p. 1). Jack Welch of General Electric provides a real-life example of employing communication to lower resistance. In his interview with Sherman (1993), Welch comments, "How do you bring people into the change process? Start with reality. Get all the facts out. Give people the rationale for change, laying it out in the clearest, most dramatic terms. When everybody gets the same facts, they'll generally come to the same conclusion. Only after everyone agrees on the reality and resistance is lowered can you begin to get buy-in to the needed changes" (p. 84). Longo (1996) emphasizes that companies generally do a poor job of communicating about change to their people. Longo states, "The second biggest problem [beyond a lack of involvement] is communication. Getting people to buy into [change] isn't easy because people put little stock in what management is selling. Senior managers dilute, filter, and distort information" (p. 69).

Experience shows that organizations need to do a better job of communicating, not only initially but throughout their efforts to integrate two companies. A good example of this comes from the acquisition of a systems-integration consulting firm by a large computer manufacturer. As the integration process of the two firms unfolded, the director of communications from the consulting company sent out information about the acquisition process only when "there was something important to tell people." This reduced communications to an average of once a month or less. The communications director kept insisting that the managers and employees within the firm "were receiving enough information and did not want to be bothered by too many communications." About three months into the acquisition process, the management of the computer manufacturer held a gathering of key managers from the acquired consulting company to welcome them to the larger organization. During the first meeting of the session, a panel question-and-answer discussion was conducted. The most telling indication of people's reactions to the limited communication was the very first question asked by a manager in the audience, "How can I tell my people what needs to be done to integrate the companies when I have heard nothing about what is going on?" This comment was immediately echoed by three other managers. The managers continued by commenting on the good communication that took place up to the closing of the deal and that they had heard nothing since— almost three months later.

Not Able

To offset the second level of the pyramid, "not able," training and education are key. Equipping people with information and new skills they need (e.g., on the other company's procedures and systems) lowers their resistance to the integration. This is reinforced by May and Kettelhut (1996) in their discussion of managing human issues during change. They emphasize training as a key component in reducing people's resistance to change and contend that, "Individuals need to feel competent and to continually develop their competence. Change generally involves new knowledge, skills or abilities, and this often places people in positions where they initially lack that which they need to feel competent" (p. 8). Although viewed as a luxury and added expense by many executives, workforce learning and development is a necessity during merger integration. No matter how similar, different companies will have different systems, procedures, rules, policies, and so on. Communication is not enough. Even when provided with necessary information, managers and employees will resist a merger as long as they do not possess the skills to integrate the two companies.

Not Willing

The third level, "not willing," implies that communication and education only begin to lower people's resistance. As Figure 2 illustrates, willingness can be increased through a solid performance-management process that includes goals, measurements, feedback, and rewards and recognition.

First, new goals and measurements must be developed. The goals of the integration effort should be clearly understood by both managers and employees. Also, measurements should be linked directly to the desired goals.

The other half of performance management, rewards and recognition, is also a key component of increasing people's willingness to make the

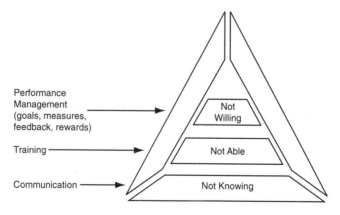

Figure 2. Actions To Take To Manage Resistance

changes needed to create a successful merger. People will work toward a goal that they are motivated to achieve. Incentives and rewards can take many forms, including cash awards, stock, trips, time off, and promotions. Recognition can be provided by means of publicity (e.g., being mentioned in the company newsletter), letters and visits from executives, thank-you memos and "pats on the back" from managers, award lunches and dinners, plaques and trophies, and so on.

RE-RECRUITING HUMAN CAPITAL

In addition to creating resistance, mergers cause people to re-evaluate their situations within an organization. This often creates an exodus of key personnel at a time when they are most critical to the future success of the organization. As was stated earlier, the first things that people think of on hearing about a merger or acquisition are their personal issues. This focus becomes paramount: my job, my pay, my security, my career. Moreover, knowing that this is the case, headhunters and recruiters from other companies increase their efforts by targeting the personnel of merging companies. Recruiters provide answers to people's issues with job offers, higher pay, security, and career changes.

Early in the integration process, a comprehensive re-recruitment strategy should be developed and implemented. Such a plan entails three major steps: 1) identify key individuals or groups within the two organizations and the potential impact of losing them, 2) gain an understanding of their motivations, and 3) develop and execute a retention action plan to motivate them to remain.

Table 2 represents a re-recruitment planning matrix that can be used to develop this strategy.

ROLE OF AN OD PROFESSIONAL

Merger integration adds numerous activities on top of an already heavy work load for managers and employees. Planning, organizing, implementing, and assessing the progress of an integration effort become overwhelming to people who are not skilled in addressing the complexities of accelerated change. As an integration process unfolds, an OD professional can play a key role by providing expertise in overall project management, integration planning,

Table 2. Sample Re-Recruitment Planning Matrix

Key People/ Groups	Impact of Loss	Motivators	Retention Actions	Responsi- bility	Timing
Top individuals: S.H. P.M. J.H.	• Schedule delay • $100M revenue	• Control • Pay • Ego	• Promote • Stay bonuses	P.S. P.D.	10/2 (one day before annnounce- ment)
Other Key Individuals: G.B. E.O. K.S.	• Schedule delay • Interna- tional markets	• Security • Career path	• Personal communi- cations • Promote	S.H. P.M.	10/3 (morning of annnounce- ment)
Key Groups: Domestic Sales R&D	• Revenue • New product knowledge	• Security • Pay	• Stay bonus • Q&A sessions	Supervisors	10/3 (morning of annnounce- ment)

implementation activities, education and training, communication, and other core integration activities.

Table 3 shows the key activities that need to be addressed from the beginning and throughout an integration effort. Organization development professionals should be well skilled in assisting organizations with the key activities identified in Table 3. For example, merger integration is a process that is best addressed organization-wide. An integration effort should contain all of the components that any large-scale, complex project would,

Table 3. Key Integration Activities

Overall merger-integration project management	Merger communications
Re-recruitment of key personnel	Merger staffing and selection
Merger training	Development of operational and functional integration plans
Cultural integration	Integration progress assessments

including: a project infrastructure (with a fully dedicated project manager), clear decision-making processes, project communications, time lines, budgets, milestones, deliverables, measures of progress, and the like. An OD professional should have the project-management skills necessary to oversee and orchestrate such a complex effort.

In addition to project-management expertise, OD professionals should possess competence in merger communications, merger training, staffing and selection, cultural integration, re-recruitment of key personnel, the development of integration plans, and integration-progress assessment—all of which are integral to the process of bringing two companies together.

As discussed earlier, frequent communications, coupled with the education of managers and employees about the processes that will be used in the newly formed organization, are critical to the success of the integration. Staffing and selection issues need to be dealt with, as functional and operational integration plans often identify personnel redundancies. This is best performed by establishing a competency-based process that identifies key work roles, including the skills and competencies needed in those roles, and selecting the people who possess the needed competencies.

Cultural integration is another necessary OD skill during a merger-integration effort. Addressing the cultural combination of two organizations through adjusting tangible "levers" (such as the ways in which people are measured and rewarded, the communication and training they receive, and the rules and policies of the companies) is crucial. Likewise, setting up a process for re-recruiting key personnel is a core skill that OD professionals should have.

Establishing time lines and templates for integration-plan development is also critical to the success of the effort. Integration plans are typically developed by task forces of managers and employees from various functional (e.g., finance, systems, or HR) and operating areas of the merging companies. Plan templates provide consistency in format and ensure that all implementation issues are addressed, including timing, communications and training needs, budgets, equipment and technical support, success measures, and so forth. Finally, as part of the integration-management process, progress assessments should be conducted periodically (e.g., every forty-five to sixty days during the first six months after the deal closes) to provide information on how the integration is progressing. In addition to the financial progress of the merger, progress assessment should be done through a brief (one- to two-week) survey and/or an interview/focus-group process that solicits feedback from a sample of managers, employees, and customers about the progress of the merger integration effort.

Summary

Mergers present a change-management challenge like no other, bringing about all of the change dynamics at the same time and in two organizations. Unfortunately, resistance to the changes brought on by mergers and acquisitions is the norm rather than the exception. The reasons for resistance are "not knowing," "not able," and "not willing." Fundamentally, this hierarchy suggests that there are specific actions management should take to work through people's resistance to change during the integration process. First, people need communication and information to feel that they know what is going on. Second, people need to be trained and educated in order to acquire the skills needed to accomplish the changes that are being asked of them. Third, people need incentives in the form of goals, measurements, feedback, and rewards to help to develop their willingness to change.

In addition to the resistance created, departures of key people and/or groups are commonplace during a merger. Addressing this fact early in an integration process—even before the general announcement of the merger is made—by developing and implementing a re-recruitment strategy will help to maintain the human capital that is critical to the success of the merged organization. These actions will go a long way toward gaining people's commitment to making a merger work.

Organization development practitioners also need a broad base of organizational and managerial skills to enable them to play key roles in the management and orchestration of such a complex change-management effort and to enable them to help managers to play effective roles in the effort.

References

Clemons, E.K., Thatcher, M.E., & Row, M.C. (1995, Fall). Identifying sources of reengineering failure: A study of the behavioral factors contributing to reengineering risks. *Journal of Management Information Systems*, pp. 9–36.

Galpin, T.J. *The human side of change*. San Francisco: Jossey-Bass, 1996.

Growing your company: Five ways to do it right! (1996, November 25). *Fortune*, pp. 78–88.

Haslett, S. (1995, November/December). Broadbanding: A strategic tool for organizational change. *Compensation & Benefits Review*, pp. 40–46.

Longo, S.C. (1996, January). Has reengineering left you financially stronger? *CPA Journal*, p. 69.

Mastering management—Part 11: Summary—Human resources management (1996, January 19). *Financial Times,* pp. III.

May, D., & Kettelhut, M.C. (1996, January/February). Managing human issues in reengineering projects. *Journal of Systems Management,* pp. 4–11.

Peck, R.L. (1995, November/December). Reengineering: Full speed ahead. *Nursing Homes,* p. 10.

Sherman, S. (1993, December 13). A master class in radical change. *Fortune,* pp. 82–90.

World Wide Web site. (1996). Frequently asked questions about organizational change: Answers to questions often asked by heads of companies. *http://www.electriciti.com/dchaudron/faq.htm,* pp. 1–2.

Timothy J. Galpin, Ph.D., *serves as practice leader for human resource strategy with Watson Wyatt Worldwide in Dallas, Texas. He has led projects incorporating the design, implementation, and evaluation of merger integration, strategic planning, change management, and cultural change for several national and multinational companies. His articles have appeared in several publications, including* Mergers and Acquisitions, Journal of Business Strategy, HR Magazine, Training & Development, *and* Human Resource Professional. *He has also written two books, both published by Jossey-Bass:* The Human Side of Change: A Practical Guide to Organizational Redesign *(1996) and* Making Strategy Work: Building Sustainable Growth Capability *(1997).*

THREE TEAM TRAPS

Sara Pope

Abstract: Many organizations use teams as vehicles for organizing work, accomplishing tasks, and completing projects. However, few of these organizations are reaping the full benefit of the time and resources invested in their teams because of three common traps that affect the performance of teams. These three traps are:

- Failure to establish and communicate a clear purpose for teams;

- Lack of leadership in setting direction and providing guidance for team activities; and

- Insufficient provision of structure, boundaries, and guidelines to teams.

This article discusses each of these traps, including the negative outcomes of each and how each impacts team success (using three cases from real organizations and what they did to refocus and redirect team efforts). It also contains ways in which organizations can eliminate these barriers to team success, including methods for avoiding the traps and advice on how to redirect team efforts that have already gone astray.

When looking at the slogans, mottos, and missions that are posted in most organizations, one is likely to see something about the power of teamwork. A great deal of money, time, and other resources go into organizational teams, be they "self-directed work teams," "project teams," or "high-performance work teams." However, many organizations are not reaping the benefits that they expect from their teams. Many teams are underperforming and draining resources, rather than adding to the bottom line. The reason for this is likely to be the three traps that ensnare organizations and affect the performance of their teams:

> Trap #1: "Who's on First?" or the failure to establish and communicate a clear purpose for teams.

> Trap #2: "Who's in Charge Here, Anyway?" or the lack of leadership in setting direction and providing guidance for team activities.

> Trap #3: "The Myth of Self-Direction" or the insufficient provision of structure, boundaries, and guidelines to teams.

WHO'S ON FIRST?

Most organizations institute the use of teams to improve business. There are numerous stories about organizational turnarounds and improvements that have been accomplished through employee involvement and teams. Managers and decision makers read these success stories and become excited about the possibilities for improvements in their own organizations. They often jump on the team bandwagon without clearly understanding or communicating the reasons for using teams. The result may be compared to the "Who's on First" story made famous by Abbott and Costello, in which both Mr. Abbott and Mr. Costello are using the same word, but with very different meanings. The skit shows comedic genius. However, when that same kind of miscommunication and frustration occurs in the workplace, there is nothing funny about it. The "who" in this case is *teams* versus *teamwork*.

Confusion Between Teams and Teamwork

When organizations make broad announcements introducing the "team concept" and herald it as the organization's new approach to work, employees may have different ideas about what it really means. Both managers and employees often confuse the concept of teams with teamwork. This is not surprising, as executives and managers often make broad statements about everyone pulling together as a team to make the organization successful. A distinction needs to be made between *teamwork* and *team work*.

"Teamwork," as it applies to the entire organization, implies values and behavioral norms that encourage respectful, cooperative behaviors. These values are critical to any organization, no matter how it is organized. An organization can promote and reward teamwork without any intention of organizing into teams. Teamwork is a very positive, commendable practice for the workplace. As a matter of fact, teams cannot operate without the principles of teamwork in place. However, simply promoting a sense of esprit de corps is not going to give an organization the kind of payoff that can be derived from a true team-based workforce, and teamwork alone is not enough to make the investment in teams pay off.

A true team is a small group of people with complementary skills who, by working together and pooling their skills, can operate more efficiently or effectively. The true team has a shared, performance-driven purpose, and members hold one another and themselves mutually accountable for meeting that purpose. Team members rely on one another for elements of their work and the realization of their objective. Teams that are performance driven, with mutual accountability, can be a smart investment. Effective teams can and will help organizations to meet the challenges of today's competitive, constantly changing environment.

Case of the Customer-Service Teams

The sales department for a major manufacturing company in the U.S. had a customer-service department that handled customer orders, shipments, and delivery. There were four regional offices; within each office the customer-service representatives carried out a number of different functions. Each employee was responsible for completing his or her tasks alone, and customers were often shuffled from one employee to another when there was a problem or issue.

After reading an article on the power of teamwork, the division manager decreed that these employees had to work as a team in order to provide better customer service. Regional managers organized employees into several teams within each office, and each team was assigned specific accounts. Employees cross-trained in all activities involved in fulfilling and following up on customer orders.

Once the cross-training was complete, the initial reports were positive. Customer satisfaction increased as customers were able to resolve a problem or receive an answer from any team member who answered the phone. However, there were few improvements in processes; issues that had always plagued the organization continued to cause problems. The managers were surprised and disappointed by the results. They felt that the investment in cross-training had not yielded the significant improvements they had expected.

The managers decided that it was time to invest in outside intervention to see what was missing. Interviews with employees revealed that most were satisfied with the results. When asked about significant achievements, most pointed to the successful cross-training, along with improved working relationships. In other words, the employees had no idea that more was expected of them. They believed that they were successful teams: they helped one another with tasks, they listened to one another, and they were all carrying their share of the load. They were practicing the values of teamwork, and it had a positive impact. However, these improvements could easily have been accomplished without the expense of cross-training and reorganizing the work. For this company to see the full benefit of the investment, the teams needed to find ways to improve processes, implement continuous-improvement practices, and solve some of the long-term issues that kept them from delivering exceptional customer service.

As soon as the managers recognized the problem, they became determined to fix it. Teams were given clear assignments and goals. Measures were set in place, and teams began having weekly meetings to focus on solving some of the long-term issues and problems. Within six months, managers began to see measurable, concrete performance results. There were substantial reductions in billing and shipping errors, along with improvements in the computerized reporting systems. The company began to see a bottom-line impact from the teams, in addition to the improvements in customer confidence and trust.

WHO'S IN CHARGE HERE, ANYWAY?

In a traditional organization, the manager's role is to establish and communicate clear, meaningful goals and to ensure that employees have the means and resources to meet those goals. In a team-based organization, the manager's role is to establish clear, meaningful goals and to ensure that the teams have the means and resources to meet those goals. In other words, the need for strong leadership committed to tangible results is just as important in a team-based organization as it is in any type of organization. When teams do not know where to look for guidance and leadership, they can, at best, give lackluster performance. At worst, they can be disruptive and wasteful. In any organization, no matter what structure is in place, employees look to the leaders for direction and governance.

Unfortunately, in many cases, managers have taken the stance that teams should be left alone. Many managers and supervisors are confused about their roles with teams. Supervisors have actually said in interviews, "I can't intervene; the team is working on it." This "hands-off" approach may set up the teams to fail. Teams may work on the wrong issues, set priorities in direct opposition to organizational priorities, or simply waste time with little or no meaningful contribution.

Where teams have been successful, managers have been willing to play critical leadership roles. This does not mean that the manager becomes a member of the team or becomes the team leader; rather, he or she sponsors the team by committing to the team's success, providing direction, removing roadblocks, and becoming the team's champion. *Webster's Dictionary* defines "sponsor" as: "one who assumes responsibility for some other person or thing, a person or organization that pays for or plans and carries out a project or activity." Synonyms include advocate, backer, champion, patron, and supporter.

Essentially, the sponsor is the person who is willing to assume accountability for devoting resources to a particular team or team activity. This sponsor is committed to the success of this team because his or her name is associated with it. It is the sponsor's job to communicate clear expectations to the team members, garner the resources the team needs to be successful, and provide guidance if the team is not accomplishing its goal. When sponsors understand this role and take it seriously, team activities are selected carefully and thoughtfully. There may actually be fewer teams but they are working on high-priority problems or issues. Most importantly, they are more likely to achieve results.

Case of the Leaderless Textile Teams

A textile-manufacturing business formed teams throughout the plant. The company used a design team to examine every process in the plant and form teams around the process. Every person in the plant had to be on a team. The company did a good job of defining measures for each process team and supplied the teams with the training and know-how to track their own measures. The teams got off to a good start; team members had excellent ideas on improving their processes and meeting their performance goals.

However, some of the teams' ideas required engineering or maintenance support. Team members tried talking to these support groups about the issues but were ignored, as these groups had their own teams and their own issues. When talking did not help, the teams tried putting the issues in their meeting minutes. But no specific managers were assigned to be the teams' sponsors, so the teams' minutes were not seen by people who could remedy the situation. The teams simply assumed that someone was taking the time to look at their logbooks. In the meantime, the plant manager was unaware of the teams' struggles. He thought that all of the teams knew that they could go to any member of the management team with their issues. Eventually many of the teams' members became frustrated and gave up. Team meetings turned into "gripe sessions" rather than problem-solving sessions, and the team members felt that the entire redesign was a waste of time.

It did not take long for the company to begin questioning the value of the investment in the teams. It had invested in a cross-functional design team over a ten-month period, reorganization of the work, and team training for the entire workforce, but was not seeing any payoff. Deciding that they needed help, the managers brought in an outside firm to conduct a team audit. Interviews, surveys, and diagnosis showed that the teams had no idea who was able or willing to make a decision, intervene, or make things happen for them. Team members were uncertain about what they were empowered to act on; therefore, they were waiting for someone else to step in and give permission or take action. Since they had no idea who that someone was, they simply continued to wait, which resulted in frustration, anger, and a sense of helplessness.

The official appointment and training of team sponsors or "champions" had an immediate impact. The teams already had unnamed sponsors: their department managers. Unfortunately, these department managers did not truly understand their roles or how to carry them out. All of the team-training efforts had been focused on the team members, with little focus on the managers and leaders of the teams. Finally, the sponsors received training on the critical aspects of team leadership, including:

- Different types of teams and how to use each effectively.
- Constructing an effective team charter.
- Evaluating team measurements and team progress.
- Coordinating the efforts of multiple teams.
- Recognizing when and how to intervene.

This training clarified the managers' roles and gave them hands-on skills for supporting the teams and their activities. Each of the sponsors met with the teams and explained the sponsor role to the teams so they would know what they could and should expect from their managers. Team members responded positively; they now knew who they could turn to when they needed resources, help, or guidance.

Although there were some immediate improvements in team activities, it did take some time to rebuild trust throughout the organization. Employees had developed an extremely negative perception of the entire concept of teams because of what they perceived as lack of responsiveness. Managers had also developed negative attitudes about the teams because they felt that teams had added little value to the organization while consuming a lot of time and resources. It was not until both groups began to see some results that the teams really were back on the right track.

THE MYTH OF SELF-DIRECTION

The term "self-directed work team" has done more to contribute to the struggles that team members and managers have experienced than has any other factor. "Self-directed" connotes that teams do not need direction from outside. Both managers and team members have fallen prey to the myth that teams do not have rules. Because of this, many teams have been formed with little to no structure, allowing team members to believe that anything is fair game. When they find out that there are limits on what they can and cannot do, frustrations and disappointments arise—making it very difficult to move back on track.

When a manager or decision maker in an organization forms a team, he or she must provide that team with structure, guidelines, and a disciplined process. The initial structure is best provided through a written document called a charter. This document clarifies expectations and communicates the purpose of the team. It specifies the team's membership and lays out the boundaries the team must operate within and the resources available. Without a charter, there is a great opportunity for misinterpretation. Team members often misunderstand their purpose or their limitations when there is no charter.

Case of Missing Direction

A company was starting up a new plant and saw it as the perfect opportunity to begin the "right way," as a team-based operation. Potential employees went through an intensive screening process that measured team skills as well as the required technical skills. The plant manager believed that because these employees came into the workplace with good team skills and the expectation of taking responsibility for themselves and their own work, there was little need for structure. There were no charters for the teams and no clear expectations of what they were to accomplish. The plant manager became the team sponsor for all the teams, because the plant was small and the selected employees were prepared to work in teams.

Team members participated in extensive technical training and received some training in effective meeting processes. The only expectation that was communicated to them was that they work in teams and meet one hour per week. Their initial meetings were well structured; they used agendas and meeting roles quite effectively. However, less than a year into the process, the plant manager was ready to give up on the concept of teams. The plant was off to a slow start. Production was not where it should have been by that point. Very few of the start-up problems had been solved. Morale on the plant floor was low, and some of the employees who had seemed to be promising performers had resigned.

The plant manager knew that something had to be done. She began looking at meeting minutes and found that one team had spent three meetings talking about people spitting in the water fountain (a bothersome problem, but not a good investment of time). The continuing waste of team time had happened because the team members were left to founder on the wrong issues during team meetings.

Once the manager realized that the teams did not have an understanding of the issues they were charged with, she saw how important it was to clarify her expectations. With consulting help, the plant manager drew up a charter for every team in the plant, clarifying the teams' job descriptions and outlining the performance expectations and the areas of empowerment, along with the limits or boundaries. The plant manager took care to ensure that the teams had significant areas over which they had control so that they would not become caught up in trivial matters. She appointed members of her management team as team sponsors, with the realization that each team needed a champion who had enough time to truly carry out that role effectively.

These steps began to pay off fairly quickly. The teams began to concentrate on the equipment and machinery problems that were slowing the start-up process. They also requested and received additional technical training, recognizing that some of the issues were due to limited knowledge of what was a new process for a majority of the workforce. Even with the slow start, this particular plant was able to meet production demands and become profitable in half the time of similar start-ups for the overall company.

Conclusion

Teams are a major investment of both time and resources. Organizations and their managers approach most investments with a plan and steps for carrying out that plan. However, that mind-set does not always carry over when it comes to establishing teams. Numerous experiences have proven that there are three basic truths about teams that will help avoid the traps illustrated by the case studies:

- The organizations must establish and communicate a clear purpose for each team;
- Leaders must play strong roles in setting direction, guiding team projects, and ensuring team successes;
- Teams must be given clear structures, boundaries, and guidelines within which to work.

Like any other major undertaking in the management of an organization, teams require an investment on the part of management and leadership. A successful transition to teams requires a plan of action, a strategy for carrying out the plan, and a great deal of coaching, directing, and guidance. The sponsor's role is critical in the success of teams. The sponsor ensures that team members are working on the right things, have the necessary resources to complete their tasks, and have meaningful measures in place to gauge their success. If that seems like a tough role to fill, simply compare it to the manager in a traditional organization. Often, the traditional manager has to determine what to do, how to do it, and who should do it. The team sponsor simply has to direct the what and who; the team generates the "how to," within its charter.

The charter is the tool that helps the sponsor carry out his or her role. The charter is a formal mechanism for providing direction and guidance. It is also an excellent vehicle for clarifying the difference between teams and teamwork. It may seem like overkill to clearly communicate the purpose of teams to the entire organization; to train and appoint sponsors for every team; to lay out exactly what is expected from the team and what its boundaries are. However, taking the time to communicate the purpose of and carefully plan teams can eliminate miscommunication, misunderstanding, and time wasted in working on the wrong issues.

Sara Pope *is a senior associate with Cornelius and Associates, a consulting firm dedicated to maximizing the performance of employee work teams. She has more than fifteen years of human resource management, consulting, and training experience. Throughout her career, she has worked in both manufacturing and service industries across the United States and Canada, providing assistance with the planning, implementation, and training of high-involvement employee work teams. Her recent work focuses on helping traditional managers and supervisors understand and carry out their roles in developing and managing the high-involvement work place. Ms. Pope has authored two books,* The Team Sponsor Workbook *and* The Team Leader Workbook, *which provide practical advice for success in team environments.*

THE A²D⁴ PROCESS FOR DESIGNING AND IMPROVING ORGANIZATIONAL PROCESSES

Neil J. Simon

Abstract: One of the greatest challenges in organizations is implementing change. Expert consultants often are engaged to help to effect change and arrive with their version of the "best" methodology to use. Unfortunately, the methodology developed within one organizational culture does not always suit another. Even if the organization is able to use it, the employees may be resistant because they have not been involved in decisions that affect how their work is done. The people who do the work determine the success of any change effort.

This article is a "road map" to be used in the design and improvement of organizational processes. The process involves employees at all levels in the design and implementation of the change initiative. As a result, employees support and sustain the change. Whether an organization is evolving, incorporating new technology, changing work systems, or improving processes, this approach addresses the needs of the people who must make it happen.

INTRODUCTION

Organizations today must have effective and efficient processes to ensure their competitiveness. Any organization that is willing to invest in itself can change or improve by utilizing a methodology that provides an opportunity for employees (those who perform the work) to design, redesign, and/or improve their processes.

The A^2D^4 model is based on the principles of sociotechnical systems, organization development, evolution, and change management. The following are the fundamental assumptions:

- Every organization is a system of interconnected parts that mutually support one another.

- Organizational work processes and practices, policies and procedures, technologies, and support systems are all interconnected.

- Organizational culture is an integral part of the organizational process.

- Technological adoption/adaption (change) is influenced by people systems, performance systems, and management systems.

The fundamental concepts of the A^2D^4 self-designing change process are:

- It integrates the needs of the organization and new or improved concepts with the existing culture, so it more easily overcomes common organizational-culture barriers.

- It focuses on the processes used to design, develop, and implement or improve what currently exists and allows organizational members to develop competencies in designing, developing, implementing, improving, and integrating organizational processes.

- It focuses on employee participation in the design, development, and implementation of processes, utilizing the knowledge of employees and their customers.

- It is a disciplined approach that builds knowledge about the organization and its membership.

- It assists in the rapid adoption or adaption of processes by organizational members by involving stakeholders in the entire process.

Employee participation is accomplished through involvement in a variety of teams (e.g., design team, development team, local work-unit team). Thus, much of the usual resistance to change does not arise because the people involved actually developed the processes. This assists in the alignment of organizational direction and creates an environment that encourages all employees to work toward common goals and objectives.

The consultant's role is as process guide, trainer, coach/mentor, and counselor.

The following is an overview of each *phase* of the process and its primary *goal*:

- **A**gree: Identify and clarify desired change with sponsor and key stakeholders.

- **A**nalyze: Analyze current state of the organization.

- **D**esign: Develop vision, goals, objectives, strategy, and transition plan.

- **D**evelop: Design implementation plan; develop support structures and materials needed for the change.

- **D**o: Execute implementation plan.

- **D**igest: Continually improve.

To launch this endeavor, a leader of the organization who will serve as sponsor of the initiative commissions a "champion" to spearhead the change process. The champion gathers a core team of key stakeholders—employees who will be impacted by the initiative—to assist in the change process. During the process, additional organizational members may participate. A consultant (or more than one) is engaged in a facilitative role to act as coach, mentor, trainer, and counselor. The consultant's first task as part of the team is to empower the team by providing the information necessary to design the planned change.

A SIX-STEP PROCESS

Following is the six-step process that the team (champion, appointed key stakeholders, any additional organizational members, and consultant) will use to fulfill its commission.

Agree on the Task

The first step in the process is to determine what the team will focus on. During this phase, discussion needs to take place between the sponsor and the team to ensure clarity about the sponsor's goals, desired outcomes, and motivation for the change effort. The team's preliminary task is to develop an agreement with the sponsor about what is needed and wanted. The sponsor often has a mental image of the path to the desired outcome. To ensure effective results, it is essential that the team understand the sponsor's mental models.

During the agreement stage, it is important to find out from the sponsor which things can be changed and which cannot. These are called negotiables and nonnegotiables. The nonnegotiables usually are based on the business strategy developed by the organization to ensure competitiveness and success. It is important that the sponsor educate the team regarding the business strategy and the boundaries or rules the team must follow. Examples of nonnegotiables are: no decreases in departmental personnel, 25 percent reduction of costs, 35 percent reduction in time from design to concept finalization, reduction of through-put time, and a total quality management (TQM) process must be utilized. Often the nonnegotiables are considered the "whats" (what must be done) and the negotiables are considered the "hows" (how to achieve what must be accomplished).

This initial work done by the team also serves as a team-building tool as members learn about one another; identify special-interest topics, passions, and skills; and learn how to work effectively together. This first phase often sets the tone of the initiative throughout the organization.

The next important things to be determined are what, specifically, the sponsor, key stakeholders (employees), and organization are willing and able to do. The discussion should focus on the resources and boundary conditions under which the change will take place. Available resources may be: financial (the money available for the change effort); tools (e.g., the availability of space, telephones, computers); and personnel (e.g., whether people can be "drafted" to assist). Resource limitations become boundary conditions. Additional boundary conditions may include such things as time factors, reporting processes, and the project delivery date.

Learn About Stakeholders and Territories

The team members must learn about the organization—its structure and culture; they must identify additional stakeholders, influencers, and "fiefdoms." Stakeholders are people or groups of people who have a major interest and/or investment in the planned initiative. They may be the workers who will be responsible for changing the ways in which work is done or a work unit that will have to give up space in order to accommodate the initiative. The key stakeholders are those with the most power and influence. Some are open to change, while others want the organization to stay the same. Fiefdoms are "territories" or centers of influence held by stakeholders who have a vested interest in the continuance of the organization as it is and who are opposed to change unless it benefits them and their areas of influence. It is important to identify the stakeholders' preliminary concerns and passions, their personal and professional agendas, and what they will use to measure success.

Build Relationships

Stakeholders must be made aware that the team exists. By developing relationships with the people who have vested interests in the change, the team often can build the requisite rapport and trust needed for support during the change. As the team gains greater clarity about stakeholders and their interests, it can plan to help them achieve their personal and professional successes; in turn, the stakeholders will support the team's endeavors. The bottom line is knowing where the team stands with supporters, fence sitters, and detractors of the planned initiative.

Document the Process

Documentation is important throughout the process. The team needs to document its assumptions, thinking processes, and methods. This written record serves as the organization's memory, and it can be used for learning what works in the organization and/or to meet certain quality-certification requirements (e.g., ISO compliance).

Analyze the System

This is the phase in which the team studies the organization and learns what makes it work and what interferes with its success. Basically, the team collects facts about the organization and the perceptions and beliefs of key people who will be involved in the change effort. The following areas are important in achieving a good organizational analysis:

Current organizational systems and processes—the existing ways of doing business. This "snapshot" of the existing organization will provide a process map of the formal and informal work system the organization uses to conduct business. A careful analysis is required of the systems and processes, the structures and substructures, and the environments in which they operate. Analyzing the whole system will also provide an understanding of how the organization is likely to respond to the planned change.

True causes of problems. If the change is meant to solve a problem, it is important to recognize the difference between the symptoms of the problem and its underlying cause(s). A true cause is often masked by symptoms such as production or service backlogs, unattained profit goals, late product delivery, and customer dissatisfaction. The challenge is to understand how the organization's system works and how the culture of the organization and the behaviors of its members contribute to the dynamics of the system. With this knowledge, the team will be prepared to isolate the systemic causes of the problem.

Where the organization is now in relation to where it wants to be. This analysis serves as the baseline data from which the team will determine what it needs to do in order to accomplish the goals established in agreement with the sponsor.

Once the team has an understanding of how the organizational system works, it is ready to identify the leverage points that will facilitate and expedite the change process. Whether one is solving a problem, instituting a change in the way in which work or business is conducted, or attempting to change people's behaviors, it is essential to understand the system to know where primary efforts need to be directed to optimize results.

Find the Leverage Point(s)

Leverage points vary. Desired outcomes need to be kept in mind. For example, to make an organization more cost effective, one can focus on cost reduction as a leverage point or one can focus on quality issues, with overall reduction of costs as a by-product of effectiveness.

The selection of the leverage point is critical for the overall success of a change effort. The organization only has so much "energy" to devote to the change process. If too little is used, the change is ineffective. If too much is used, the system's resources are drained and the overall process is often hurt. It is important to initiate only as much change as the organization can bear without losing its integrity or creating uncontrollable chaos.

Identify Norms and Cultural Issues

Identifying the formal and informal norms and the cultural issues in the organization is an important step in understanding what will and will not work. Such issues often determine what people are willing to do. For example, the culture may not promote cooperation or the sharing of knowledge across departments or it may be an unspoken rule that people are not asked to work on Saturdays.

Design the Intervention

Once the current organization is understood, the team moves into the phase of exploring options, eventually settling on the design of the intervention. With a clear picture of the organization, the team can work on creating a different image that can be used to help the organization grow.

Define Where the Organization Wants To Go

A clear direction, with everyone moving together in that direction, is critical for change. It is important that the team plan a change strategy that is compatible with the sponsor's and stakeholders' desired outcomes.

Often a technique such as benchmarking the best-in-class operations of other companies can assist the team in generating ideas. Ideas that come from other organizations need to be adapted to the current organization's culture.

During this step, it is important that the team not over-design the results. The major job is to identify the specific aspects of the organization and its processes to be changed or the behaviors of people that need to be changed. This design information is often expressed as minimal critical specifications, those key critical requirements that provide the basic structure and boundaries to the defined outcomes.

In identifying minimal critical specifications, there are two classes of things to be considered. First are those things that are nonnegotiable. For example, a corporate directive may be issued for a 15 percent cost reduction. Second are those things that are negotiable, such as "how" to achieve the change. A cost reduction may take place by reducing inventory expense, decreasing labor cost, or by creating more effective or efficient production or delivery processes. The team can negotiate how it will achieve the desired 15 percent reduction.

Create an Image of the End Result

The team's next task is to develop a vision of what the end result will be. The vision then becomes the model that all can buy into—one that is aligned with and contributes to the organization's vision. For example, if the organization's vision is to be the world's leading manufacturer of quality drill presses, utilizing state-of-the-art technology, the work unit's vision might be to produce best-in-class gearing for the drill presses.

It is important that this image reflect the minimum amount of specifications required to make the change happen. In the above case, the only specification is to produce best-in-class gearing. This allows those involved in effecting the change to have input in *how* the change will be accomplished. Personal contributions from organizational members create feelings of ownership and "buy in."

Define Desired Results and Establish Goals

Now that the team has determined where the organization is and where it wants to be, a gap analysis can be performed to determine what needs to be done to achieve the vision. The team develops a series of clear goals and objectives that will guide the change. The goals and objectives should focus on the performance of the particular system(s) and people that the change will impact. Often the goals focus on things such as:

■ The effectiveness of the system (making sure the right things are done).

■ Efficiencies of effective systems (making sure the right things are done in the right ways).

■ The performance behaviors of the people within the system (making sure the systems are useable and friendly to the workers and support the service or production efforts).

Develop a Transition Plan

Once it has determined what needs to change to bring about the desired outcome, the team is in a position to recommend a transition plan and to develop a methodology. A minimum of five basic areas must be addressed and documented in the transition plan:

■ Where you are.

■ Where you want to go.

■ How to get there.

- What you need to get there.
- What success will look like.

    A transition plan includes:

- The vision (what the change/outcome will look like).
- The strategy (a statement expressing how the team will achieve the vision).
- A requirement definition (the final specification around which the change in the system is to be developed).
- The boundary conditions (negotiable and nonnegotiable guidelines the team needs to follow).
- Goals and objectives (a sequence of initiatives or mini-leverage points and the stages of progress that need to be achieved in order to attain the vision).
- Success measures (quantifiable measures that will be used to determine success).
- A project-management plan (a plan that states what is due when used to measure progress and hold the team members accountable in terms of timeliness).

    The transition plan is shared with the sponsor and all key stakeholders who are impacted by the change initiative. To ensure that an accurate portrayal has been created by the team, it is important to set up a system for feedback from organizational members.

Develop a Strategy, Plan, and Materials

During this phase, the team has an opportunity to directly involve other people in the process of developing a strategy, plan, and the materials that will be used to bring about the change.

Additionally, all members of the organization need to be made ready to accept the change and adjust to the efforts made. The transition plan outlines the big picture of the transition. During this phase, the team develops an implementation plan. This plan is shared throughout the organization. The following are the key tasks at this point:

Develop an Implementation Plan

- Identify key resources.
- Identify key personnel who are able to assist in the development of support structures as well as the rollout requisites (funds, management programs, employee programs, information, and transition materials).

- Identify the supporters of the initiative and those who do not want change to occur (it is useful to identify those detractors who will be challenged to become allies; unless the team identifies the people to implement the change, the effort will not work).

- Clearly transmit minimal critical specifications and requirements. Transmission of the vision, strategy, goals, final specification and requirements, success measures, and boundary conditions is an important step. As with laying a new path, the forms need to be laid to define the new direction.

- Develop sequenced steps. Developing a written plan, using a project-management methodology, allows for orchestration and monitoring of the implementation and coordination of activities. Dates serve as a guide for the timing of each sequence of the implementation plan. This assists the organization in creating a time frame for implementation.

Set Expectations of Roles and Responsibilities

Leaders need to explicitly prepare the organizational members for the upcoming events and changes. Included in this step is clearly communicating the roles and responsibilities of leaders and employees. There are three sets of responsibilities: first, leaders must clearly state the direction; second, employees need to understand the direction being taken and how they will incorporate the changes; and third, leaders and employees need to assist one another in the transition and in making behavioral changes.

Effecting behavioral change takes time, assistance, coaching, and reinforcement. This is often best accomplished with a team effort.

Develop Materials, Methods, Tactics, and Tools

Before the change effort is launched, materials need to be developed to familiarize organizational members with the change. These include orientation materials, training materials, and leadership materials.

Specific tactics and tools may need to be developed to assist organizational members in creating change in their local work units.

It is important to include information on how the change may affect the organizational members and what they can do to assist themselves in the transition process. Often orientation materials cover the facts of the change but do not address the "people" aspects (e.g., changes in reporting structures, the effects of new learning, the effects of new leaders, frustrations caused by problems with a new computer program, the stress of trying to keep business going as usual while incorporating new procedures).

Create Leadership Buy-In

The next critical effort is to create an environment in which all leaders "buy in" to the implementation of the planned change and its associated strategies. Leaders need to contribute to the process and develop minimal critical specifications for their units and employees, which are then rolled out so that others can buy in as well.

Develop Training Materials

The team will need to provide orientation (knowledge, skills, and behavior) training to the sponsoring executive and other leaders. This training should address the fundamentals of the change and assist the leaders in defining and carrying out their roles. A discussion of expectations regarding their contributions to the transition and ultimate change is also necessary.

Orientation and training materials also should be provided to all the members of the organization who will be involved in or affected by the change.

Develop Performance Measures

Organizational and individual performance measures need to be developed to assist in the clarification of expectations. These measures will assist in gauging the success of the endeavor. Additionally, the team can use the measures as a feedback tool to communicate with those individuals or work units involved in the change initiative.

Train Leaders to Assist Employees to Achieve Success

The awareness and support of organizational leaders is critical to the success of the endeavor. Leaders have an important role in assisting the employees in achieving success. Therefore, they need to be trained in how to do this.

Leaders need to have personal mastery in fundamental knowledge areas such as group dynamics, process and system concepts (including business, work/production, and people management), organizational and team development, assertiveness, and conflict resolution. Additionally, leaders need skills in facilitation, meeting management, coaching and mentoring, empowerment, and effective communications (listening, providing feedback, and developing presentations).

This fundamental knowledge and the skills assist in creating an environment in which the team members can contribute their own knowledge, skills, and experience for the betterment of their work unit and the organization as a whole.

Establish Accountability

In order for any change effort to be successful, a system of accountability needs to be established. Specifically, leaders and followers must maintain their agreements and assume their responsibilities to make the effort work. Accountability systems should specify such things as the performance agreement between followers and leaders, recognition and reward systems, consequences for nonperformance or failure to achieve performance agreements, problem-solving and conflict-resolution methods, and a plan to incorporate change of direction.

Accountability systems often are designed to be punitive. However, systems that are supportive and that assist people in making the transition from old to new behaviors are far superior to those that are punitive.

Do (Implement)

The implementation phase is the "doing" phase. This is where "the rubber meets the road." Involvement, struggle, pain, and eventually success are all part of this phase. Whatever the leverage point and resulting change strategies or actions, organizational personnel will need to adjust and, ultimately, accept the new way(s) of doing things. Strategies that lead to improved performance can be successful only when employees buy in and incorporate the change; thus, a crucial task of the team is that of coaching the change process.

During this phase, the team's role is basically that of:

- Keeper of the mission
- Feedback giver
- Obstacle remover
- Coach
- Cheerleader

The following substeps are essential for implementing successful and sustainable change:

Determine the Steps Involved

Each unit (organization, division, business unit, or work team) needs to understand the desired outcome, determine a way to achieve it, implement the requisite change, and develop a feedback process so that it can self-correct. This planning process is used throughout all levels of the organization.

Conduct Training

The training that was developed earlier should be rolled out as the first step in the change process. This training will empower the organizational members with the information necessary to transition or transform.

Guide, Coach, and Share Knowledge and Skills

Those involved in the change process need to work with the employees sharing their expectations and nurturing the transition/transformation. Leaders need to work on methods of feedback so they are made aware of employees who require skill training or help with changes in behavior.

Design/Redesign and Implement Work Flow

At the local work-unit level, leaders need to assist in the transition to new behaviors. This often is accomplished by having the members of the work unit design or improve its work flow.

Reinforce Roles and Responsibilities

It is important that leaders and workers work together during the transition/transformation. Often leaders will be inclined to micromanage, rather than allow people to define their own roles. Such behavior creates dependencies that can impede the creativity of the process.

Additionally, it is important that all organizational members assume their rightful responsibilities. This includes learning from failures and successes. The sharing of learning assists in the reinforcement of change.

Ensure Leadership Support

The primary responsibility of top leadership is to support the transition process. This effort involves "carrying the torch" for all to see, giving honest feedback, and using authority to remove barriers. Sustainable change depends on top leadership's ongoing support.

Digest (Institutionalize and Improve)

People need time and experience to become comfortable with any change before they can further learn, develop, and continually improve the organization. The following are the final steps in the A^2D^4 process of change.

Ensure that Work Systems Are Going in the Same Direction

During this phase, it is important to ensure that the focus of all change is concentrated in the same direction. Agendas, initiatives, goals, and outcomes all must be aligned. When change is introduced, some chaos is normal. People have to let go of the old and embrace the new. As the change becomes part of the organizational system, behaviors and processes will align with it.

Ways do need to be set up, however, to address process problems such as inconsistencies, confusion, lack of clarity, and noncompliance. Methods must be supportive and, at the same time, definitive.

Create a Vehicle for Ongoing Monitoring

Activities such as a "lessons learned" session allow the organization to observe its path and evaluate its degree of success.

The development of a continuous-improvement program, both to refine the new process and to create organizational learning, is important for the long-term success of the project. It allows the system to correct errors, miscalculations, and misassumptions. A "learning organization" has the advantage of being able to continually improve its processes and procedures through sharing of knowledge and learning, an ongoing feedback mechanism, and employee awareness of the continuous-improvement process.

THE LAST STEP

When the change initiative has been completed, it is important that everyone involved be acknowledged and given feedback. A useful and celebratory tool is to have an organizational debriefing at which the efforts of key players in the design, development, and implementation stages are recognized specifically. All who were affected by the change also should be commended for their part in it.

The following chart is a summary that can be used as an overview of the different phases of the process.

Checklist for the A²D⁴ Self-Design Organization Approach

Phase	Goals	Major Tasks	Benefits
AGREE	Identify & clarify desired change with sponsor & key stakeholders	Gain clarity on what is needed or wanted	Needs and wants identified
		Identify specifically what the system is willing to do	Significance of each issue understood
		Develop knowledge about the territory	Focus, scope, and boundary conditions identified
		Develop knowledge about key stakeholders—their concerns, passions, agendas, & measures of success	Mutually supportive work relationships established
		Build relationships	
ANALYZE	Analyze current state of the organization	Identify where the organization is now	An understanding of corporate culture developed
		Study the system; identify organizational patterns	Structural and cultural assisters and barriers identified
		Determine the leverage point(s) for needed change	Symptoms separated from causes and leverage point(s) identified
		Identify goals & objectives	Change guided by clear goals and objectives

Checklist for the A²D⁴ Self-Design Organization Approach (continued)

Phase	Goals	Major Tasks	Benefits
DESIGN	Development of vision, goals, objectives, strategy, & transition plan	Identify where the organization wants to go	Change strategy compatible with organizational direction
		Create an image of what the end result(s) will be	Ownership in change process created by shared vision
		Determine the difference between the two states (gap analysis)	Everyone works in the same direction
		Define the desired results & create the vision	Lets everyone know what they need to do
		Establish the goals & objectives, & create the strategy	Creates organizational expectations
		Develop the transition plan & measures of success	
		(Note: Document this entire process.)	
DEVELOP	Implementation-plan design, development of support structures & materials needed for the change	Identify key resources	Plan is thought out and assists in capturing all significant processes of the planned change to:
		Transmit minimal, critical specifications & requirements	reduce surprises and ensure success
		Create leadership buy-in	smooth out implementation timing
		Train leaders to assist employees in achieving success	work out issues
		Develop sequencing of steps	involve everyone

Checklist for the A²D⁴ Self-Design Organization Approach (continued)

Phase	Goals	Major Tasks	Benefits
		Prepare expectations around roles & responsibilities Set up system of accountability	Create basic support structures for transition
DO	Execution of the implementation plan	Implement plan Determine substeps Guide, coach, train employees Reinforce roles & responsibilities Ensure leadership support	Development of procedures by employees Organizational involvement Employees appropriately utilized Employees empowered
DIGEST	Continuous-improvement process	Process established to ensure working systems going in the same direction Vehicle developed for ongoing monitoring process to correct the system	Achieving desired results Ongoing quality improvement

Neil J. Simon *is president of Business Development Group, Inc., based in Ann Arbor, Michigan. The firm specializes in process-design engineering to optimize organizational performance through systems design. Mr. Simon's methodology is a self-design process that produces meaningful, sustainable change in departments, divisions, or entire organizations. Mr. Simon conducted his post-graduate studies at the Fielding Institute in Santa Barbara, California. He holds staff appointments at several colleges and universities.*

CREATING THE DYNAMIC ENTERPRISE: STRATEGIC TOOLS FOR HRD PRACTITIONERS

Lisa Friedman and Herman Gyr

Abstract: The profound and accelerating changes faced by organizations today call for "dynamic enterprises" that can respond rapidly and successfully to dynamic environments.

Strategic thinking and change implementation are no longer just the responsibility of the CEO or senior management team. People throughout the organization must be able to take part. Human resource development (HRD) professionals play a critical role in creating the dynamic enterprise; they can provide the assistance that people need to perform this critical, strategic work.

Enterprise development (ED) integrates six strategic-thinking and change-implementation practices into one comprehensive framework—an overview of what is needed to create the dynamic enterprise. HRD practitioners can use this model to enable their clients to "see the big picture," to identify which changes are most critical, and to clarify what is needed to implement them. In addition, ED offers common-sense concepts and a common language for strategy and change that enables people to communicate about the challenges they face.

DYNAMIC ENVIRONMENTS CALL FOR DYNAMIC ENTERPRISES

In today's rapidly changing, global business climate, organizations are facing constant and often profound, multidimensional change: from the marketplace, competitors, advancing technologies, and growing customer expectations. Most workers and teams are pressured to deliver performance faster, cheaper, and smarter. The increasing demands for cost containment and new products, when combined with a sense of urgency, produce a pressured, complex atmosphere.

Entire industries are in transition. Frequently, changes in one industry exert new pressures on and offer new opportunities for other related industries. This cascading, interactive network of change is unleashing forces that have thrust many organizations into disarray just at a time when they need to deliver high performance.

From all indications, the current levels of change are just the beginning. Changes in the workplace are occurring at an accelerating pace. As each change enables or necessitates a change in another area, changes increase exponentially.

Leaders and managers find themselves facing challenges for which their education and business experiences provide no precedent. Previous practices (generally for managing a single major change initiative or for managing a large-scale but unidimensional change) are inadequate for facing today's challenges. Often, no other organization can provide an adequate or time-tested benchmark.

Human resource development professionals must be able to help organizations find clear directions among constantly shifting priorities. They must be able to help people throughout an enterprise to work together in responding to and anticipating changes.

The "dynamic enterprise" is capable of rapid and successful response to a dynamic environment. It enables people to navigate the challenges of continual, exponential change; to turn chaos into shared strategic direction and clarity; and to transform complex change into momentum to move toward the desired future.

Definition of a Dynamic Enterprise

The dynamic enterprise continually transforms the multitude of changes occurring around it into coordinated strategic actions by its people to further the development of its products and services.

A work group of any size or scope can become a dynamic enterprise. The concepts apply to global corporations, divisions or departments within a company, or cross-functional project teams. In addition, a dynamic enterprise can include a group of strategic partners, a supply chain or "value chain" of customers and suppliers, or a network of alliances crossing many companies.

A Dynamic Enterprise Is People-Driven

The responsiveness, adaptability, and imagination essential for survival in today's business environment can be found only in its most responsive, adaptive, and imaginative element: its people.

In the traditional, hierarchical organization, the structure is designed to focus people, to determine their actions. In a predictable environment, structured job descriptions and stable performance criteria are adequate to guide people in their day-to-day work.

In the dynamic enterprise, it is people, rather than the organizational structure, that guide the strategic choices to be made. People have a much larger role to play in integrating diverse input, in making strategic decisions, and in coordinating with others. Existing organizational forms and job descriptions are not sufficient to guide the array of choices to be made. People are needed because dynamism requires choice, imagination, and courage.

In a dynamic environment, people need a new set of skills to help them navigate the complexities of the changing enterprise. They need to be able to translate emerging data into meaningful information that can guide their actions. They need to be able to collaborate with others in this effort, to develop team and work-group strategies that align with the strategies of other teams and the larger enterprise. Just as important, they need to know how to turn these strategies into real performance and coordinated action.

TRANSFORMATION OF THE HRD FUNCTION: ENABLING THE DYNAMIC ENTERPRISE

The HRD function, more than any other, can and must take responsibility for ensuring that people have the skills and tools needed to create the dynamic enterprise. Their role in enabling the creation of the dynamic enterprise can be called "performance support."

All stakeholders need to be involved in creating the dynamic enterprise. They need to understand what they are facing together and need to be able to communicate with one another—throughout the enterprise—about upcoming changes. In order to effectively facilitate strategic thinking and change implementation, HRD practitioners must enable people:

- To see the big picture—to understand the complexity of the forces impacting the enterprise, so they can choose the best strategic direction.

- To engage all key stakeholders—to build a sense of ownership and responsibility among all relevant stakeholders so that they can contribute their best thinking and be willing to put their plans into action when the time comes.

- To enable ongoing dialogue and coordinated change throughout the enterprise.

These tasks are not easy to carry out in the midst of an already busy work schedule. (One group described this as needing to change the tires while still riding the bicycle.)

STRATEGIC THINKING TOOLS FOR HRD PRACTITIONERS

People need tools to help them to think strategically and to coordinate the changes they will need to implement. They need a way to reduce complexity into a manageable number of categories and to understand how these categories relate to one another.

When given a common-sense model with clear language, people are able to describe the complexity around them. This enables them to think clearly about difficult issues, to build shared views and maps with others, to communicate about complex issues, and to work collaboratively. This promotes a sense of predictability in an otherwise unpredictable environment.

In times of great change, the most helpful tools are those that provide:

- A manageable number of basic building blocks.

- Straightforward connections between the building blocks.

- Concrete, common-sense language and a shared vocabulary for change.

- A map to clarify the big picture.

Enterprise-Development Framework

"Enterprise development" (ED) is an integrated set of tools for strategic thinking and change implementation that HRD practitioners can use to enable their clients to create and maintain dynamic enterprises. The ED Framework provides steps for people to use to move their enterprise into the future.

Six Competencies of the ED Framework

The creation of the dynamic enterprise requires six developmental capabilities or core competencies. These carry the enterprise from strategizing and changing, engaging key people in strategy, design, and implementation, through to evaluating whether the planned changes were actually implemented. The six practices in the ED Framework that help build the core competencies are:

1. Seeing the whole system.
2. Creating a shared future.
3. Seeing the past and current enterprise honestly and accurately.
4. Understanding the nature of the change.
5. Mobilizing and aligning the essential drivers.
6. Implementing the change.

The Enterprise-Development Map serves as an integrating, comprehensive framework for the essential elements and steps in building a dynamic enterprise. Each area of the map corresponds to a particular core competence. The six areas relate to one another and form an integrated whole. Figure 1 shows the basic template for the map.

The map functions as a strategy and organizational change tool in itself, providing several benefits:

- It clarifies how each core competence links to the others.
- It graphically illustrates the essential concepts of enterprise development in a way that makes them easier to remember.
- It provides a clear image that can be used to communicate ideas to others.
- It provides a practical mapping tool.

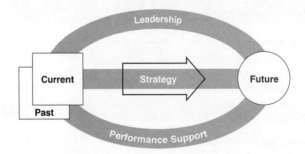

Figure 1. Template for the Enterprise-Development Map

Using the template, members of an enterprise can write in the most important data from each component of their change process: the past and current conditions, where they are going, and changes and activities that will need to occur along the way. For each of the steps, the most critical agreements can be written to provide a customized development map. Members often create large wall maps, which can be reduced to provide notebook-sized handouts or which can be posted on a computer network. Some enterprises create an enterprise-wide map and then encourage departments or teams to create their own maps (in alignment with the larger enterprise strategy).

Creating this map helps to keep the development process visible to all members of the enterprise. It also provides a dynamic picture that changes as the ED process progresses. Documenting shared agreements as they are made helps to build common ground for the work ahead.

Competence 1. Seeing the Whole System

It is important to define the terms "business" and "organization" in order to avoid confusion and problems. An enterprise is made up of a business supported by an organization. The *business* is the enterprise's *function*: it delivers products and services into an external environment (made up of a marketplace with opportunities, competition, a culture, economic pressures, government regulations, resources, partners, and other forces or groups that can impact the enterprise). The purpose of the *organization* (the enterprise's *form*) is to help the business to succeed within its environment. As the environment changes, the business and the organization may both have to change. If the business and organization are not aligned, the enterprise will find itself in trouble.

For example, businesses frequently try to implement *organizational* solutions (restructuring the organizational chart, downsizing, or team building) when a new *business* strategy is required. However, if the product or service no longer fits market conditions, no organizational fix will help the enterprise to thrive. Similarly, if the business product or service is on track but the organization is poorly designed to deliver it, no amount of market research or strategic positioning of the business will help the organization.

Human resource development practitioners can help their clients to distinguish whether a problem comes from business conditions or from the organization. In almost all cases, the ultimate solution will need to incorporate both perspectives. Form follows function.

The enterprise system can be described in terms of five components (STEP) that interact dynamically with one another (see Figure 2):

- *The Structure:* The structural elements of the organization, such as the formal organizational chart, job descriptions, physical facilities, information systems, management policies, human resource policies, and incentive systems.

- *The Task:* The products and services that the business offers to the marketplace.

- *The Environment, both internal and external:* The internal environment includes the internal culture and organizational climate. The external environment includes elements such as marketplace opportunities, competition, suppliers, the culture, the economy, regulations, resources, and potential venture partners.

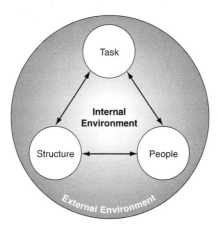

Figure 2. Dynamic Interaction Among Elements of the Enterprise System

- *The People.* The skills and talents of the people, how they get along and communicate with one another, and the quality and effectiveness of their working relationships.

It is important that the members of the enterprise understand the fundamental elements of the business and organizational systems and how they impact one another. When these are clear, as a new force enters from the external environment or from an internal change, the expected impacts on the whole enterprise can be mapped.

The STEP Model works well as a stand-alone tool that HRD practitioners can use to help clients identify their enterprise systems and to highlight where strategic interventions most need to occur.

An Example: Good and Solid Toy Company

For two generations, the Good and Solid Toy Company has manufactured a traditional line of toy cars. Parents often bought the same types of cars for their children that they had played with as youngsters. Although competition always existed, the Good and Solid Toy Company had captured a consistent and predictable market share.

For a long time, the tasks of the company had consisted of straightforward manufacturing and distribution processes. These processes had been perfected over many years and changed only incrementally. Given the predictable environment and highly routinized tasks, the management structures were systematized, traditional, and authoritarian—designed for efficiency and quality control. The majority of the employees did not require much formal education or training. They appeared comfortable with the routine nature of the work and the traditional management hierarchy. There were many long-term employees who considered themselves part of a loyal and stable family, and morale was generally high. Employees saw themselves as turning out a good, high-quality product. On the other hand, they did not look to their work for meaning in life; their primary identities and most of their interests lay outside work.

Then the offshore-manufactured Super-Duper, Laser-Powered Turbo Turtle Transporter came along. With an innovative microchip, it was voice-activated to produce movement, sound, and light. It was less expensive than a Good and Solid toy car. It was featured on a popular children's television program and also bore promise of interconnectability to an arcade-type video computer, with virtually unending potential for futuristic game playing.

The *external environment* of the toy-car market had changed dramatically. Customers of all ages waited in line for the new product, while Good and Solid cars remained on the shelves. Good and Solid's *internal environment* responded immediately: morale plummeted. Employees wondered how the owners of the firm could have been so blind to technological developments. To remain unchanged was basically a choice to go out of business.

The dramatic shift in the market significantly impacted the other elements of the enterprise (*structure, task, and people*). It questioned the relevance of the company's primary task (i.e., did a market still exist for the traditional toy car?). The leaders of the company considered options: having products manufactured in Eastern Europe, capitalizing on existing distribution channels by selling children's products from other companies, and engaging in a joint venture with a local microchip manufacturer to try to beat Super Duper at its own game. Whichever was chosen, the mission of the enterprise would be significantly altered.

In order to accommodate any of these choices, the organizational structure would have to change dramatically. The company might need to establish a research and development department that would be characterized by open, collaborative, and more autonomous management systems. New and more complex tasks would require more training and staff development. If the company chose to become a sales and distribution organization, it would need to add new systems and processes while dismantling others.

The people who worked for the Good and Solid Toy Company would also be affected. New skills would be required. Job descriptions would continue to change as the company became more innovative and responsive to the changing market. New and more highly educated employees would be brought on board, altering long-standing relationships and potentially increasing conflict. Because of possibly increased demand for people to work collaboratively in teams, the organization would need to establish transition processes designed to help people address the interpersonal needs that would surely arise.

As this example shows, the STEP analysis is a simple but powerful tool that allows its users to sift through seemingly complex and confusing enterprise data. It provides a focused view of the most essential elements of the enterprise, clarifying ways in which it can rebalance the dynamic interplay between its components. As a result, people throughout the enterprise are increasingly able to make informed, meaningful, and strategic choices about the future directions of their business and organization.

Competence 2. Creating a Shared Future

The dynamic enterprise is a system driven by the opportunities of the future. In order to capitalize on those future opportunities, people need to be able to look forward and anticipate what the future business environment will most likely be and what the future enterprise system will need to become. Figure 3 shows where this view of the future is represented on the ED Map.

A Comprehensive Enterprise Vision. Many people think of "vision" as the "softer" side of the enterprise (its values and principles, the hopes of the people, and the work culture they want to create). However, a powerful and compelling vision must include all STEP elements. The vision must project a clear picture of the future enterprise, including details such as:

- What kind of external business environment is predicted for the future?
- What will the competitive business advantage be?
- What type of organization will best support its business?
- What systems and structures will be required?
- What kinds of people will be needed, what must they know, and how will they work together?
- What type of internal environment, culture, and values will be desirable and necessary for success in the envisioned future?

A comprehensive enterprise vision helps leaders and stakeholders create a clear picture of both the business and the organization they must build together. Creating a clear and compelling shared vision of the enterprise gives

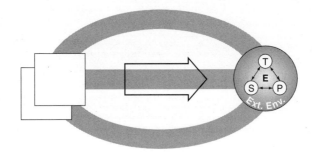

Figure 3. Future STEP

people confidence in their ability to successfully compete in the marketplace of the future. It appeals to their hearts and spirits and imparts a higher purpose to the work they do. It creates a sense of direction and focus for their business, orients their actions, and gives them a sense of predictability about upcoming changes.

Competence 3. Seeing the Past and Current Enterprise Honestly and Accurately

Just as individuals need a clear, shared vision of where the enterprise should go, they also need to agree on where it has come from and where it is currently positioned. If some members think the enterprise is almost where it needs to be while others believe that it is off target, it will be difficult to achieve agreement on a common path. It is also important that the picture of the current state of the enterprise be honest and "unflinching," so that development can begin from a realistic basis.

Figure 4 shows where the information about the past and current enterprises can be filled in on the ED Map.

Competence 4. Understanding the Nature of the Change

Once people have agreed on where they want to go and from where they are starting, they need to discuss how to get from "here" to "there." This requires further negotiation and agreement. It involves filling in the arrow in the ED Map (see Figure 5).

Strategic Pushes and Pulls. First, members of the enterprise must identify the predominant strategic "pushes" from current and past conditions. What are the issues that demand resolution, that motivate action? Then they must

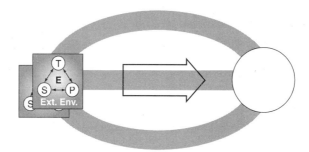

Figure 4. Past and Current STEPs

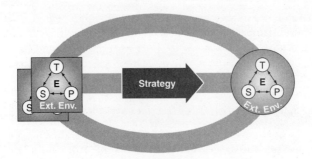

Figure 5. Strategic Development Path

explore opportunities and identify the strategic "pulls" toward the future. What are the compelling opportunities that excite people, that mobilize a willingness to make dramatic change? Identifying the most compelling issues in the vision are essential for success and can help people to focus their energy.

When the pushes and pulls have been identified, people can negotiate and agree on key change strategies and on the specific actions and commitments necessary to connect the current enterprise to its desired future.

Business and Organizational Life-Cycle Models. In addition to understanding what needs to change to get from here to there, it is also important to understand the magnitude of the change and the particular type of change required.

Businesses and organizations progress through a series of natural phases of development. Understanding life-cycle phases can help people to predict the conditions they are likely to encounter in the development of their enterprises and can help them to proactively frame the next steps they need to take. Human resource development practitioners can use the life-cycle analysis to help their clients understand which developmental activities and behaviors would be most effective in each phase. They also can help leaders to understand which leadership actions are most critical at each phase, in order to guide the enterprise toward its desired future.

Business Life Cycles. Knowing where the business is in its life cycle helps people to determine the changes that need to occur. A business life cycle typically is represented by a bell-shaped curve (see Figure 6). This curve describes phases of development. A business begins with slow (or even negative) growth in its start-up phase. If the business succeeds in its markets, it moves into a phase of accelerated growth, which then levels off as the busi-

Figure 6. Business Life Cycles

ness matures. Some businesses progress toward a choice point, where they either move into decline and potential demise or make a strategic "leap" toward breakthrough and renewal—an entirely new way of doing business.

Enterprises that are facing a need for transformation often discover that they are dealing with overlapping life cycles. Such enterprises may need dual strategies, one for the existing business and another for the new ventures that are created to carry the enterprise into its future.

Organizational Life Cycles. For every stage of the business life cycle, there is a form in the organization that either supports the business at that time or works against it (see Figure 7).

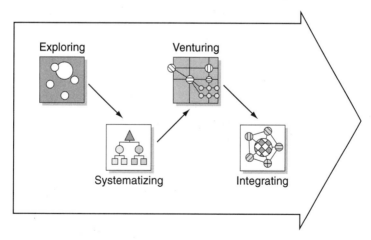

Figure 7. The Organizational Life-Cycle Model

It is the HRD professional's role to identify the developmental requirements of its client organizations and to help their leaders and stakeholders
understand the challenges they face.

The Exploring Organization. In the early stages of the business life cycle,
the organization is generally loosely structured, often with a charismatic
leader or team of leaders who had the original idea for the business. The
leaders are excited about the potential of the product or service and encourage similar excitement in others. People are chosen to join in the venture,
not necessarily for their competence in doing tasks (these are not yet well
defined), but because they are enthusiastic or know a member of the venture. Job descriptions are loose, and everyone may do a bit of everything.
Systems are quite flexible and are created or changed as needed. Given its
drive to succeed, its flexibility, and its lack of pre-established internal systems, the organization is generally quite close and responsive to its external
marketplace. This is an "exploring" organization.

The Systematizing Organization. Once the enterprise has found its market, discovered its successful products, and achieved steady business growth,
the need for stabilization emerges. This stage is "systematizing." Formal systems and structures emerge during this period in response to a more defined and well-bounded business environment. People move into more
clearly defined roles and relationships. The culture supports clarity, quality,
and predictability.

The Venturing Organization. As the business matures, a time may come
that requires a reopening of the established boundaries, norms, and rules, so
that the enterprise can begin to explore new variations of its original ideas.
This gives people a chance to expand their horizons and their freedom to
act. The enterprise develops a capacity for authorization of new activities.
Systems are put in place that set boundaries and guidelines for teams, promote empowerment, encourage organizational learning, and test new ventures. The culture values performance, and people are chosen for positions
based on the competence of their work. The organization is "venturing."

The Integrating Organization. Once people have become successful and
competent in their work, a new drive often emerges: the need for greater
meaning in work. This type of organization is responsive to its external marketplace but responds to a given set of values in relation to it. It promotes
venture in service of values and is driven by vision and strategic intent. This

kind of organization may combine levels of responsiveness, systemization, and venturing to deal effectively with high levels of complexity and discontinuity in its environment. This is an "integrating" organization.

Understanding the life-cycle phases of both the business and the organization helps members of an enterprise to predict the conditions they are most likely to encounter in a change initiative or development effort. Anticipating what lies ahead can help them to proactively identify the next steps that may be required.

Competence 5. Mobilizing and Aligning the Essential Drivers

People create the dynamic enterprise. Three groups of people, in particular, are essential in driving an enterprise toward its envisioned future: leaders, stakeholders, and performance-support team members. These three groups (see Figure 8) must be in ongoing communication and collaboration with one another if they are to guide implementation of strategy together.

Leaders may be informal as well as formal leaders and may include people from outside the enterprise. Senior leaders and key managers must be committed to the ongoing change and development of the enterprise, not just to the performance of current business tasks. Development of the enterprise must be considered part of the work, not as an extra task that occurs in the spaces between "the real work." Change and development *is* the real work. This shifts the role of leader from leading in the service of current core and administrative activities to being responsible for the ongoing change and development of the enterprise.

Many people have a stake in the success of a development effort. In addition to employees, stakeholders may be customers, suppliers, legislators, community members, and strategic partners. Even though some stakeholder

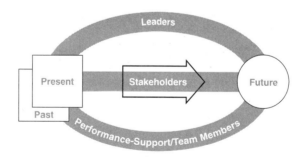

Figure 8. The Three Drivers

groups (e.g., employees) may be larger than others, all stakeholders will influence the development effort.

Stakeholders must become the owners of the development process. If they do not take ownership, it does not happen. Stakeholders cannot be passive; there is a great deal for them to do in the development process. They act as the key designers and implementors of change. Stakeholders are the ones who live through the transitions, letting go of old practices and learning new ways of doing things.

Performance support is still a new and unfamiliar function in many enterprises. However, this function is essential for executing large-scale, complex change. The existence of ongoing support for a development effort often makes the difference between success or failure in implementing planned change.

This function is increasingly taken up by newly transformed HRD departments. In a large utility company, the HRD department, having automated or outsourced most of its more routine, transactional work, formally changed its name to "Performance Support" and provided a number of needed consultative and support services.

The Role of Performance Support. Performance support usually is provided by a team of internal and external change agents who watch over the general aspects of the change process and help to keep it on track. Although leaders authorize the development process needed to reach the desired future, stakeholders must actually design and implement the changes needed to get there. Performance-support personnel coordinate details and support the stakeholders by making sure that they have the training, skills, information, systems, tools, resources, and support that they need to do the job.

Performance-support team members:

- Are responsible for overall coordination, project management, and logistics support.

- Create and shape systems to support the new vision.

- Facilitate engagement, collaboration, and stakeholder participation.

- Promote communication and visibility of the development process.

- Provide emotional support to the leaders and stakeholders in the transition process.

- Attend to the inevitable breakdowns to ensure that the development effort stays on track.

Tests: Critical Catalysts for Implementation. Once the requirement for change has been clarified, members of the enterprise begin to test the resolve of all those involved. Human beings do not seem to be able to move forward into unknown futures without questioning and challenging each step of the way. They double-check what is demanded of them. They listen to what they are told and then "test" the words with their behavior. They watch for responses (not always consciously) and act on the implied messages.

Each of the three groups of drivers—leaders, stakeholders, and performance-support team members—will be tested during the change process in different ways.

Leaders are tested for commitment (whether they mean what they say). If they lapse into old behaviors, stakeholders are also unlikely to change. When leaders fail to respond in ways that demonstrate their own commitment to the development of the enterprise, members inevitably see this as a signal to abandon the effort. On the other hand, if leaders respond successfully to tests, they reveal their personal commitment to the intended changes and help to generate the momentum that drives the dynamic enterprise.

Stakeholders are tested for responsibility. When stakeholders fail to "own" (take responsibility for) the development of the enterprise, the change efforts lose focus and become impractical.

Performance-support team members are tested for competence. If performance support fails to provide the resources required for particular developments to occur, stakeholders may be incapable of delivering the necessary skills and behaviors, even if they are motivated and committed to change.

Understanding and anticipating tests can help to prepare each type of driver to respond successfully, in ways that further the positive development of the enterprise and stabilize the intended strategy.

Competence 6. Implementing the Change

The Enterprise-Development Work Plan outlines the implementation of an ED intervention, a process for planning, monitoring, and mapping dynamic and large-scale change. The purpose of the work plan is to turn understanding into focused planning and, ultimately, into performance.

The work plan contains six phases; the actions in each lead to sustainable performance. Although the phases are shown in the approximate sequence in which they occur, they can occur in parallel or as an iterative process that moves between one phase and another (see Figure 9).

Each enterprise can produce its own customized work plan. At each step of the way, members are asked to supply content from their specific situations. Customized work plans typically include details of how each work group

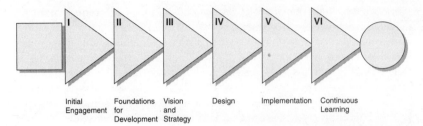

| Initial Engagement | Foundations for Development | Vision and Strategy | Design | Implementation | Continuous Learning |

Figure 9. Six Phases of the Enterprise-Development Work Plan

will implement the development process, including: the key objectives, the scope of the process, who will be involved in each step, the time frame, the budget, how specific plans link to other plans or actions that are part of the development process, and the ultimate performance to be delivered.

Phase I: Initial Engagement. During the initial engagement, the highest-priority issues in the enterprise are identified and work begins on the first outline of the needed changes and future strategies. The initial phase is a once-over-lightly process, in which key leaders, stakeholders, and performance-support team members use a broad overview of the enterprise to visualize the possible change effort from beginning to end.

Phase II: Foundations for Development. With commitment to an ED change initiative, it is time to build the foundations for the development effort. Project initiators identify the primary work teams and alliances, agree on the general work plan and on processes for development, begin to build the collaborative networks that will be needed, and establish the communication vehicles that will be used throughout the process.

Phase III: Vision and Strategy. During this phase, the participants look to the future to create a compelling picture of the desired enterprise, using tools such as business scenarios, systems planning, and values and vision clarification. Assessments of the enterprise's external and internal environments help to unfreeze old assumptions and develop understanding of current realities. Critical gaps between the present situation and the desired future are identified. The result is an integrated set of strategies for creating the desired future.

Phase IV: Design. When the members of the enterprise know what they want to do, designated work teams begin to design specific activities and tasks for implementing the strategy. Work is assigned, standards and commitments for performance are negotiated, and issues that arise over the course of the transition are addressed. The design work typically occurs in three subphases, as follows:

- *Process Assessment:* An initial review of key business and organizational processes and systems is conducted. High-level performance indicators and measures are established. Necessary bridging actions are identified.

- *Conceptual Design:* Selected processes are assessed; comparisons are made with available benchmarks; and new processes are designed. Policy, infrastructures, and other systems requirements are identified, and cost-benefit analyses are conducted. Transition and implementation planning begins.

- *Detailed Design:* Necessary policies and procedures are defined. Organizational designs (including new job descriptions, roles and responsibilities, policies, and systems and technology requirements, as well as the communication, collaboration, and work culture needed) are developed, reviewed, and authorized. Prototypes are drafted and tested.

Phase V: Implementation. Although there should have been significant engagement from many parts of the enterprise in the earlier phases, during this phase everyone who will be impacted by the changes must participate. Transition events are conducted, followed by the rollout of restructured business processes, new procedures and control mechanisms, and new organizational arrangements. Service-level agreements are established as part of performance contracts and measurements linked to the new organization.

Phase VI: Continuous Learning. The performance-support group helps the leaders and stakeholders to build systems and processes for ongoing evaluation and adjustment of the development process, in order to ensure that the new systems work well and in harmony and produce the desired outcomes. At this time, many groups establish lasting systems to support continuous learning.

CONCLUSION: A STRATEGIC-THINKING DISCIPLINE

In order for HRD professionals to be capable of assisting the critical and continuous strategy formulation of their clients, they must acquire a set of strategic-thinking tools and techniques. Enterprise development offers a comprehensive framework that integrates six tools for strategy development and implementation, which HRD practitioners can use to enable their clients to create dynamic enterprises.

Because ED offers a framework for clarifying some of the toughest challenges that emerge in the midst of complex change, it tends to engender trust, buy-in, accountability, and action from stakeholders throughout the enterprise. It provides straightforward language and concepts that allow all members of the enterprise to think together, to negotiate with one another, and to contract clearly for the actions they will take to support the strategies most vital to them and their work groups. It allows all stakeholders to participate in revisioning and redesigning the enterprise to achieve sustainable performance in the future. In the hands of committed HRD practitioners, it can engender the needed focus and commitment to reach agreement on the current state and future direction of an enterprise. The process enables leaders and teams to redesign their work, commit themselves to a desired future, and accelerate the rate of change in their enterprise.

Lisa Friedman, Ph.D., and Herman Gyr, Ph.D., are co-founders of the Enterprise Development Group, an international consulting and training firm for strategy development and change implementation. They specialize in working with leaders, key stakeholders, and teams to build dynamic enterprises—those work groups whose members collaborate to deliver high performance under complex and rapidly changing conditions. They have worked across a wide range of industries, including high-tech companies, universities, health care, oil and gas, manufacturing, utilities, financial services, the military, and fisheries. Their work has included the "harder" areas of strategy, planning, and change-management issues, in conjunction with the "softer" side of change—the culture change, communication, and team building often required to bring the strategy to reality. Drs. Friedman and Gyr are also the co-authors of The Dynamic Enterprise: Tools for Turning Chaos into Strategy and Strategy into Action *(Jossey-Bass, 1997).*

A New Way of Guiding
Large-Scale Organizational Change

Laura Hauser

Abstract: Organizations need to have the resources, skills, knowledge, and support to effect change. Gaining a competitive advantage through large-scale organizational-change (LSOC) efforts requires a new way of thinking—a shift from the old, mechanistic view to an organic view of organizations. It requires a new way of leading, and the subsequent design and implementation of interventions based on these new ways of thinking and leading. This article defines large-scale organizational change and distinguishes it from routine change. It presents a practical model, the LSOC Cycle, to illustrate the elements involved in large-scale organizational change and the new ways of thinking and leading. It discusses these elements and presents the pitfalls that accompany each. The article also introduces the four new roles required of leaders who will be guiding large-scale organizational change and explains how organizational change agents and leaders can fulfill those roles. Finally, it discusses the implications for selecting interventions that will bring about effective organization-wide change.

INTRODUCTION

The prosperity and the survival of U.S. organizations depend on their ability to effectively plan and implement large-scale organizational change. During these turbulent times, many organizational leaders are responding to the chaotic business environment by attempting to implement deep, pervasive organizational change through downsizing, mergers, and reengineering of business processes, in the hope of gaining a competitive advantage by improving the quality of services or products and, therefore, productivity and profit.

Unfortunately, many of these organizational-change efforts are falling critically short of their objectives. Simply installing new techniques and programs such as employee involvement, just-in-time inventory control, reengineering, total-quality-management methods, and leadership training has proved to be a disappointing path to improvement. Nicholas Horney (Horney & Koonce, 1995), a managing associate with Coopers & Lybrand, points out that "Despite the media attention, the verdict on many reengineering efforts today is mixed at best. In fact, a recent business survey by a leading human resources consulting firm suggests that nearly two-thirds of all restructuring efforts are clear failures."

These change efforts, which usually are launched with great enthusiasm and fanfare, typically run into serious resistance and impediments during implementation and produce disappointing financial results. Many do not last more than eighteen months. The unintentional results of these efforts often include high employee turnover, dangerously low morale and productivity, and a workplace atmosphere of fear and discomfort. People view the change initiative as the "fad of the year" (Veltrop, 1991, p. 3).

For example, a CFO of a major food-distribution company related the following story about his company's failed change efforts:

> This company has made money, has been profitable, just doing gangbusters, up until 1992. We lost a lot of money in 1992 and then made money in 1993 and 1994 but, relatively speaking, it's half of what we made before. And we have only accomplished that through eliminating jobs, eliminating people, finding smarter ways to do things, and we are doing more work with fewer people. It's great creative stuff, and it is necessary. But the change in the culture and the change in the organization and the [fact that the] pace has picked up so dramatically has stymied the people. People are so busy doing

the tasks, it leaves them shell-shocked, so they can't be there emotionally a lot of the time. I think they have a bit of an empty feeling inside as a result of it. I know I do.

We didn't understand the implications of the changes. We (the executives) were making decisions about how we were going to start the changes, but we didn't look at the long-term implications. It ended up costing us a lot of money, and we had to go back to the original structure and begin again.

A NEW WAY OF THINKING

The CFO's situation is typical of the many problems that leaders express about organizational change. The story illustrates that designing and implementing changes based on traditional thinking and leading is failing. The key, therefore, to gaining a competitive advantage through LSOC efforts is a new way of thinking, a new way of leading, and the subsequent design and implementation of interventions based on these new ways of thinking and leading.

Traditional thinking about how organizations operate is not helping to achieve today's desired results. As Hammer and Champy (1993) point out, the problem is that U.S. business is entering the 21st Century with organizations designed during a different century. Organizations are trying to navigate a 20th-Century world with a 17th-Century map. The work of Sir Isaac Newton, Emil Descartes, and Sir Francis Bacon laid the foundations for the last three hundred years of organizational progress. These entrepreneurs of the 17th Century established ways of thinking that many of us still hold dear—that the world is a great machine and that we can best understand this machine by analyzing its parts. Scientists and managers have hoped that by understanding the workings of this great machine, we could then predict everything. But we now know from history and from personal experience that we cannot predict everything, nor can we make organizations work perfectly.

Based on mechanistic thinking, managers have been taught to divide their organizations into separate parts, and these often are subdivided into departments or functions. Managers have been taught that operations should run smoothly, like machines. Managers also have been taught to treat workers like machines, i.e., assigning their roles and tasks; making them accountable for bottom-line results; providing feedback on observable facts; and ignoring their abilities, emotions, and beliefs. Simply implementing changes based on the tangible side of business, such as short-term objectives, profitability, and productivity, is not succeeding in achieving either the formal, desired results of profitability or the less formal—but equally necessary—conditions requisite for personal satisfaction and productivity.

Mechanistic thinking creates cumbersome bureaucracies and complex hierarchies that simply do not work when things need to be done quickly in an environment that changes constantly. The result is the dissatisfaction of workers and managers alike. Employee morale is depleted. Low morale diminishes productivity, which causes the monetary losses that management was trying to avoid in the first place.

According to the literature on organizations and new authors such as Wheatley (1992), the challenge of our times is to invent and discover organizational forms that can be as resilient, adaptive, and healthy as most living organisms. We need to expand our thinking and change our ways of creating and engaging in business from a mechanistic point of view to an organic point of view. We must view organizations as living, breathing organisms rather than as parts of a machine.

Because the role of change agents, such as line managers, human resource professionals, consultants, and trainers, is to help organizations plan and implement complex organizational change, they must consciously help themselves and their organizational members to expand their thinking along the following lines:

- from separate parts to connectedness and wholeness,
- from results to process,
- from outer resources to inner resources,
- from sameness to diversity and plurality,
- from control over society to reinstilling spirit into society,
- from observable facts to intuitive wisdom,
- from profit/productivity to higher purpose/vision,
- from a material age to a relationship age.

The concept of a shift in thinking is not new, but, until recently, U.S. organizations could ignore it and still be profitable. As Hammer and Champy (1993) point out, when organizational costs were high, they could be passed on to customers. If customers were dissatisfied, they had nowhere else to turn. If new products were slow in coming, customers would wait. If employees were dissatisfied and left, they would simply be replaced. The managerial job was to manage growth, and the rest did not matter. Now that customers and workers are more sophisticated, and now that growth has flattened out, the rest matters a great deal. U.S. businesses are feeling mounting pressures to embrace the new way of thinking.

Figure 1 illustrates the notion of expanded thinking.

From Traditional Thinking	To Expanded Thinking
• Newtonianism	• Quantum physics, Chaos theory
• Mechanistic	• Organic
• Separate parts	• Connectedness/wholeness
• Results	• Process
• Outer resources	• Inner resources
• Science	• Spirituality
• Sameness	• Diversity/plurality
• Control over society	• Respiritization of society
• Observable facts	• Intuitive wisdom
• Profit/productivity	• Higher purpose/vision
• Materialism	• Relationships

Figure 1. Old and New Ways of Thinking

A NEW WAY OF LEADING

Successfully guiding organizational change in today's chaotic marketplace requires not only a new way of thinking but also a new way of leading. Leaders need to update and expand their leadership maps. Existing beliefs about leadership in organizations were influenced by years of mechanistic thinking. For example, traditional leaders pride themselves on "getting the job done," they recognize individual performance, they are preoccupied with power and politics, and they focus on short-term results—even when this negatively impacts long-term performance. They make decisions based on external data, taking into consideration only the observable facts and "rational" information. They look for ways to "treat" organization ills; they try to "fix the broken parts" of the system. They align structures and systems to maximize profits and efficiency even when it is at the expense of human needs. Traditionally, a leader's personal development is aimed at gaining external knowledge and skills, such as "five quick steps in giving feedback," or "three easy steps to recognizing results."

The traditional ways have served the purpose of allowing leaders to get the organizational results they have gotten so far. But they are no longer sufficient to enable organizations to survive in a changing world. Managers who rely on traditional forms of leadership will continue to face dilemmas such as the CFO's in the story at the beginning of this article.

In order for change agents' views of leadership to be congruent with the new way of thinking, which will prepare them to lead in a rapidly changing business environment, they must expand their perspectives. It follows that change agents who embrace the new way of thinking also must seek meaning in the work that they and their employees perform, and must seek the true value that their product or service contributes to their customers and to society. They must not only value individual performance, but also must value team performance. They must search for purpose, values, and ethics in their lives, including their personal lives. They must not focus only on short-term results, but also must have a long-term business orientation that does not compromise their values and principles. They must make informed decisions, not by relying only on external data, but also by taking into consideration internal data such as their intuition or "gut feelings." They must align structures and systems in a way that maximizes not only profit but organizational and human potential as well. The leaders must not only develop themselves from the outside, by doing such things as attending traditional classes and seminars; they must develop themselves from the inside, doing their personal work. They must seek their internal wisdom and values and peel away layers of former mechanistic thinking to get at the essence of who they are. This will allow them to act with authenticity and integrity as leaders.

Figure 2 illustrates the contrast between the traditional and expanded ways of leading.

From Traditional Leadership	To Expanded Leadership
• Need to get the job done	• Need for meaning
• Reward individual performance	• Reward team performance
• Preoccupation with power and politics	• Preoccupation with purpose, values, and ethics
• Short-term orientation at all costs	• Long-term orientation without compromising values and principles
• Decision making based on external data, such as observable facts	• Decision making includes data from internal sources, such as intuition
• Treatment	• Prevention
• Fix the current system	• Create the future
• Align structures and systems to maximize profit and efficiency without regard for human needs	• Align structures and systems to maximize organizational and human potential
• Professional development focusing on external knowledge and skills	• Personal development focusing on internal wisdom and values

Figure 2. Old and New Ways of Leading

Just as the shift in thinking is not really new, the shift in leading is not new. These perspectives have been known in the field of organization development for years. What is new is the mounting pressure, generated by both the external environment and personal imperatives, to implement the new way of leading. It needs to be enacted on a day-to-day basis and applied in the design and implementation of interventions for achieving deep, pervasive organizational change.

LARGE-SCALE ORGANIZATIONAL CHANGE

Based on the new ways of thinking and leading, the design and implementation of large-scale organizational-change interventions should:

1. Be based on environmental realities and the future direction of the organization;

2. Take into consideration the organization's ability to implement the change and how the intervention will impact the organization and its key stakeholders, such as employees, customers, suppliers, and communities;

3. Inspire the commitment of managers and employees to act on the intervention; and

4. Support continued learning, thereby encouraging individuals, groups, and the organization to rise to higher levels of success and satisfaction.

A pressing dilemma for change agents who are charged with LSOC initiatives is the lack of practical models and tools to help their client systems effectively design and implement LSOC and to reduce potential pitfalls. There is a limited amount of design and implementation of LSOC and resultant documented research because it is a relatively new field. This has led the author to develop some practical models. In order to understand the LSOC model presented in this article, it is necessary to understand the differences between large-scale organizational change and routine, incremental change.

The Differences Between Large-Scale Organizational Change and Routine, Incremental Change

Large-scale organization change is a deep and pervasive change in the character of an organization that significantly alters its performance (Mohrman, Mohrman, Ledford, Cummings, & Lawler, 1990). Depth of change refers to shifts in organizational members' basic beliefs and values and in the way the organization is understood; such shifts are often emotionally intense. LSOC is in contrast to small-scale, routine changes that are made to "fix the problem" or organization or fine-tune organizational subsystems; these often focus on continuous improvement of existing structures, systems, and technologies, and have a trivial effect on system performance (Mohrman et al., 1990). "Pervasive" means that the change permeates the entire organization; it eventually affects the whole organization, including subunits and individuals. Implementing such change affects both the psychological and strategic aspects of an organization (Kilmann, 1989).

Given the preceding definition, the following general concepts apply to LSOC:

Complexity: LSOC is a complex process and does not lend itself to simple prescriptions or programmed approaches.

System-wide: LSOC requires a system-wide, holistic approach, focusing on all aspects of organizational health. It combines a business perspective with a people perspective to foster organizational change.

Ongoing: Change is an ongoing organizational process, not a periodic event or program.

Embracing Change: Organizations need to embrace change rather than attempt to control it.

Time: The more deep and pervasive the change, and the larger the size and complexity of the organization, the longer it will take to achieve the change. It spreads throughout the organization at different rates of absorption because of different capacities for learning and changing (Kilmann, 1989).

Integration and Alignment: Large-scale change efforts must be integrated and aligned. The efforts among individuals and groups must be integrated, and they must be designed and aligned with the current and future purposes, needs, and direction of the organization and its key stakeholders.

Large-Scale Organizational Change as a Cycle

Designing and implementing LSOC initiatives also requires a new way of thinking, which is different from traditional, programmatic, incremental, compartmentalized change. Large-scale organizational change must be viewed as a cycle—a living, breathing, ongoing process that continually needs to be adapted to the internal and external demands of the organization. Figure 3 shows the LSOC Cycle, a practical way to visualize and integrate the concepts of LSOC.

Figure 3. The LSOC Cycle

The figure shows that environmental pressures surround and impact organizations and their key stakeholders. During times of uncertainty and turbulence, leaders must anticipate and cause effective organizational change. LSOC demands not only fluid adaptability to environmental changes, but also a bold vision and a commitment to that vision. Commitment evokes action. As a result of action, breakdowns naturally occur, and the learning that results from the breakdowns helps the organization and its members. Seeing new possibilities and committing to a vision leads to action to fulfill the vision. In the process of dealing with the inevitable breakdowns, people learn.

This cycle, which is critical to understanding and keeping up with the rapid pace of change, must ultimately occur at all levels of the organization. The breakdowns and learnings must be rewarded, not punished; they must be celebrated, not mourned.

The LSOC Cycle, therefore, encompasses and integrates the following components: stakeholders, environmental pressures and requirements, the perceived (and understood) need for change, a vision of the future and of what it takes to make these changes, a commitment to change, action (based on the vision), and the learning that results from what happens when changes are implemented. The learning then is applied to the ongoing cycle of designing and implementing change.

Stakeholders

At the center of the model are the stakeholders. Key stakeholders include employees, managers, executives, customers, suppliers, community, and any other person or group that is significantly impacted by the large-scale organizational change. The implementation of a large-scale organizational-change initiative affects every key stakeholder. When designing an LSOC initiative, it is critical to take into consideration the impact on each of the stakeholders and to plan how to best meet the needs of the stakeholders.

Commitment at all levels in the organization is a critical factor in the successful implementation and maintenance of complex change. Change requires a combination of top-down, bottom-up, and horizontal direction.

The Environment

Internal and external environmental pressures create a perceived need for change. Change is registered and anticipated by the organization in many ways, such as through economic pressures, new opportunities, technological imperatives, legal constraints, and cultural pressures (Mohrman et al., 1990).

A common pitfall in planning an LSOC initiative is using a simplistic model to diagnose and implement complex change, and hastily designing a future plan without paying attention to the environment and the key stakeholders.

A Perceived Need for Change

A perceived need for change usually is accompanied by a sense of urgency. When this occurs, an organization often responds in one of two ways: either by focusing its attention and action on fixing the current system or by creating a new system to respond to current and future needs.

The ability to create a new system based on current and future needs (rather than old problems) requires that organizational members understand and experience the need for change. This involves experiencing discomfort and dissatisfaction with the current environment and the status quo in order to become sufficiently motivated to try new strategies and new behaviors.

The following methods can help to generate a genuine and urgent need for change (from management to the newest employee):

- Sensitize organizational members to the pressures of change by revealing the discrepancies between the current and future states of the organization,

- Convey the personal and organizational benefits of change,

- Convey the negative consequences of not adapting and changing.

Managers should not attempt to insulate their employees from the reality of the situation; this is inappropriate in times of true upheaval and change. If organizational members do not feel a sense of urgency to change the way they are doing business, the "bottom of the box" syndrome occurs, and the change interventions they are asked to implement do not seem important and become low or nonexistent priorities. They may even be seen as "just more work," and employees may become unnecessarily obstinate in the face of the required changes.

It is very important—in addition to being straightforward about the necessity for change—to communicate realistic, positive expectations about the changes and the important roles all members of the organization play in determining the success of the outcomes.

Vision

A new mind-set is needed to create a vision based on what is possible in the future, rather than looking only for ways to fix problems within the existing system, which is based on old assumptions. The new of way of thinking enables people to focus on new possibilities. Fisher and Selman (1993) call this new mind-set "committed inquiry." Such inquiry is not looking for answers; it encourages people to look creatively and innovatively for new potentials (and new questions), thus creating a new vision. The new, visionary mind-set frees people to discover and pursue a broad range of transformational possibilities that would otherwise be invisible (Veltrop, 1991).

Once there is consensus about the new vision, leaders and employees can look at what currently exists within the organization that is congruent with the new vision—what is in place that will support the vision and what is in place that will impede the vision. They can identify any gaps and, thereby, create an effective transition plan to help move the organization toward its new vision. This type of response is inclusive, rather than exclusive; it creates a new system that incorporates the best of the existing system into the new system, while removing things that no longer serve the organization well.

The process of developing a vision is heavily weighted by existing values and preconceptions. People think they know what the organization should look like and how it should function. The concept of "vision" conjures up ideas and hopes of what the organization can become. Unfortunately, dreaming about the future is often discouraged in organizations, because it involves creative and intuitive thought processes that have no crisp borders and that take time. This conflicts with the rational, analytical methods commonly used in organizations. To counteract this, leaders must create special conditions and communication forums to unleash people's potential for creating vision and innovations and to guide people in generating productive visions, rather than escapist or pie-in-the-sky ideas.

There are three common pitfalls associated with vision and LSOC:

1. Managers do not link (or integrate) the business side of change with the people side of change.

2. People are actually designing and implementing interventions that are solutions to yesterday's problems, rather than supporting the vision of the present and future strategic direction of the company.

3. Changes are incongruent with the organization's vision and values. The lack of congruence (actual and perceived) between current changes and future vision results in frustrated employees and a loss of managers' credibility in the eyes of employees.

Commitment

Having a new mind-set and envisioning transformational possibilities is not enough to create and sustain needed change. Mobilizing energy and support for change is one of the most important steps in the critical path to change. It is imperative to the organization's success and it is a step that many organizations ignore.

Meaningful action will not be taken until members of the organization are seriously committed and willing to bring about the changes that will make major differences. Once committed, the workforce will perpetuate the key elements of success more effectively than any external control measures, such as policies, procedures, and supervision.

An organization must first diagnose its situation and identify the one or two things it can do well and successfully, e.g., product innovation, customer service, or low-cost production. Stakeholders at all levels should be involved in this diagnostic activity to discover what needs to be done to achieve the vision. When commitment to fulfilling the vision is present, inventing new and original interpretations and models that are useful for empowering people to generate a different future then follow easily and naturally.

Clearly, achieving commitment requires a new management viewpoint, one that includes a willingness to see formerly invisible possibilities and the fearless involvement and empowerment (rather than controlling) of employees during the change process.

The most common pitfalls encountered during the commitment phase are:

1. Changes are imposed from the top but do not involve or develop the capabilities of the managers and employees who are affected by the changes.

2. The application of traditional, bureaucratic styles of management to LSOC efforts that stifle the creativity, innovation, and spirit of people.

3. There is reluctance by employees and managers to confront the difficult relationship and power issues that are associated with the dynamics of change and that underlie traditional, control-oriented management practices.

Action

When an organization is committed to fulfilling a vision, individuals put their energy and heart into their work, teams do the right things, and a strong sense of undivided and clear direction occurs (Goldman & Nethery, 1991). When people are committed to fulfilling a vision, innovative responses and unprecedented actions necessary to solve problems will occur.

Innovative and creative actions must be in alignment with the key stakeholders and the organization's future purpose, direction, and needs. Some of these actions are the development and implementation of an organizational strategy, the education about and design of structures and processes that support the vision, attention to the current culture and the required future culture, development of people's skills and competencies, and the allocation of resources that are critical to fulfilling the vision.

Some common pitfalls during the action phase of the LSOC Cycle are:

1. Lack of resources to implement the interventions;

2. Lack of integration between functions and departments;

3. An attempt to change everything at once (and expecting it to be done yesterday);

4. Lack of employees' and managers' skills or knowledge and commitment needed to effect change interventions.

Learning

Organizations must become learning organizations. This means that joint inquiry and experimental learning must occur, rather than simple transference of knowledge. Learning is the principal process by which innovation and creativity occur at all organizational levels. Senge (1990) and Strata (1989) state that learning is the only sustainable competitive advantage, especially in knowledge-based industries.

Effective LSOC requires a shift from the traditional "learn first, then decide, then act" model to a "commit first, then act, and then learn in the process of dealing with breakdowns" model. The greatest leverage point for learning occurs while actions are taking place, specifically when breakdowns occur.

Moreover, learning needs to take place in a reciprocal way. Successful transformations involve reciprocal learning across the organization, between the top and the bottom, and between the periphery and the core (Kilmann, 1989). If reciprocity does not develop, the LSOC initiative will stray from its critical path.

IMPLICATIONS FOR LEADERS WHO GUIDE CHANGE: FOUR NEW ROLES

A key implication for leaders who guide organizational change is that their roles must expand from simply those of planners, organizers, staffers, directors, and controllers to more sophisticated functions: visionaries, servers, warriors, and merchants. These roles are defined below.

A second key implication for leaders is the need to assess their levels of skill and effectiveness when taking on and enacting these new roles and the commitment to continually educate and develop themselves. As Bennis and Goldsmith (1994) say, "It is not what great leaders do that makes them extraordinary, but . . . who they are as human beings."

We know that certain elements exist in organizations, such as vision and values, leadership styles, power and politics, people, skills, structures, and systems. We also know that humans in general need a sense of meaning and purpose, affiliation and inclusion, and control and achievement.

Given these elements and needs, there are certain leadership principles that exist and certain roles that must be enacted. The leadership principles are as follows:

1. Organizations are whole systems;

2. Leaders must care for their people and support relationships among people and teams;

3. Leaders must have the courage to take action and the free will to make choices; and

4. Leaders must understand that survival is based on the reality of the internal and external environment.

These principles led to the development of the four roles that are imperative for leaders to enact in today's changing and complex world. These are:

- the visionary,

- the server,

- the warrior, and

- the merchant.

Figure 4 links organizational elements, human needs, leadership principles, and leadership roles.

Organizational Elements	Human Needs	Leadership Principles	Leadership Roles
Shared vision and values	Sense of meaning/ purpose	Vision: seeing the whole system	Visionary
Style/people	Affiliation/inclusion	Heart: caring for people	Server
Power/politics	Control	Action: having courage and free will	Warrior
Systems, structures, skills	Achievement	Reality: focusing on survival	Merchant

Figure 4. Implications for Leadership: New Roles

Many organizational leaders, trainers, and consultants were taught in college business classes that the primary roles of the leader were those of planner, organizer, recruiter, director, and controller. These roles focus on the "tangible" side of business, emphasizing action and survival in the marketplace. These roles served leaders well when they responded to an environment that called for the traditional, mechanistic way of thinking and leading.

However, the new ways of thinking and leading needed to bring forth deep and pervasive change demand that leaders also enact roles that focus on the "intangible" side of business, such as communicating a clear vision of the future and inspiring people to follow that vision. Leaders also must pay attention to other intangibles, such as people's hearts, hopes, and dilemmas. By combining the tangible and intangible dimensions of business, organizations can spark the energy necessary to fully use their potential, which, in turn, will provide the much-needed competitive advantage.

There are four key roles that leaders must consciously enact if they wish to effect successful changes in their organizations. The four roles incorporate both the tangible and intangible sides of business. The roles that incorporate the intangible are the *visionary* and the *server*. The roles that incorporate the tangible are the *warrior* and the *merchant*. These roles are supported by the work of Koestenbaum (1991), Arrien (1993), Bennis (1994), Schutz (1994), Block (1993), Beckhard and Pritchard (1992), Covey (1990), and McClelland (1965), just to name a few.

The Visionary

The visionary clearly sees the big picture, the entire landscape. Rather than viewing life from the ground like a mouse (nose to the grindstone), the visionary soars like an eagle who sees the whole landscape with sharp eyes and who sees how parts of the whole interrelate. The visionary sees not only the current situation but also a whole range of new possibilities. The visionary uses the gifts of intuition and creativity to create the future. The visionary speaks passionately of vision in a way that honors personal values and maintains personal authenticity and integrity. Walt Disney, an exemplary visionary, said, "If you can dream it, you can do it." The visionary consistently and inspiringly communicates the vision to help unleash the hidden creativity and spirit already present in the organization.

To cite an example: The vice president of human resources for a major U.S. producer and distributor of grocery-store products was to design and facilitate an offsite session to deal with the pain of change (downsizing, restructuring, and changed roles) and to help build cohesion and provide direction within the splintered human resources group. During the workshop, she catalyzed the group when she powerfully invited them into her vision: "We have the opportunity to do something here that has never been done before in this group. We have the opportunity to create our future, to proactively structure ourselves and work in a way that best serves the needs of our customers and, to that end, to positively impact the success of this organization. We can begin now and do it together." By communicating her vision and inviting others into that vision, she built the momentum and energy to fuel change.

The Server

The server pays attention to what touches the heart and what has meaning in peoples' lives. The server reaches out to people and acts in caring service to others, including himself or herself. The server realizes that there is more to people than meets the eye; he or she studies and understands what is under the surface of self and others. The server seeks to understand the mysteries of the human heart and of relationships. The server knows the power of love and acts on that wisdom. The server actively seeks to see another person's point of view. The server acts as a coach and catalyst to others by drawing out, nurturing, and celebrating the gifts found in others and the growth they achieve. By these means, the server helps people tap into their internal, innate gifts. The server also understands teamwork and the fact that tasks are accomplished best through people working well together. The server helps others find meaning in their work, which inspires loyalty and commitment. Both add significance and worth to a person's work and existence.

The Warrior

The warrior is action oriented, but not in a vicious way. Rather, the warrior has the courage to take action on a vision and the courage to act in service to others. According to Koestenbaum (1991), "Courage is the foundation of leadership. All other leadership values are brittle unless reinforced with the steel of courage." The warrior is a like a tree that is firmly rooted in its vision and values, yet is able to bend and be flexible in how it takes action to enact the vision. The warrior takes charge of his or her own life before taking charge of the organization. The warrior taps inner resources and personal power in order to initiate, act, and risk. The warrior defines true power as self-mastery, not as a club to be wielded over others. The warrior acts with sustained initiative. The warrior's presence is felt by others in a way that causes them to hear and respond to the vision. As Arrien (1993) says, "The power of presence means bringing all four intelligences forward: mental, emotional, spiritual, and physical." The warrior not only understands the marketplace but responds, for example, by designing and introducing new products. The warrior has independence of thought, takes the initiative, and is a self-starter.

The warrior takes responsibility for his or her own actions, even if that means standing alone. The warrior tolerates ambiguity and manages anxiety constructively, knowing that confusion and anxiety often precede break-throughs in personal and organizational growth. Courage creates energy, which a warrior needs to be fueled to lead the charge. The warrior understands the notion of freedom of choice—freedom to act—and takes responsibility for his or her choices and actions.

Warriors are not dismayed by obstacles, because they know that leading successful organizations means that frustrations and obstacles continually crop up. Their satisfaction comes from the challenge of finding winning solutions. Challenge energizes them.

The Merchant

The merchant focuses attention on survival. The merchant is like an animal in the wild, fighting fiercely for survival in the marketplace, for both himself or herself and for members of the organizational "family." The merchant responds to the marketplace, to facts, and to the bottom line. The merchant is objective, pragmatic, rational, detailed, and result oriented. The merchant understands the internal and the external environments, the organization, its customers, its suppliers, its community, and its stockholders. The merchant is aware of the acceleration of change and makes decisions about how to expend time and money within the context of absolute reality and within the vision. The merchant uses his or her skills to plan, staff, direct, organize, and maintain control measures that are necessary to implement changes.

Four Roles as Part of the Whole

All four of the new leadership roles are already present in each of us. In analyzing our leadership skills, the question is "How much do we access these roles and how congruent are we when enacting these roles?" Are our actions consistent with our vision? Are we serving those who are important to our vision?

For example, the president of a mortgage banking company learned through a reengineering initiative that having a vision, taking action on that vision, and focusing on bottom-line results was not enough. Something was missing. He said, "Without the team interventions, I think we would have been at only 80 percent of our financial goal. More important is the positive change in the satisfaction rating of our major customer base and our increase in market share. I think what we realized is the power of the human spirit in the equation. The first half year, I was talking to people's heads by emphasizing the numerical targets, but my message just wasn't sinking in. I said to myself, 'I have to switch; I have to talk to their hearts'" (Hauser, 1996).

Leaders who guide change must take into consideration each of the roles, and the roles must be consistent and congruent with one another. If any one of the roles is missing, problems will result. For example, if a leader does not act as a server, he or she will not gain the personal commitment to fuel the change, and the change effort will become a "bottom of the box" priority for organizational members. If a leader does not assume the role of visionary and share a clear vision that is consistent with his or her own values (displaying integrity and authenticity), the change effort may start fast but will quickly fizzle out. If the leader does not assume the role of the merchant and allocate adequate resources to enable people to implement the desired changes, the people will experience anxiety and feel incompetent and frustrated in their attempts to effect the changes. Finally, if the leader does not take meaningful action on his or her vision, the organization will experience costly, haphazard efforts and false starts. These relationships are illustrated in Figure 5.

Leaders must assess their own strengths and weaknesses in terms of their effectiveness in enacting these roles. They must consciously and continually develop themselves. Bennis and Goldsmith (1994) say, "The process of becoming a leader is much the same as becoming an integrated human being."

Leadership is not a teachable set of skills that can be learned by sitting passively in a classroom where facts, numbers, and concepts are presented. Nor can leadership be achieved by memorizing a list of seven habits or twelve characteristics. At best, these methods can provide a roadmap for growth and development. True leadership comes from an inner process of personal development that can only be supported externally through encouragement, mentoring, and skill building. Leaders must nurture and train themselves and others in the mind and heart of leadership. The development of the heart and mind is a lifelong task. But commitment to developing oneself into a whole, healthy, complete person can begin immediately.

Just as the new ways of thinking and leading have implications for the leaders who guide LSOC efforts, there are also implications for the assessment of whether or not large-scale organizational changes should be implemented at all and, if so, for the selection of interventions that are most likely to bring about successful, organization-wide change.

IMPLICATIONS FOR SELECTING INTERVENTIONS FOR LARGE-SCALE ORGANIZATIONAL CHANGE

The term "intervention" refers to a set of planned activities that are intended to help an organization increase its effectiveness, based on a thorough diagnosis

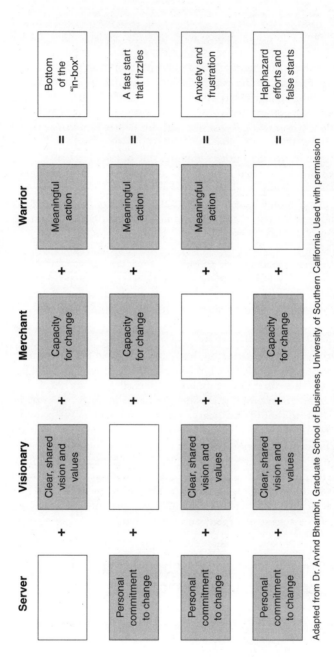

Figure 5. When Any of the Four Roles Are Missing from the Change Process

Adapted from Dr. Arvind Bhambri, Graduate School of Business, University of Southern California. Used with permission of that organization. Large-scale organizational-change interventions are aimed at effecting deep and pervasive change in the character of the organization, significantly altering its performance, and changing members' basic beliefs and values. The scope of such change is large; the experience is often emotionally intense. The change eventually permeates the entire organization, reaching all subunits and individuals. Therefore the implementation of LSOC affects both the psychological and the strategic aspects of the organization. Complex, system-wide, ongoing change requires commitment; takes time; requires integration among individuals and groups; and must be aligned with the future purposes, needs, and direction of the organization and its key stakeholders. Large-scale organizational changes should be thought of as gradual and ongoing transformations.

Four criteria are basic to the planning and implementation of LSOC interventions:

- readiness,
- starting points,
- change-agent skills, and
- sequence of interventions.

Readiness

The criterion of readiness refers to the assessment of the organization's level of readiness to undertake the LSOC intervention. The conditions that signify readiness for change are noted in the LSOC Cycle:

- Key stakeholders must feel pressure from the environment and must feel dissatisfaction with the status quo.
- There must be a compelling vision that engenders a firm commitment to the change by the key stakeholders.
- There must be sufficient resources and support available to take meaningful action.

The cycle implies that readiness begins at the individual level. Therefore, interventions should be selected that can tap into the hearts of individuals, inspiring them to commit to the changes. Because a critical mass is needed of people who are committed to change and who have a passionate belief that things must be different, there is a need to develop pools of people who can bring others along. Without this human recruitment of others, the change initiatives end up at the bottom of people's in-baskets.

Of course, the assessment and commitment process takes time, and time is one of managers' most precious and coveted commodities. But management impatience breeds failure. Beer, Eisenstat, and Spector (1990) warn against this impatience:

> Pressured managers are tempted to leap ahead; tempted to build a vision before energy for change has been mobilized, tempted to force renewal without a process that ensures support, fit and consistency, tempted to consolidate by making structure and system changes before the intricacies of the task are understood or people have the motivation and skills to make them work. We caution against such impatience because the sequence by which the critical path (of successful LSOC efforts) unfolds is as important to successful revitalization as the specific content of the interventions.

Starting Points

This criterion involves identifying aspects of the organization that are particularly amenable to change. Change is best started by targeting small, isolated, peripheral operations that are ready for change before targeting large, central-core operations. Organization-wide introduction of a change can start with a pilot project in a small, contained area of the organization in which the need for change is highly focused and the change can be readily implemented. This might mean reengineering one process in a business (e.g., the billing process of an insurance company or the funding process of a mortgage company). The power of targeting smaller operations to begin a change effort is in the fact that, as it proceeds, it actualizes and exemplifies commitment and action based on a new vision, which enables the organization to learn from the experience and begin the cycle again in other sectors of the organization.

By beginning in a place in the organization that is ready for change, one targets a manageable arena for the application of the LSOC Cycle. At its conclusion, learning takes place and is applied to the next step in the LSOC initiative, such as reengineering another business process in the organization. It is often not wise to implement all change initiatives at once; in fact, to do so could be devastating to the health of the organization and to the heart and soul of its organizational members.

Change-Agent Skills

The criterion of change-agent skills implies both the level of skills and the understanding of the process at hand. It assumes that the change agent (internal or external) has the skills and expertise to guide the implementation of any required interventions. Failures in interventions often arise when change agents attempt to use methods beyond their levels of competence and understanding. The key point is that change agents must have internalized the new ways of thinking and leading before they attempt to design or guide the implementation of LSOC. If they have successfully embraced the new ways of thinking and leading, they will travel down the right path, despite normal setbacks. They will learn from the process itself and infuse their learning into the next step of the LSOC Cycle. Again, the change process must begin with building the capabilities and commitment of leadership; otherwise all strategies will be rudderless.

The actual intervention(s) selected will vary, depending on the values held in the organization, the levels of awareness engendered by various organizational and environmental issues, and the political system in place (Mohrman et al., 1990). The nature of interventions is not as important as the understanding of leaders of the new ways of thinking and leading, which will guide them in choosing and implementing appropriate interventions.

Sequence of Interventions

There is a general sequence of implementing formal and informal interventions, using key leverage points (at the individual and group levels as well as the organizational level), that develops the optimum commitment, competence, and coordination necessary for LSOC efforts to succeed. The driving force for change is the commitment developed in the earliest stages, which energizes employees to take meaningful action toward the vision. So the place to start in the sequencing of interventions is with the necessary (intangible) precondition of evoking vision and commitment at all leverage points (individual, group, and organization). Only with that accomplished can one move into the more tangible areas of changing informal behaviors and changing formal structures and processes.

The power of the sequence, using the key leverage points, is in the fact that each group of interventions creates the necessary conditions—levels of motivation, skills, information, etc.—to allow the organization to move to the next step of the change process (Beer, Eisenstat, & Spector, 1990).

Figure 6 illustrates the framework for implementing interventions, emphasizing the tremendous importance of engaging the intangibles that underlie the new ways of thinking and leading.

Sequence and Leverage Points

Tangible Dimension	Organization	Individual/Group
Informal: interventions that seek to modify informal behaviors	1. Redefinition of roles, responsibilities, and relationships	2. Coaching, counseling, training, process consulting, team building
Formal: interventions that seek to modify formal structures and processes	4. Compensation system, information systems, organizational structure, measurement system	3. Replacement, recruitment, career pathing, succession planning, performance appraisal

Preconditions and Foundation

Intangible Dimension Interventions that seek to spark organizational energy toward change	Vision and values clarification Commitment to vision through communication that speaks to both the head and the heart; use of emotional language, stories, metaphors, and symbols Participative planning and decision making

Adapted from Beer, Eisenstat, and Spector (1990), *The Critical Path to Corporate Renewal,* Harvard Business School Press. Used with permission.

Figure 6. Planning and Implementing LSOC Interventions

Figure 6 shows how important it is—when using the interventions shown in each of the four quadrants—that the foundation of vision and commitment be kept alive and well at all leverage points, from individual to organizational, during each sequential step. This is needed to sustain the energy for the change process. When this occurs, the general sequence of implementing interventions develops the levels of commitment, energy, support, resources, and capability needed to create and sustain large-scale organizational change. As action and learning take place, and as people are rewarded for their behaviors and results, the LSOC Cycle repeats itself, having an upward spiraling effect.

CONCLUSION

This article is not intended to provide prescriptive, formulaic definitions of large-scale organizational change methods and practices. The major point of this article is that a shift in thinking is occurring in our society and is mirrored in our organizations. We may call it a transformation in thinking. This shift requires a new way of leading. There are important implications for the roles of leaders and change agents in organizations and for how they design and guide the implementation of LSOC interventions.

Organizational change starts with personal change. The leader has the opportunity and the responsibility to personally develop so that he or she can help the organization to develop. Change begins with inspiring individual energy that can then inspire organizational energy toward new possibilities for the future.

Successful leadership begins at the personal and individual level and spreads to the organization. The key, therefore, is to understand not only how to reengineer and retool during times of change, but how to create and sustain an inspired, caring, courageous, and profitable organization. The LSOC Cycle provides a framework from which to embrace the new ways of thinking and leading.

A natural cycle of events occurs during successful organizational change. Certain pressures and preconditions exist that create a dissatisfaction with the status quo and a sense of urgency to change. A vision of a new future is formulated. When both the tangible and intangible dimensions of change are integrated, a sense of commitment is engendered in leadership and key stakeholders. This commitment carries the momentum that causes people to take meaningful actions toward their new vision of the future. They then experience the effects of their actions, learn from them, and infuse that learning into the ongoing cycle of change. The process continues to cycle in a spiraling effect. The result is deep and pervasive change that creates an organizational awareness that serves as a mirror to keep the businesses creative, to solve problems as they appear, and to enable the cocreation and realization of a desired future.

References

Arrien, A. (1993). *The four-fold way.* San Francisco, CA: HarperCollins.

Beckhard, M., & Pritchard, W. (1992). *Changing the essence: The art of creating and leading fundamental change in organization.* San Francisco, CA: Jossey-Bass.

Beer, M., Eisenstat, R., & Spector, B. (1990). *The critical path to corporate renewal.* Cambridge, MA: Harvard Business School.

Bennis, W., & Goldsmith, J. (1994). *Learning to lead: A workbook on becoming a leader.* Reading, MA: Addison-Wesley.

Block, P. (1993). *Stewardship: Choosing service over self-interest.* San Francisco, CA: Berrett-Koehler.

Covey, S.R. (1990). *Principle-centered leadership.* New York: Simon & Schuster.

Fisher, L., & Selman, J. (1992, September). Rethinking commitment to change. *Journal of Management Inquiry, 1*(3).

Goldman, K., & Nethery, K. (1991, October 26–30). *The power line: An integrated approach to organization change.* Paper presented at the Organization Development Network National Conference, Los Angeles, CA.

Hammer, M., & Champy, J. (1993). *Reengineering the corporation: A manifesto for business revolution.* New York: HarperBusiness.

Hauser, L.L. (1996). *The new bottom line: Bringing heart and soul to business.* San Francisco, CA: New Leaders Press.

Horney, N., & Koonce, R. (1995, December). The missing piece in reengineering. *Training and Development Journal,* pp. 37–43.

Kilmann, R.H. (1989). *Managing beyond the quick fix.* San Francisco, CA: Jossey-Bass.

Koestenbaum, P. (1991). *Leadership: The inner side of greatness.* San Francisco, CA: Jossey-Bass.

McClelland, D.C. (1965). Toward a theory of motive acquisition. *American Psychologist, 20,* 321–333.

Mohrman, A.M., Jr., Mohrman, S.A., Ledford, G.E., Jr., Cummings, T.G., Lawler, E.E., and Associates. (1990). *Large-scale organizational change.* San Francisco, CA: Jossey-Bass.

Schutz, W. (1994). *The human element.* San Francisco, CA: Jossey-Bass.

Senge, P.M. (1990). *The fifth discipline: The art and practice of the learning organization.* New York: Doubleday/Currency.

Strata, R. (1989, Spring). Organizational learning—The key to management innovation. *Sloan Business Review,* pp. 63–74.

Veltrop, B. (1991, June). *The tool kit: Theory, models, and definitions prepared for the gamma learning expedition.* Paper presented at the Ecology of Work Conference, Pittsburgh, PA.

Wheatley, M.J. (1992). *Leadership and the new science.* San Francisco, CA: Berrett-Koehler.

Laura L. Hauser is the founder of Leadership Strategies International (LSI), a change management consulting and training firm in Santa Clarita, California, that specializes in the development of leaders from the inside out. Her expertise is derived from twenty years of work with various organizations and her degrees in communication and organization development. Her recent work and research focuses on a new way of thinking and leading that results in powerful leadership strengths and a healthier organization capable of dealing with unrelenting change. This work involves strategic planning, team building, leadership training, and one-on-one executive coaching. Ms. Hauser also is a published author and a speaker in the area of leading personal and organizational change.

COLLABORATIVE CONTRACTING: A KEY TO CONSULTING SUCCESS

Homer H. Johnson and Sander J. Smiles

Abstract: The contracting phase is one of the most critical parts of the consulting process. Here an agreement is reached about the purpose and outcomes of the project, how it will be implemented, and the responsibilities of both client and consultant. This article provides a general process for effective contracting, outlining the tasks of the contracting phase, clarifying the terminology, providing a model for a collaborative contracting interview, suggesting how to write an effective proposal, and describing how to follow up after the proposal has been submitted.

The consulting process begins with a client and a consultant discussing a problem or a project that is of concern to the client. In this *entry* phase, they explore whether there is a fit between what the client wants done and the consultant's capability and interest.

Given that both decide, at least tentatively, that there is a good match, the *contracting* phase begins. The two parties discuss, and usually commit to writing, the details of the project, covering such general questions as:

- What is to be accomplished?

- What methods will be used?

- What will the consultant provide and what will the client provide?

- What will be the time frame for the project?

- What will the project cost?

- How will the client and consultant work together?

Following the initial discussion, the consultant is usually asked to submit a proposal that details the major points on which they agreed. If the client accepts the proposal as submitted or as amended, and if both parties acknowledge their agreement to the proposal or to a formal contract, the consultant then has a legal agreement to begin the assignment. An agreement ends the contracting phase, and the project begins.

It is often difficult to specify where the entry phase ends and the contracting phase begins. For example, in the initial conversation with the client the consultant may have outlined his or her approach to the problem. The client may have responded by indicating that this is the approach that he or she would like to take. Thus, client and consultant reached a tentative agreement on a major piece of the contract before they even thought about formalizing the arrangement.

Signing a formal agreement will not mean that all discussion about the details of the project ends. Indeed, there is constant discussion and "contracting" throughout the project. The contract may have stipulated that thirteen business units were to be involved, but only ten chose to participate. Perhaps a new president is hired part way into the project and wants to emphasize something different. Perhaps there is a labor strike at one of the facilities. Any of these events may necessitate a contract amendment, agreed to by both parties.

LEGALITIES AND QUESTIONS

Some of the legal technicalities of contracting and the more frequently asked questions are covered below.

Legal Conditions

A contract between two or more parties is only legally valid if two conditions are met:

- *Mutual consent:* Both sides must enter the agreement freely and by their own choice. One party cannot decide what the other will do without his or her freely given agreement. A contract is not legally binding if one of the parties was coerced or misled, or simply never said yes.

- *Valid consideration:* A contract is not binding unless each party receives something that a court of law would determine has value. In the consulting business, the usual exchange of value is that the consultant provides some service to the client, and the client provides financial remuneration to the consultant.

Oral Contracts

Oral contracts can be as valid as written contracts. Indeed, many of the "contracts" in everyday life are oral. The person who cuts grass or cleans house probably has an oral contract to perform that service and, in exchange, will be paid a specific amount of money.

Many consulting contracts are oral, particularly those that occur inside an organization. Suppose that a consultant is working in an internal OD department and the general manager of customer service asks for help planning and facilitating a three-day "retreat" for the senior officers of the division. The assignment is accepted and is completed. No written agreement is ever made. The consultant's remuneration (usually regular salary) comes from the unit, and so neither the consultant nor the manager contracts for payment.

Although contracts for internal consulting assignments in the past were usually oral, this is changing. The recent emphasis on an internal exchange of payment for services has increased the use of internal written contracts considerably.

Oral contracts are fraught with problems. Sometimes people just do not remember what they agreed. They remember that they agreed to something in January, but it is now June and they do not remember the details. Or perhaps the person who made the agreement left the company in March.

For these reasons it is best if all agreements (formal or informal) are put in writing, whether as a short internal memo; a letter of agreement; a more formal proposal submitted for approval; or perhaps a lengthy and formal contract drawn up by the legal department. Both parties should acknowledge acceptance of the agreement and have copies.

The major advantage of a written agreement is that it forces both parties to put down in writing exactly what they want from the project and what they expect from each other. It provides a document that each party can study, circulate among the key players, discuss, and change if necessary. Once the contract is signed and the project begun, if a change is necessary then a memo signed by both parties will clarify any changes and will satisfy any legal challenge.

Legal Recourse

Another frequently asked question is what kind of legal recourse consultants have if the verbal or written contract is not being honored. Of course, the first step is always to try to work it out with the client. If that is unsuccessful, the consultant can hire an attorney to protect his or her interests. However, consultants rarely pursue the legal route, deciding that it takes too much time, effort, and money for legal fees.

CLARIFYING TERMINOLOGY

The terms "proposal," "contract," and "letter of agreement" are used quite loosely and can add more confusion than clarification. The *contracting phase* is that part of the consulting process that begins when the client and consultant begin to seriously discuss the possibility of working together; it ends when both sign some form of contract or a letter of agreement that acknowledges that they will be working together.

During the first part of this phase, the two parties discuss the details of the work to be done. As a result of their discussion, most clients will ask the consultant to submit a *proposal*, which outlines the proposed project, including time lines and fees. A proposal may be in the form of a brief memo, a letter, or a lengthy document.

The client may accept the proposal as is, ask for changes, or reject it. If the proposal is accepted outright or as amended, and if both parties somehow acknowledge their agreement (usually by signing the proposal), then the proposal becomes legally binding on both parties (a *contract*).

Usually, only lengthy documents drawn up by an attorney, filled with legal language, are thought of as contracts. Clients use this form of contract more often than do consultants, especially if there is an in-house legal department. In some cases a client will take the proposal, rewrite it in legalese, and send it back to the consultant for approval. Or a client may discuss the project with the consultant and, without asking for a proposal, have a contract written based on that discussion. However, a contract becomes effective only if both parties agree to the terms and sign the document.

As an alternative to a contract, either party could use a *letter of agreement,* which is usually much shorter in length than either a formal contract or a proposal. The letter is usually written on the consultant's letterhead and is one or two pages in length, although it may have some additional information in an appendix. Again, both parties have to sign the letter before it becomes binding.

TYPES OF CONTRACTS

Consultant Written

A contract can be put together in a variety of ways. One way is for the consultant to take the information that he or she gathered in the earlier discussions and to write a proposal or a contract, then send it to the client for approval or rejection. Consultants who use this approach assume that they have the expertise to plan an intervention that is in the best interests of the client. (Implicit in this approach is the hope that the client will recognize the consultant's expertise.) Although this approach is often used, a more effective method of contracting is "collaborative contracting."

Collaborative Contracting

In collaborative contracting the consultant and client jointly develop a contract. They do not write the actual proposal together, but discuss and agree on the key points. This approach has several significant advantages:

1. It produces a proposal that the client is favorably disposed to accept, because he or she has contributed or agreed to the key points.

2. The client is more committed to the project, because he or she has had a major role in designing it.

3. The project becomes more "do-able," because the consultant has the benefit of the client's knowledge of the company.

As the key points of the contract are discussed, the consultant's expertise and the client's ideas of what is needed blend together into a workable course of action.

The collaborative contracting approach is not without drawbacks:

■ It usually takes more time and effort from both consultant and client. It may mean more trips to the client's place of business; more meetings; and more uncomfortable discussions over points that were not initially agreed upon.

■ Some clients will not want to use this approach, but just want to give the consultant the pertinent information and expect the consultant to write the proposal.

However, the advantages outweigh the disadvantages. With some practice, a consultant can become quite adept at collaborative contracting. The description of a contracting meeting that follows is based on the collaborative model.

THE CONTRACTING MEETING

Preparation

The consultant needs to have a "game plan." Several phone calls probably have been exchanged, and he or she probably has an initial idea of the client's problem. The consultant must remember that he or she has been called because the client either does not have an answer to the problem or wants a more comprehensive solution that has not yet been approved by higher management.

The consultant also needs to learn as much about the company and its current business environment as possible. This allows him or her to understand the situation better and to design an intervention that will meet the client's needs. The next section covers what the consultant needs to discuss at the meeting.

What To Discuss

Several important points must be covered in any contracting meeting, with the objective being to achieve consensus on each.

The consultant will usually take the lead by providing an agenda for the meeting and making sure that each key point is discussed. However, if contracting is to be collaborative and the objective is to reach a consensus, then there must be plenty of give-and-take. Rather than telling the client what to do, the consultant suggests procedures and elicits input about their probable effectiveness and best ways to implement them.

Key discussion points to be covered in the meeting are:

- *Definition of the problem or the project.* The consultant has probably discussed this with the client several times before, but the success of the contracting session, and the entire project, depends on both parties talking about the same thing. So the consultant must review the problem or project again to make sure that they agree on its definition and scope.

- *Expected outcomes of the project.* Again, this is probably something that has been discussed many times, but the success of the contracting session, and the project, rests on them agreeing about what should be accomplished.

- *General strategy or approach to take.* The consultant suggests what should be done, whether team building, a new software program, or a reorganization of the sales force, and explains why this approach will produce the desired outcomes.

- *Key factors needed for the project to succeed.* The people and units involved, members of the design team, extent of the training, employee time needed, and so on.

- *Overview of the plan.* More detail is given about the recommended plan, step by step, with a general time line and an outline of the major activities from beginning to end.

- *Overview of the consultant's responsibilities.* A fairly detailed listing of the services and the materials that will be provided by the consultant.

- *Detailed listing of what the client will provide.* The resources (people, equipment, space, time) that will be provided by the client organization.

- *Working relationship of consultant and client.* Less formal aspects of the client/consultant relationship must be covered. Some of these will be clear during earlier discussion of responsibilities, but they must talk about the relationship again, particularly to outline the amount of collaboration that is expected, frequency of meetings, etc.

- *General costs of the project.* Some consultants feel uncomfortable discussing their fees and other expenses directly with the client and prefer detailing the costs in a contract letter or proposal. However, if contracting is to be collaborative, the fees must be discussed openly. The consultant may not have a detailed account of the costs prior to the meeting; however, he or she does know the usual fees and will have a rough idea as to the number of billable days that the project will take. Giving the client a "ball-park figure" is still possible, and it might be helpful to hear the client's reaction. If the costs seem high, they can jointly redesign the project until the costs are acceptable.

The Process

If the consultant has done an effective job during the entry phase, he or she will have a good idea as to how the project can be implemented successfully, which will become the basis of the contracting discussion. The consultant sets the agenda to cover all the key points.

Three suggestions for the process follow:

- The consultant should take the lead in this meeting. He or she has gathered preliminary data concerning the problem and will be in a position to, at least tentatively, recommend ways to handle it.
- Even though the consultant takes the lead, he or she does not dictate to the client how the project should be done but discusses how best to accomplish the objectives.
- It is important for the consultant to explain the logic of the recommended approach, as well as to explore the rationale for alternative approaches.

Sample Meeting Outline

An abbreviated version of a contracting meeting follows:

1. *First, thank the client for taking time to meet.* Review the *purpose, agenda,* and *time* (PAT) of the meeting. Indicate that the purpose of the meeting is to decide the best way to put the project together; that you would like to start by reviewing the problem and making some suggestions based on previous discussions; and that the meeting should take about an hour and a half. For example:

   "Thanks for meeting with me today. I would like to go over some of the details of the project. Based on our previous discussion, I have some ideas, but I'd like your input. I think that if we work on this together, we will have a plan that is much stronger than anything either of us could develop alone. I would like to go through the key points in the next hour or hour and a half and decide how best to proceed."

2. *Next, review the problem or the project:* "I understand that the problem is in the reservations area. A new, more decentralized structure was put into place and there seems to be a lot of dissatisfaction with the changes. I talked to some of the supervisors, who indicated that there was a lot of confusion as to who had responsibility for both the information and the scheduling. They seemed to think that the new structure was workable, but that some changes were needed. They also indicated that the reservation agents had the most problems with the new system. Is that your understanding of the problem?"

3. *Be sure that mutual agreement exist on the objectives:* "We first want to find out what the problems are with the new structure and to make some recommendations of ways to eliminate them, which will be reviewed by the Operations Committee and then implemented. The overall objective is to eliminate the problems and allow the new structure to operate effectively. Is there anything we should add to this objective?"

4. *Give an overview of the suggested approach to the problem:* "Let's discuss a strategy for getting at the problem. During our last conversation, we talked about interviewing a cross section of the reservation agents and supervisors to find out what types of problems they were having. I would write up a report to summarize the issues, then have a group of agents and supervisors analyze the list and propose ways to manage the issues. Their proposed solutions would go to the Operations Committee for approval and implementation. The people who are most affected by the problems would be involved in finding ways to eliminate them. How do you feel about that strategy now? What are the advantages and disadvantages of using it?"

5. *Move to the detail level.* One obvious detail is who conducts the interviews and who is interviewed. The consultant might say: "Let's discuss the interviews now. I recommend that consultants from our firm conduct all interviews. That way, respondents will be talking to a neutral party who has been trained to be professional and objective. Does that sound alright to you?

"How many interviews would you like us to conduct? There are eight locations throughout the U.S., with about twenty-five people per location.

One option is to go to four of the locations, interviewing about half the people at each. That would give us a good sample of both locations and employees and would be less expensive than going to all locations. What do you think about that idea?"

6. *Continue to discuss details.* Some details from the example would be: "What people in what locations would be interviewed?" "When would the project start?" "When does it need to be finished?" "How will the group meet to make recommendations?" "Who should be in this group?"

7. *Outline the services provided.* Some services in the example would include:

   - Conduct interviews at four sites with about twelve people at each site.

   - Summarize the data from the interviews in a report.

   - Present the report and its findings to a representative group of agents and supervisors.

   - Facilitate the group's analysis of the results and assist them to develop recommendations for dealing with issues.

8. *Be clear about your needs.* These can be introduced by a statement such as: "Every consulting project has specific factors that contribute to its success. I want to share some of those with you but, first, do you see any key areas that we must address or be aware of to make this project successful." (Wait for a response and then share your success factors. Some examples are listed below:)

   - Senior management must be completely behind these efforts.

   - We must be clear on what a successful project looks like. Afterward, we should be able to refer back to our criteria and determine if your needs and the company's needs have been met. We will spend a few minutes defining "success" before we finish our meeting.

   - The participants must understand completely the reason for the project and the importance of their honest and sincere participation.

   - The data obtained must be anonymous.

   - The Operations Committee must report back to the participants in a timely manner.

   Be sure to ask for feedback and for any other points the client wishes to make before proceeding.

9. *Summarize the key points that have been discussed and check to see that any agreements have been recorded accurately.* Block (1981) makes the point that the

consultant should not leave the meeting without knowing how the client feels about the project, the meeting, and the consultant. If there are problems in any of these areas, they need to be settled quickly or the proposal either will not be accepted or, if accepted, the project will get off to a shaky start.

10. *Discuss fees at the end of the meeting.* By this time the client has a good overview of what the project will entail; has a good idea of how useful the project will be to the company; and has also tentatively agreed to the details and procedures.

The following is an example of what to say about costs:

"I would like to briefly discuss the costs of the project with you before we close. In the proposal I will estimate the number of consulting days needed and give you a rough figure for direct expenses such as travel, hotel, and materials.

"My consulting fee is $1,200 per day, which includes preparation time, interview time, time spent on-site, and time spent writing a follow-up report. Each set of interviews will take two days, plus half a day for travel. Reviewing forty-eight interviews and writing the report will require two days. Preparing and conducting the debriefing will be two days. Assisting the Operations Committee to prepare its presentation will take one day. My estimate of the total number of days needed for this project will be fifteen days, or $18,000 plus direct expenses.

"This investment is an important step in addressing the problems you are facing in such a critical area of your business. Are the costs what you expected?"

It is best to deal with any objections now before leaving the client's office. If more than one consultant has submitted a proposal, you may ask for feedback about how this proposal compares to others.

11. *End the meeting by thanking the client.* State that the plan is much stronger because you have both worked on it. Give the client an indication of when to expect the proposal from you. Make it soon to show your interest in, and eagerness to work on, the project.

ASPECTS OF THE PROPOSAL

Form and Length

The next step in the process entails writing a proposal covering the points discussed during the contracting meeting. To ensure that it is accepted, the consultant should go over the proposal with the client, preferably face-to-face, to make sure that the proposal accurately reflects what was agreed on. Any required changes to the proposal can then be made.

A considerable diversity of opinion exists as to the form and the length of a proposal. A few consultants prefer to work without a written proposal or a written contract. Usually, they have established such a solid relationship with the client that a verbal agreement is good enough for both parties.

Geoff Bellman, another successful consultant, thinks that the formal contract can get in the way of the relationship that evolves as the project evolves. His preference is to use an informal memo that clarifies what the project will entail and how the project will be planned (Kimmerling, 1995).

At the other end of the spectrum are those who insist on having a formal contract drawn up by an attorney. For example, Felicia McAleer (Cohen, 1996) states that "the first rule is to get an ironclad contract. Hire a tough attorney, someone who specializes in this industry and copyright issues. It's important to have clear written and verbal communications with your client" (p. 44).

What is the correct form[1] and the correct length? Assuming that one uses a proposal, how long should it be? Some proposals are two paragraphs long, some two pages long, and others are from 100 to 200 pages. There are three ways to decide:

- *Find out what the client prefers.* Many clients expect a certain format and length, so the consultant can ask the client what information must be included and in how much detail or ask to see a previous example. (This request is seldom granted. However it may be worth a try.)

- *Consulting firms usually prefer a certain format.* Consultants employed by a firm may already have a standard model. Even internal consulting groups are beginning to standardize their contracts.

- *Many published examples of consulting proposals and contracts exist.* Shenson (1990) has written a very helpful *Contract and Fee-Setting Guide* that covers

---

[1]It is this author's philosophy that all agreements or proposals must be put in writing. Placing all agreed-to objectives, resource requirements, fees, and time lines in writing fosters communication between the parties and provides a reference to which all can refer later.

the steps of proposal writing, complete with sample proposals and contracts, as well as how to determine fees. Greiner and Metzger (1983) also have some excellent examples of proposals covering a variety of areas of consulting practice.

Content

Minimally, the topics that were discussed in the contracting meeting must be covered, but the proposal should also cover the following points:

- *Why the proposal has been submitted.* This is a definition of the challenges being faced by the client and the desired outcomes from the project—the benefits for the client.
- *The work to be performed.* This is the core of the proposal, describing activities or tasks that will be undertaken to accomplish the desired outcomes.
- *Consultant responsibilities.* Given the work to be done, what tasks will the consultant complete.
- *Client responsibilities.* What type of support will the client provide? Will some of the client's personnel be assigned to the project? What actions will the client take to help the project?
- *Time line of the project.* When will it start? How long will it take?
- *Confidentiality and/or anonymity issues.* Anonymity is the assurance that the sources of information will not be revealed. Confidentiality refers to the assurance that the consultant will not disclose any information that he or she learns about the company.
- *Reporting procedures.* What written reports are expected from the consultant and who will receive these reports? Is the consultant expected to provide periodic progress briefings? How often and to whom?
- *Fees and costs of the project, as well as the schedule for payment.*

Less frequently, a proposal or contract might cover such topics as:

- Why and how one or both parties can terminate the contract.
- Who has the legal right to materials and instruments produced as part of the project.
- Information about the consulting firm and/or the key consultants who will work on the project, showing prior experience with projects of this type.

An example of a letter of agreement is shown in Figure 1, below.

Continuous Improvement Systems, Inc.
Bringing People and Technology Together

April 15, 1998

Ms. Sue Morin, Director of Operations
Direct Marketing Nationwide, Inc.
Reservations Center
Omaha, Nebraska

Dear Ms. Morin:

Thank you for the opportunity to discuss the challenges facing Direct Marketing Nationwide and to help you and your Reservations Center with its continuous-improvement efforts. You face a highly competitive market, and we recognize how important it is for you to run an efficient and effective reservations center.

Goal and Objectives:

CIS understands that your main objective is to eliminate the current problems in your Reservation Centers across the country and to have your new organizational structure operate effectively.

Background Information:

Our understanding is that DMN has been a very effective direct marketing company whose business has grown significantly in the last few years. DMN responded to this growth by decentralizing to respond better to its customers. The decentralization has not gone well, and confusion exists on roles and responsibilities at many of your sites. The old system also functioned poorly and was not designed for the current growth or expected growth over the next few years. Decentralization has worked well for other industries, but your organizational culture has not had enough time to absorb and adapt to the new systems and procedures.

Proposed Plan

DMN and CIS agree that the success of the Reservations Centers lies in the hands and hearts of the people who run them. People who work in the centers must be the source of any solutions.

CIS proposes to meet DMN's needs by conducting interviews with a cross section of agents and supervisors at four representative sites. From this information a report will be developed, then reviewed at a debriefing meeting of a representative group of agents and supervisors. The group will be led through an innovative problem-solving session whose goal is to propose solutions and procedures to make the system work. The group's proposals will be presented to the Operating Committee for final approval.

Project Scope and Costs

The key aspects of this project include:

- Conduct interviews at four sites with twelve people at each site (eight days)
- Review interviews and prepare report (two days)
- Travel to four sites (two days)
- Prepare for and conduct problem-solving session (two days)
- Assist in writing Operating Committee presentation (one day)

Total = 15 days at $1,200 a day for a total of $18,000, plus direct expenses for travel, hotels, meals, and meeting-related materials. Invoicing will be monthly.

CIS will be able to begin this project as soon as the agreement is signed. Assuming that we are able to schedule the interviews and meetings in a timely manner, it is anticipated that the project will be completed within four weeks from the start date.

CIS Qualifications

CIS has worked with several companies in DMN's industry group. (References are attached.) CIS has over twenty years' experience in interviewing and innovative problem solving and understands the necessity for practical business solutions. Continuous improvement efforts succeed through creativity, not capital.

We look forward to working with Direct Marketing Nationwide and helping you in your continuous-improvement efforts as we have helped other clients.

Sincerely yours,

Don Jones

Direct Marketing Nationwide agrees to the project as outlined in this letter of agreement.

_____   _____
Sue Morin, Director of Operations   Don Jones, President

Figure 1. Sample Letter of Agreement

The Question of Fees

One of the most frequently asked questions is how much to charge and what basis to use to set these charges. Shenson (1990) provides a detailed explanation of this topic, but a few of several methods are covered below.

Most consultants bill on an *hourly or daily rate,* plus the direct expenses associated with the project. The daily fee charged varies considerably, and therefore an appropriate fee is difficult to suggest. Consultants who work with churches may charge as little as $150 to $300 per day. In the private sector, a daily fee of $800 to $1,200 is common, with the better-known consultants billing at $1,500 to $2,500 per day. A few premier consultants charge considerably more.

Direct expenses such as travel, hotels, and materials (all of which are nontaxable) are usually billed separately. These expenses are usually itemized, and the consultant may be required to submit the original receipts.

Another frequent method of billing is *the fixed fee.* Using this approach, the consultant contracts to complete the entire project for a single fixed fee. If the project is completed on schedule, the consultant can make a nice profit. However, if time or cost has been miscalculated, the consultant could end up losing money. Apparently, this does not happen too often with experienced consultants, as Shenson (1990) reports that consultants who use a fixed fee report higher income and profits than those who use hourly or daily fees.

Fixed fees are based on the consultant's estimate of how much time it will take to complete the project multiplied by the hourly or daily fee that the consultant would like to receive. Such costs as office overhead, insurance, and desired profit are added in. Some consultants include direct expenses such as travel and hotels as part of the fixed fee. Others prefer to bill the client separately for direct costs because items such as airfare are not predictable. In either case, the consultant has to be quite adept at estimating time and costs.

Shenson discusses several other approaches to setting fees, including performance contracts and cost-plus contracts. However, the majority of consultants use daily or hourly fees of a fixed-fee approach.

What Happens Next?

The client may accept the proposal as is or as amended. If the client accepts the proposal, or will accept it with certain amendments, he or she should indicate so in a formal (written) manner. Some consultants ask the client to

The 1998 Annual: Volume 2, Consulting/© 1998 Jossey-Bass/Pfeiffer

sign the proposal to indicate approval. Others request a formal letter of acceptance. In other cases, the client or the consultant will draw up a formal contract written in legal language that covers the same points as the original proposal. This document is then signed by both parties.

Conversely, the client may not accept the proposal but would be receptive to a revised one. In this case the consultant should meet with the client to determine what changes are required. If the consultant thinks that the project still can be carried out successfully, given the changes suggested by the client, the proposal should be amended to meet the objections and resubmitted (quickly) to the client.

FOLLOW UP ON UNSUCCESSFUL PROPOSALS

Sometimes the client rejects the proposal outright. He or she may have solicited proposals from other consultants and decided to award the contract elsewhere. It is helpful in this case to receive some client feedback on the proposal: What were the strong points or weak points, and what made the other proposal so attractive?

Consultants often learn more from unsuccessful proposals than from those that are accepted. The lack of success forces the consultant to critically examine his or her approach and presentation. This, in turn, leads to better proposals and to increased business. Some clients will be quite willing to provide this feedback, others will not (and may not return phone calls). In all cases, the consultant should send the potential client a note of thanks for reviewing the proposal and ask to be kept in mind for future projects.

References

Block, P. (1981). *Flawless consulting.* San Francisco, CA: Jossey-Bass/Pfeiffer.

Cohen, S. (1996, October). Shortcuts to starting a consulting practice. *Training & Development Journal,* pp. 39–44.

Greiner, L.E., & Metzger, R.O. (1983). *Consulting to management.* Englewood Cliffs, NJ: Prentice-Hall.

Kimmerling, G. (1995, June). How to start a consulting business. *Training & Development Journal,* pp. 22–28.

Shenson, H.L. (1990). *The contract and fee-setting guide for consultants and professionals.* New York: John Wiley.

Homer H. Johnson, Ph.D., *is a professor in the Center for Organization Development at Loyola University in Chicago, where he teaches and consults in the areas of continuous improvement, strategic planning, change management, and consulting skills. He is the co-author (with Sander Smiles) of the forthcoming* Consulting Skills Fieldbook.

Sander J. Smiles, M.S.O.D., *is an internal organization development consultant for Fel-Pro, Inc., where he trains in the areas of continuous improvement, KAIZEN methodologies, self-managed teams, performance management, change management, customer satisfaction, and technical skills training.*

INFORMAL REWARDS AS A PERFORMANCE-MANAGEMENT TOOL

Bob Nelson

Abstract: This paper calls attention to the merits of informal rewards and explains why they need to be better understood and utilized by management as a complement to formal reward systems. Guidelines for implementing an informal reward system are outlined, with examples and implications for the future.

This paper focuses primarily on those informal rewards that can be controlled by management actions: recognition, personal contact with management, and nonmonetary rewards such as time off.

Management has long underestimated the importance of informal rewards for the achievement of organizational goals. At a time when formal reward and recognition systems are increasingly ineffective, the use of informal rewards could provide just the right combination of relevance, immediacy, and individual value to warrant their use. Considering that a reported 33 percent of managers would rather work in another organization in which they could receive better recognition (Schneier, 1989), the time is ripe.

DEFINITIONS

A *reward* "is an outcome that results in increased satisfaction of individual needs" (Anthony et al., 1989, p. 57). It is something special—a special gain for special achievements, a treat for doing something above-and-beyond (Kanter, 1986). An *informal reward* is one that stems from the informal relationship between the parties involved. Examples include intrinsic rewards related to performance and stature, recognition, and personal contact with management (Maciariello & Kirby, 1990). Leisure time, access to information, social approval, and status are also powerful reinforcers in an organization (Nord, 1974).

The *informal reward system* parallels the formal reward system in every company. Informal systems come about as a result of interactions among people, relationships that are often independent of their organizational roles. Barnard (1968) defines this informal organization as "the aggregate of the personal contacts and interactions and the associated groupings of people" (p. 115).

Informal systems serve several indispensable functions, as noted by Barnard (1968): (1) communication, (2) maintenance of cohesiveness through regulating the willingness to serve and the stability of objective authority, and (3) maintenance of the feelings of personal integrity, of self-respect, and of independent choice. In addition, as Maciariello and Kirby (1990) indicate, informal systems supplement the formal controls by increasing the organization's ability to make adaptive responses. Although less frequently discussed in management literature, in part due to its intangible nature, the informal system is an important and viable complement to any organization—and an effective resource for managers who know how to use it.

THE IMPORTANCE OF INFORMAL REWARDS

Informal rewards are of increasing importance for managers today for two reasons. First, traditional rewards such as compensation and promotions—although still important—are becoming less and less effective in recognizing high performance or in motivating employees. Second, informal rewards work!

Traditional rewards are increasingly inadequate in U.S. business. Consider these facts (Schneier, 1989):

- 81 percent of workers say they would not receive any reward for productivity increases.

- 60 percent of managers feel their compensation will not increase if their performance improves.

- 3 percent of base salary separates average from outstanding employees.

Clearly, our traditional system of rewards is in crisis if it fails to differentiate high performance on such a widespread basis. To make matters worse, rewards that are still in place are losing effectiveness. As Drucker (1974) points out:

> Economic incentives are becoming rights rather than rewards. Merit raises are always introduced as rewards for exceptional performance. In no time at all they become a right. To deny a merit raise or to grant only a small one becomes punishment. The increasing demand for material rewards is rapidly destroying their usefulness as incentives and managerial tools. (p. 239)

Material rewards such as cash have even been found to have a demotivating effect in some cases. Explains Cecil Hill (1989), corporate manager of improvement programs at Hughes Aircraft Company:

> I found certain aspects of the cash awards approach would be counterproductive at Hughes Aircraft. For example, cash awards would reduce teamwork as employees concentrated primarily on individual cash gains. We also found that United Airlines had dropped its long-time cash awards system because of litigation problems. Other companies pointed out a negative boomerang effect whenever ideas were turned down, while many firms reported an ongoing problem with timely response, and others noted disagreements on determining dollar amounts and conflicts regarding what constitutes "a part of

normal job performance." We have also found instances where "pay" for certain types of intellectual performance tends to denigrate the performance, and remove it from the intellectual achievement category, which elicits pride and satisfaction, and reduces it to a more mundane "pay-for-performance" concept. In short, cash awards seemed to have an overall demotivating effect." (p. 161)

Kanter (1986) summarizes the problem and need for better rewards well: "In this time of corporate hierarchy-shrinking and organizational layer-removal, companies cannot afford the old-fashioned system in which promotion was the primary means of recognizing performance. Greater accessibility to rewards—at all levels—is a necessity when employees stay in place longer; and recognition is an important part of this" (p. 19).

Although they are given little or no attention in management literature and practice, the truth is that informal or nontraditional rewards work. The effectiveness of such rewards can be traced back to fundamental principles of positive reinforcement. Positive reinforcement is efficient for several reasons. First, it increases the probable reoccurrence of the desired response. Second, the adverse emotional responses associated with punishment and extinction are apt to be reduced and, in fact, favorable emotions may be developed (Nord, 1974).

To illustrate the power of positive reinforcement on individual behavior in an organization, Daniel Boyle (1987), vice president and treasurer of Diamond Fiber Products, Inc., describes the impact on an employee of being given a nylon and cotton jacket as an employee recognition reward called The 100 Club in his company:

> You might think this is a trivial thing, but it means a lot to the people who earn a jacket. A teller at a local bank told me once that a woman came in and proudly modeled her baby blue 100 Club jacket for bank customers and employees. She said, "My employer gave me this for doing a good job. It's the first time in the 18 years I've been there they've recognized the things I do every day."
>
> During those years she had earned $230,000 in wages, which had paid for cars, a home mortgage, food, other essentials, vacations, college educations. In her mind, she had provided a service for her earnings. The money wasn't recognition for her work, but the 100 Club jacket was. (p. 27)

Think of the impact recognition would have had on this employee if it had been used on a daily basis, instead of once every eighteen years! As the example illustrates, many informal rewards cost relatively little or no money, so are very cost effective. According to Merchant (1989), "The corporation can provide meaningful rewards at the lowest possible cost if it tailors the rewards to employees' preferences" (p. 28).

When the positive reinforcement is done by members of an informal work group, the results can be even more dramatic. Because rewards and punishments from the informal group are apt to be administered immediately and frequently, they are very powerful in controlling behavior (Nord, 1974).

CHARACTERISTICS OF INFORMAL REWARDS

What makes informal rewards effective? Informal rewards are most effective when some simple guidelines are followed:

1. *Directly reinforcing of desired behavior.* "The crucial variable in distributing any reward is contingency" (Nord, 1974, p. 398), that is, the reward needs to be clearly a response to the desired behavior.

2. *Immediate in their use.* Informal rewards need to be given as soon as possible after the desired behavior occurs. As Nord explains, "Most rapid conditioning results when the desired response is 'reinforced' immediately. In other words, the desired response is followed directly by some consequence. In simple terms, if the outcome is pleasing to the individual, the probability of his repeating the response is apt to be increased. The process of inducing such change in the response rate is called operant conditioning. In general, the frequency of a behavior is said to be a function of its consequences" (p. 385).

3. *Delivered personally.* Part of the power of informal rewards comes from having them personally delivered. Because time is a limited, precious resource for most managers, taking time to recognize or praise an employee underscores the importance. Time taken by a peer to recognize a colleague has an equal or greater effect in that it is both unexpected and unrequired.

4. *Valued by the individual.* A final guideline for effective informal rewards is to be sure they are valued and meaningful to the individuals who receive them. According to Locke's theory of motivation, "results-dependent rewards should be sufficiently meaningful to offset other incentives employees have to act contrary to the corporation's best interest" (Merchant, 1989, p. 27).

The rewards that are meaningful to a particular employee, however, depend on personal circumstances and tastes. For example, some employees are interested in immediate cash bonuses, whereas others are interested in increased autonomy, in better promotion possibilities, or merely being recognized for doing a good job (Merchant, 1989). The best way to find out what employees value in terms of rewards is to ask them!

Seven Principles of Informal Rewards

Kanter (1986) outlines seven principles that are useful when using informal rewards:

1. *Emphasize success rather than failure.* You tend to miss the positives if you are busily searching for the negatives.

2. *Deliver recognition and reward in an open and publicized way.* If not made public, recognition loses much of its impact and defeats much of the purpose for which it is given.

3. *Deliver recognition in a personal and honest manner.* Avoid providing recognition that is too "slick" or over-produced.

4. *Tailor your recognition and reward to the unique needs of the people involved.* Having many recognition and reward options will enable managers to acknowledge accomplishment in ways appropriate to a given situation, selecting from a larger menu of possibilities.

5. *Timing is crucial.* Recognize contribution throughout a project. Reward contribution close to the time an achievement is realized. Delays weaken the impact of most rewards.

6. *Strive for a clear, unambiguous, and well-communicated connection between accomplishments and rewards.* Be sure people understand why they receive awards and the criteria used to determine them.

7. *Recognize recognition.* That is, recognize people who recognize others for doing what is best for the company.

IMPLEMENTING AN INFORMAL REWARD SYSTEM

Individuals tend to be more strongly motivated by the potential to earn rewards than by the fear of punishment, which suggests that management control systems should be reward oriented. Here are some guidelines for implementing an informal reward system within the organization:

Link to organizational goals. To be effective, informal rewards need to support behavior that leads to the attainment of organizational goals. Management must see to it that the consequences of behavior increase the frequency of desired behavior and decrease the frequency of undesired behavior (Nord, 1974).

Individuals respond to many kinds of rewards, tangible and intangible, on the job and off the job. Tying these rewards to controls is not simple. Consequently, a careful review of the reward system should be made along with any major redesign of the control system. Insofar as flexibility permits, rewards should be clearly and explicitly related to desired performance as reflected by the controls (Newman, 1975).

Define parameters and mechanics. Once the behavior to be reinforced is identified, specifics of a reward system need to be defined. The rules for awarding incentives must be clear and understood by all. This can make an incentive system powerful and make a clear connection between the level of performance and the awarding of the incentive (Pritchard et al., 1989).

Obtain commitment and support. Once the mechanics of an informal reward system are clear, the program needs to be communicated and "sold" to those who will be using it. This can usually be done in a group setting by presenting the program as a positive, fun activity that will benefit everyone as well as the company.

Monitor effectiveness. Any program is only as good as its implementation. Informal reward systems must be monitored to see if they are being used and to see that the desired results are being obtained. Even the best informal reward program will be apt to lose its effectiveness over time, as one of the attributes of a reward is that it is special. Old programs often lose their specialness.

Link to formal rewards programs. A challenge for management is to ensure that informal rewards are in line with the formal reward structure (Marciariello & Kirby, 1990). This can most easily be done by having informal rewards become a subset of larger, more formal reward programs that are in place. For example, a company award (a formal reward) could be given to the employee who submits the greatest number of letters of praise (an informal reward) from fellow employees, management, or customers over the course of a year.

An Informal Reward System Inventory

The Bulova Watch Company outlined the following checklist of questions to help a company determine if it would benefit from a recognition program (*Personnel Journal*, 1986, p. 68):

1. Does your company have a *systematic* way of letting people know that you value their contributions?

2. Does your company publicly single out those people who do something right, rather than those who do something wrong?

3. Has your company established one, or at most two, fundamental attributes, e.g., pride of workmanship, dedication to customer needs, to be best at—and continually reinforced that goal?

4. Does management believe your company's assets are primarily its machines, products or money, rather than its people?

5. Do you encourage performance competition among workers in a way that is nonthreatening?

6. Do you offer rewards that are strictly monetary (salaries, bonuses) and fail to provide symbolic awards as well?

7. Is management as totally committed to its people and their well-being as they wish their employees to be toward the company and its goals?

8. Is top management visibly involved in the recognition of employee achievement *at all levels?*

9. Does management recognize and reward only the few top performers and ignore the remaining 80 percent or 90 percent?

10. Has management tried various incentive programs in the past and given them up because they "just don't seem to work?"

Two Examples

Following are descriptions of two programs that fit the criteria just described for an informal reward system.

The Winning Edge Award. At the Honeywell Technology Center in Minneapolis, management implemented a recognition program entitled "The Winning Edge" for superior performance "above and beyond" the job. The program was open to any employee to submit a brief statement recommending another employee for the award. A committee reviewed the recommendations, and winning individuals were awarded $100 cash and a certificate presented at a periodic ceremony. In addition, all award winners had their names mentioned in the company's newsletter.

The program was considered a success in getting employees to pay extra attention to helping others with their needs, recognizing those who were committed to excellence, and increasing the general morale and excitement of the work environment. The program ran its course over about a year and was discontinued after it was felt that a majority of the employees had received the award. Although there were some program costs, it was generally felt that the benefits of the program considerably exceeded the program costs.

The Eagle Award. At Blanchard Training and Development in San Diego, The Eagle Award was established to recognize "legendary service" to customers—one of the organization's strategic objectives. The program was initially announced and explained at a company-wide meeting. The program was open to any employee, who could submit the name of another employee who had gone out of his or her way to help satisfy a customer request. The name was submitted with a brief description of the activity that was considered exceptional. Typical examples included staying late to ship materials, helping a customer locate a lost order or resolve a billing problem, rearranging trainer schedules to deliver a last-minute training request by a customer, and so forth.

The recommendations were reviewed by a committee, primarily to screen out items that were an expected part of someone's job. The accepted individuals were surprised by a visit from "the Eagle Committee," who took a picture of the person holding "an Eagle Award"—one of several eagle statues that rotated around the company. The photo was displayed on a bulletin board in the company's lobby with a brief description of the activity that was being recognized. The individual kept the eagle statue on his or her desk until it was needed for a new recipient—typically a week or so. An "Eagle of the Year" award was given at the end of the year by a vote of previous eagle award winners. The winner was given an engraved clock at the company's annual celebration program.

This program was one of several that was credited with making "legendary service" an established part of the company's culture. It was implemented at virtually no cost. The only criticism the program received from some employees was that it favored those individuals who dealt with customers on a daily basis. The program was revamped and revised after about a year to focus more on internal customer service, a new priority for the company.

IMPLICATIONS FOR THE FUTURE

There are at least three trends favoring the increasing use of informal reward systems today and in the future (Mintzberg, 1979):

1. *The trend toward fixed compensation.* A major trend in employee compensation today is toward fixed compensation systems in which salaries are

frozen and merit increases are paid only on a bonus basis. Such changes place pressure on organizations to find other ways to reinforce desired behavior. Informal rewards can help accommodate this need.

2. *The trend toward empowered employees.* Empowered employees have increased responsibility and autonomy to act in the best interests of the company. With those new responsibilities comes the need to be able to influence others. The challenge for management is be adaptable, providing each individual with more flexibility and freedom to innovate while concurrently directing their activities toward the common purpose of the organization (Maciariello & Kirby, 1990). This need can be achieved in part through the use of informal rewards.

3. *The trend toward increased uncertainty.* U.S. business is experiencing change at a faster and faster rate. The nature of effective rewards is changing as well. Management must use a more flexible, less formalized mechanism to meet whatever business needs come up and be flexible to the needs of people as well.

Informal systems work better during times of uncertainty. Informal systems can help to stabilize operations. During times of crisis, management utilizes informal structures more quickly to meet organizational demands that the formal system cannot handle. As Maciariello and Kirby (1990) explain, "The association between the informal and formal changes with the degree of uncertainty. As stability and predictability increase, the use of formal systems increases. In times of major change, the informal system should be the dominant management system. The formal system, that is, the policies and procedures that applied to the past products and customers, may actually be looked upon by management as a potential barrier" (p. 15).

Informal rewards also have increased potential for use with executive management. According to Greenberg and Liebman (1990), "In today's business environment, the critical motivational needs of executives and, therefore, the effectiveness of most incentive schemes are undermined. In a climate characterized by debt-laden companies, changing ownership, corporate downsizing, flattening organizational structures, and a $375 million outplacement industry, there is less certainty, loyalty, and stability. This environment undermines the needs for belonging, security, and control. Most executives have usually satisfied their basic financial needs. While stock options or additional bonus dollars play a role, personal incentives, such as recognition or achievement, become more important" (p. 9).

The challenge is to design management controls that simultaneously encourage continuous improvement and stability to current operations and adaptation to major discontinuities in the environment (Maciariello & Kirby, 1990). Informal reward systems can do just that.

Conclusion

Managers must consider some intangible tools and approaches for obtaining results in an organization that only a few years ago might have been considered too qualitative, abstract, and undefined. Foremost among these approaches is the use of informal rewards for motivating and encouraging individual performance that corresponds with the organization's goals.

Informal rewards are personal and flexible and thus can be more widely used. They can have greater impact in motivating more people and in helping to reinforce more formal organizational systems. With relatively little effort and expense, management can reap the benefits from an informal reward system that works in harmony with more formal reward programs to obtain maximum individual performance and productivity for the organization.

References

Anthony, R.N., Dearden, J., & Bedford, N.M. (1989). *Management control systems* (5th ed.). Burr Ridge, IL: Irwin Professional.

Barnard, C.I. (1968). *The functions of the executive.* Cambridge, MA: Harvard University Press.

Boyle, D.C. (1987, March-April). Ideas for action: The 100 club. *Harvard Business Review,* p. 27.

Dalton, M. (1959). *Men who manage.* New York: John Wiley.

Drucker, P.F. (1974). *Management: Tasks, responsibilities, practices.* New York: Harper and Row.

Greenberg, J., & Liebman, M. (1990, July-August). Incentives: The missing link in strategic performance. *Journal of Business Strategy,* p. 9.

Hill, C.F. (1989, Spring). Generating ideas that lower costs and boost productivity. *National Productivity Review, 8*(2), 161.

Kanter, R.M. (1986, December). Kanter on management. Holiday gifts: Celebrating employee achievements. *Management Review,* pp. 19, 21.

Maciariello, J.A., & Kirby, C.J. (1990). *Adaptive control using formal and informal systems.* Unpublished manuscript.

Merchant, K.A. (1989). *Rewarding results: Motivating profit center managers.* Boston: Harvard Business School Press.

Mintzberg, H. (1979). *The structuring of organizations.* Englewood Cliffs, NJ: Prentice Hall.

Newman, W.H. (1975). *Constructive control: Design and use of control systems.* New Jersey: Prentice Hall.

Nord, W.R. (1974). Beyond the teaching machine: Operant conditioning in management. In H.L. Tosi & W.C. Hammer, (Eds.), *Organizational behavior and management: A contingency approach.* Chicago: St. Clair Press.

Pritchard, R., Roth, P., Watson, M., & Jones, S. (1989, May). Incentive systems: Success by design. *Personnel,* p. 68.

Sathe, V. (1985). *Culture and related realities.* Burr Ridge, IL: Irwin Professional.

Schneier, C.E. (1989, March-April). Capitalizing on performance management, recognition, and rewards systems. *Compensation and Benefits Review,* p. 23.

Staff. (1986, December). Recognizing reward programs. *Personnel Journal,* p. 68.

Bob Nelson, M.B.A., *is president & founder of Nelson Motivation, Inc., San Diego, California, and author of the best-selling* 1001 Ways to Reward Employees *and* 1001 Ways to Energize Employees. *He has been a vice president for Blanchard Training & Development, Inc., as well as a management trainer for Norwest Banks and Control Data Corporation. Nelson received his M.B.A. in organizational behavior from UC Berkeley and is a doctoral candidate in the Executive Management Program of The Peter F. Drucker Graduate Management Center at The Claremont Graduate School in Los Angeles.*

CONTRIBUTORS

Heather Jean Campbell
620 North Lakeshore Drive
Ludington, MI 49431
(616) 845–6185
fax: (616) 639–1548

Heidi Ann Campbell
620 North Lakeshore Drive
Ludington, MI 49431
(616) 845–6185
fax: (616) 639–1548

Dave Francis, D.Litt.
Leader, Innovation Consulting Group
Center for Research in Innovation
   Management
University of Brighton
Falmer, East Sussex BN1 9PH
UK
   44–1–273–600900
   e-mail: david_l_francis@
     compuserve.com

Lisa Friedman, Ph.D.
Principal
Enterprise Development Group
930 Roble Ridge Road
Palo Alto, CA 94306
   (415) 855–9440
   fax: (415) 855–9987
   e-mail: friedman@
     enterprisedevelop.com

Timothy J. Galpin, Ph.D.
Watson Wyatt Worldwide
2121 San Jacinto, Suite 2400
Dallas, TX 75201
   (214) 978–3489
   fax: (214) 978–3650
   e-mail: tim_galpin@watsonwyatt.com

Barbara Pate Glacel, Ph.D.
CEO
VIMA International
5290 Lyngate Court
Burke, VA 22015
   (703) 764–0780
   fax: (703) 764–0789
   e-mail: bpglacel@vima.com
   website: http://www.vima.com

Herman Gyr, Ph.D.
Principal
Enterprise Development Group
930 Roble Ridge Road
Palo Alto, CA 94306
   (415) 855–9440
   fax: (415) 855–9987
   e-mail: gyr@enterprisedevelop.com

Laura Hauser, M.S.O.C.
President
Leadership Strategies International
15555 Bronco Drive, Suite 101
Santa Clarita, CA 91351
   (805) 251–0641
   fax: (805) 251–5062

Markus Hauser
Max L. Hansen Consulting
Ausserhoferstrasse 1
Schwaz 6130
Austria
 011–43–664–2600035
 fax: 011–43–664–2697409

Nancy Jackson, Ph.D.
Principal
Nancy Jackson & Associates
592 South Victor Way
Aurora, CO 80012
 (303) 363–1930
 fax: (303) 337–8842
 e-mail: nansolo@aol.com

Bonnie Jameson, M.S.
Consultant
1024 Underhills Road
Oakland, CA 94610
 (510) 832–2597
 fax: (510) 832–2597

Homer H. Johnson, Ph.D.
Professor
Center for Organization Development
Loyola University Chicago
820 North Michigan Avenue
Chicago, IL 60611
 (773) 508–3027
 fax: (773) 508–8713

H.B. Karp, Ph.D.
Personal Growth Systems
4217 Hawksley Drive
Chesapeake, VA 23321
 (757) 483–9327
 fax: (757) 483–9327
 e-mail: pgshank@aol.com

M.K. Key, Ph.D.
Principal
Key Associates, LLC
1857 Laurel Ridge
Nashville, TN 37215
 (615) 665–0846
 fax: (615) 665–1622
 e-mail: keyassocs@nashville.com

Andrew Kimball
Managing Director
Qube Learning, LLC
7 Ross Common
Ross, CA 94957–0371
 (415) 925–8900
 fax: (415) 925–8936
 e-mail: akimball@qube.com

Ginger Lapid-Bogda, Ph.D.
Organization Development Consultant
Bogda & Associates
2396 Nalin Drive
Los Angeles, CA 90077
 (310) 440–9772
 fax: (310) 472–2381
 e-mail: lapidbogda@aol.com

Jean G. Lamkin, Ph.D.
Corporate Training Director
Landmark Communications, Inc.
150 West Brambleton Avenue
Norfolk, VA 23510
 (757) 446–2913
 fax: (757) 446–2985
 e-mail: jlamkin@lcimedia.com

Bob Nelson
Nelson Motivation, Inc.
12687 Gibraltar Drive
San Diego, CA 92128
 (800) 575–5521
 fax: (619) 673–9031
 e-mail: bobrewards@aol.com

Jennifer Nordloh
3123 Diana Court
Bloomington, IN 47401
812–336–7982

Sara Pope
Senior Associate
Cornelius & Associates
631-G Harden Street
Columbia, SC 29205
(803) 779–3354
fax: (803) 254–0183

Robert C. Preziosi, D.P.A.
Professor of Management Education
School of Business and
    Entrepreneurship
Nova Southeastern University
3301 College Avenue
Fort Lauderdale, FL 33314
(954) 262–5111
fax: (954) 262–3965

Wayne Reschke
Principal
Center for Organization
    Effectiveness, Inc.
6515 Grand Teton Plaza
Suite 145
Madison, WI 53719
(608) 833–3332, ext. 24
fax: (608) 833–3363
e-mail: wreschke@
    greatorganizations.com

Emile A. Robert, Jr., Ph.D.
COO
VIMA International
5290 Lyngate Court
Burke, VA 22015
(703) 764–0780
fax: (703) 764–0789
e-mail: chumrob@vima.com
website: http://www.vima.com

John Sample, Ph.D.
Principal
Sample & Associates
2922 Shamrock South
Tallahassee, FL 32308
(904) 668–1067
fax: (904) 668–1067
e-mail: sampleassoc@nettally.com

Neil J. Simon
President
Business Development Group, Inc.
122 Miller
Ann Arbor, MI 48104
(734) 741–4150
fax: (248) 552–1924
e-mail: njsimon@aol.com

Sander Smiles
Fel-Pro, Inc.
7450 North McCormick Boulevard
Skokie, IL 60076–8105
(847) 568–2585

Michael Lee Smith
48 Andover Lane
Aberdeen, NJ 07747
(732) 566–8721
e-mail: msmithhr@aol.com

Michele Stimac, Ed.D.
Professor
Graduate School of Education and
   Psychology
Pepperdine University
400 Corporate Pointe
Culver City, CA 90230
   (310) 568–5613
   fax: (310) 568–5755
   e-mail: mstimac@pepperdine.edu

Karen Vander Linde
Director
Center of Excellence for Learning
   Systems
Coopers & Lybrand, L.L.P.
1530 Wilson Boulevard
Arlington, VA 22209–3051
   (703) 908–1517
   fax: (703) 908–1695
   e-mail: karen.vanderlinde@
      us.coopers.com

Jeyakar Vendamanickam
Senior Faculty
Hindustan Aeronautics Ltd.
   Staff College
Vimanapura
Bangalore 560 017
India
   011–91–80–5263133
   fax: 011–91–80–5266598

Patrick J. Ward, Ph.D.
Principal
Organization Analysis & Development
915 Northside Drive
Mount Dora, FL 32757
   (352) 735–0551
   fax: (352) 735–0551
   e-mail: pat.bette.ward@prodigy.com

Contents of the Companion Volume, The 1998 Annual: Volume 1, Training

*See Experiential Learning Activities Categories, p. 5, for an explanation of the numbering system.